SOUTH–SOUTH TRADE IN GLOBAL DEVELOPMENT

*To my parents
for their unconditional love
and support.*

South–South Trade in Global Development

ELIZABETH PARSAN

Avebury

Aldershot • Brookfield USA • Hong Kong • Singapore • Sydney

Published by
Avebury
Ashgate Publishing Limited
Gower House
Croft Road
Aldershot
Hants GU11 3HR
England

Ashgate Publishing Company
Old Post Road
Brookfield
Vermont 05036
USA

Typeset by
Neville Young
49 Muswell Avenue
London N10 2EH

A CIP catalogue record for this book is available from the British Library

ISBN 1 85628 432 8

Printed and Bound in Great Britain by
Athenaeum Press Ltd., Newcastle upon Tyne.

Contents

Figures and tables

Foreword

South–South trade is the missing link in global trade. The fifteen per cent or so of the world's population in the industrial countries do about two-thirds of global trade with each other, while the developing countries, with the bulk of the world's population, do less than ten per cent of global trade with each other. The explanation of this gap is therefore of great importance in locating opportunities for the future growth of global trade.

Elizabeth Parsan has studied this problem in depth, both as a general problem and for the specific case of linkages between Trinidad and Tobago and Brazil, with special reference to trade in petrochemicals. The book covers a range of issues including the potential and benefits of South–South trade, the design of trade policy, institutional barriers and the policy changes required for their removal. The most interesting features of the book are contained in the concrete example of Trinidad and Tobago–Brazil trade, where it is shown that despite existing barriers, possibilities exist for trade in both goods and services between countries at different levels of development, and in a sector where trade has been traditionally North–South. Further, the benefits from this trade are more dynamic and greater than for South–North trade. This detailed case study makes Elizabeth Parsan's work an important contribution to the international debate on the prospects for South–South trade, a debate that undoubtedly has demonstrated the need for this type of empirical research. Her book can be recommended to all students of development and trade problems.

Sussex, England
October 1992

Hans Singer

Acknowledgements

I wish to express my gratitude to the numerous people who directly or indirectly contributed to this book. The Department of Economics at the University of the West Indies, Trinidad equipped me with the foundation skills necessary for analytical research, and provided warmth, encouragement and support during the preparation of the first draft. Special thanks are due to Prof. Compton Bourne, Dr. Eric St. Cyr, Dr. Trevor Farrell and Dr. Ralph Henry.

This book is an outgrowth of my DPhil thesis, completed at the University of Sussex in 1988. Of the many people there who gave advice and encouragement, I wish to thank Prof. Hans Singer and Dr. H. D. Evans for their intellectual and close personal support throughout the entire writing of the book. They gave willingly of their time to reading various parts of the study, and I benefited tremendously from their criticisms and constructive comments. The case study depended greatly on the assistance of officials in the petrochemical industry in Trinidad and Tobago and Brazil, and I wish to express my deep appreciation to them for the time they took to discussing various aspects of the industry with me. In particular, I owe a huge debt to Dr. Amilcar da Silva Filho of Petrobrás Química, who provided invaluable guidance during my stay in Brazil, and gave enthusiastic support to my initial ideas at a time when they seemed unrealistic to most.

Finally, I wish to thank my family in Trinidad and Tobago and my many friends, both from the South and from the North, who provided the underlying emotional support for this study that was so vital to enable its successful completion.

Abbreviations and explanatory notes

APEC	Associaçâo Promotora de Estudos da Economía
c.i.f.	cost, insurance and freight
CR$	Brazilian cruzeiros
EC	European Community
ECLAC	Economic Commission for Latin America and the Caribbean
ESCAP	Economic and Social Commission for Asia and the Pacific
FAO	Food and Agricultural Organization of the United Nations
f.o.b.	free on board
GATT	General Agreement on Tariffs and Trade
GDP	Gross Domestic Product
GNP	Gross National Product
IBRD	International Bank for Reconstruction and Development
ILO	International Labour Organization
IMF	International Monetary Fund
ISIC	International Standard Industrial Classification of All Economic Activities
OECD	Organization for Economic Cooperation and Development
OPEC	Organization of Petroleum Exporting Countries
Petrobrás	Petróleo Brasileiro S/A
Petroquisa	Petrobrás Química S/A

R & D	Research and development
SITC	Standard International Trade Classification
t/d	tons per day
t/y	tons per year
TT$	Trinidad and Tobago dollars
UN	United Nations
UNCTAD	United Nations Conference on Trade and Development
UNCTC	United Nations Centre for Transnational Corporations
UNDP	United Nations Development Programme
UNESCO	United Nations Educational, Scientific and Cultural Organization
UNIDO	United Nations Industrial Development Organization

'Dollars' ($) refer to United States dollars, unless otherwise stated.

A dash (-) indicates that the amount is nil or negligible.

Two dots (..) indicate that the data are not available or are not separately reported.

All tons are metric tons, unless otherwise stated.

Part One
South–South Trade: Theoretical, Empirical and Policy Issues

1 Introduction

Objectives of the study

Ever since Arthur Lewis[1] proposed a strategy of South–South (S–S) trade or trade among developing countries (DCs) for promoting industrialization and development in the Third World, the subject has fuelled intense debate.[2] Critics have pointed to the alleged 'failure' of regional integration schemes, the serious debt problems of the DCs and highly protectionist trade regimes maintained by them, as strong arguments against a policy of S–S trade. Along another line they have argued that in view of the relatively larger markets offered by the industrialized countries (ICs) and the greater scope for labour intensive trade with them, the gains associated with South–North (S–N) trade are greater than for S–S trade. Neither of these arguments however, pose a challenge to the fundamental case for S–S trade which rests upon the underlying need to explore the vast underexploited and underdeveloped resources in the South, especially its human resources, for the enhancement of its growth and development.

The need for increasing S–S trade is a particularly urgent one in the light of current global changes which are likely to affect traditional S–N trading opportunities in the future. The slowing down in the growth of the ICs is expected to lead to a reduction in the rate of Northern imports of goods and services from the DCs; and the increasing trend in protectionism in the ICs implies reduced access for DCs' goods in Northern markets. Indeed, over the past decade or so the tendency within the ICs has been towards the adoption of increasingly restrictive measures, especially 'new' nontariff barriers (NTBs) such as voluntary export restraints, orderly marketing arrangements and health and quality regulations. This tendency coupled with the emergence of regional blocs such as the European Single Market have fuelled fears of increased protection in the ICs in the future. Further, it is now being recognized that the

3

Uruguay Round of World Trade Negotiations which is aimed at liberalizing world trade is not expected to bring substantial gains to developing countries.

In the light of the above the objectives of this study are two-fold: (a) to undertake a comprehensive evaluation of the salient issues involved in a strategy of S–S trade, and (b) to demonstrate the actual potential and problems of S–S trade through a case study of trade between Brazil and Trinidad and Tobago. In pursuing the first objective certain key questions are addressed: is there a basis for S–S trade? in which areas is the potential for trade greatest, and to what extent can existing trade policy barriers prevent the realization of such trade? how important are other barriers such as those present in the system of finance, shipping, marketing and distribution? Is S–S trade 'better' than S–N trade and if it is, what types of policies are required to facilitate its promotion?

The case study which involves trade between Brazil and Trinidad and Tobago in petrochemicals is a particularly interesting one from both a country and industry point of view. The two countries being considered are at different levels of development. Brazil belongs to the group of newly-industrializing countries (NICs),[3] while Trinidad and Tobago is one of the less industrialized countries (LDCs) of the South. However, as will be seen later, they exemplify the possibilities for trade in both goods and services, between those two groups within the South. The micro level analysis of trade in petrochemicals permits a detailed examination of a range of issues relevant to a S–S trade strategy. Over the past two decades or so many oil rich DCs have developed a strong comparative advantage in petrochemicals production. This has enabled them to compete effectively in the ICs' markets as well as in those in the South where demand for these products is projected to grow more rapidly in the future. Further, whereas the ICs are adopting increasingly protectionist measures against petrochemical imports from Southern countries, the latter are now gradually dismantling their trading barriers. This investigation into the petrochemicals sector therefore provides an opportunity to examine pertinent issues such as the competitiveness of S–S/S–N trade, the trade creating rather than trade diverting aspects of S–S trade and the influence of trade policy barriers.

The emergence of a South–South trade strategy

The espousal of S–S cooperation as an internationally accepted approach to development took place only in the late 1970s, following discussions for the creation of a new international economic order.[4] At a meeting of the Group of 77 held in Mexico City in 1976, a resolution was adopted regarding the need for strengthening economic cooperation among developing countries (ECDC).[5] S–S trade formed an integral part of the ECDC programme, the details of which were outlined at a subsequent conference held by the group in Caracas in 1981.

S–S trade is not, of course, an entirely new phenomenon. During the 1960s and 1970s the majority of DCs entered into various types of regional economic arrangements in an attempt to boost their intra trade. The first such arrangement, the Latin American Free Trade Association (LAFTA), was established in 1960 by Argentina, Brazil, Mexico, Paraguay, Peru and Uruguay, and later joined by Ecuador, Venezuela, Bolivia and Colombia.[6] It consisted of a free trade area involving the abolition of tariff barriers on intra area trade. This was soon followed by a multiplicity of other arrangements such as common markets and fully fledged economic communities in Latin America, Africa and Asia. Other attempts were made to foster linkages at the bilateral and subregional levels, particularly among countries from different regions. In the 1960s for example, Egypt, India and Yugoslavia formed a Tripartite Trade Expansion and Economic Cooperation Arrangement to strengthen economic linkages among themselves; and China, Cuba and India launched substantial technical assistance and financial cooperation programmes.

The above arrangements succeeded in generating a substantial amount of trade among DCs and played an important role in promoting industrialization within the South. However, countries have not been able to reap the full benefits of regional integration because of two fundamental problems – the lack of complementary production structures in member countries and the reliance on highly protectionist, trade diverting policies. Many integration groupings have involved countries at similarly low levels of industrialization and this has placed limits on the scope for intragroup trade, especially in manufactured goods. More importantly however, in many instances high cost producers within the union were protected from outside competition through high tariff barriers, and member countries often found that they had to purchase goods from within the union at higher prices than obtainable elsewhere. Indeed, numerous studies on the static effects of economic integration have shown that regional integration schemes have often involved costly trade diversion.[7]

The 'new' approach to S–S trade differs from past arrangements in at least two respects. First of all, rather than being confined to subsets of countries it embraces all DCs and is located within the broadest framework for cooperation among DCs – that of collective self reliance. Secondly, it emphasizes trade creating policies under more liberal trading regimes. Inclusion of a larger number of countries in the group increases the chances of incorporating lower cost producers and therefore maximizes the potential for trade creation. Further, a removal of trade policy barriers among a wide range of DCs will undoubtedly stimulate greater competition within the group and, in general, encourage the exploitation of more fruitful, trade creating opportunities.

Building on the indigenous needs, capabilities and resources of the South is a central feature of collective self reliance, but the concept itself is a much wider one. Sauvant (1982) explained it as follows:

5

Self-reliance seeks ... to de-emphasize the predominant reliance of the developing countries on linkages with the developed countries in favour of a greater selectivity in traditional linkages and better mobilization of indigenous resources for primarily indigenous needs. In its collective dimension, joint actions by developing countries – especially through economic and technical cooperation – for the purpose of strengthening their own autonomous capacities in all areas are the cornerstone of this approval (p. 12).

Collective self reliance refers therefore not only to the harnessing of the South's resources for its development, but to a reduction of dependence on traditional linkages with the North. Unfortunately however, the concept is often mistakenly associated with the notion of 'de-linking' from the North. The current emphasis of a S–S trade strategy is to develop linkages with the North selectively and intensify those with the South. The strategy envisages a kind of global interdependence in the world economy where S–S trade is seen as complementary to S–N trade. An expansion of S–S trade (absolutely and as a share of total South trade) within a liberal trading order implies increasing overall trade. N–S trade can then increase absolutely (though decline relatively) and both parties can reap gains in the long run. As pointed out by Singer (1983) it is equally in the interest of the North to encourage S–S trade as it is in the South to promote its development. Therefore, S–S trade has an important role to play in the promotion of global development.

The case for South–South trade

Factors both external and internal to the South provide strong arguments for the promotion of trade among DCs. The external ones are largely market related and although in the past their role has been somewhat downplayed, they now assume great significance in the light of current global economic and political changes. In general though, it is the internal factors which provide the 'core' arguments for S–S trade since they are related to the fundamental need for exploring the South's unexploited human and natural resource potential. For according to Helleiner (1990) 'whether or not the North is experiencing booms or depressions, there will be a need for detailed thought and policy prescription on the means for economic cooperation among developing countries in various spheres and geographical areas' (p. 59).

External factors

One of the main reasons for the promotion of S–S trade relates to the slowing down in the growth of the ICs, an argument advanced by Lewis (1980). According to Lewis, during the years up to the early 1970s the ICs experienced nearly three decades of high and sustained economic growth. This rapid growth of the ICs permitted large exports from the DCs which, in turn, fuelled growth in those countries. Indeed, the expansion of the NICs during the 1960s and 1970s was largely facilitated by the huge expansions in NIC–IC trade, especially in manufactured goods. Since 1973 however, the ICs have entered a protracted period of much lower annual growth rates than before, and projections indicate a continuation of this trend in the future. If, as posited by Lewis, there is a close link between growth of the North and growth of the South via trade, then this trend has adverse implications for DCs. A slowdown in the growth of the ICs implies a decline in the rate of growth of exports from the DCs, and hence a slowdown in the rate of growth of those economies. Given such a scenario, the promotion of S–S trade can assist not only in decreasing the vulnerability of the DCs to changes in the North, but also in creating their own 'engine of growth' quite independent of growth in the North.

The rapid growth of protectionism in the North and the likelihood of its reinforcement in the future is another strong reason for DCs to increase trade among themselves. The surge of protectionism which began in the early 1970s has accelerated in recent years, and this has had a strong negative impact on both the agricultural and manufactured exports of DCs. For example, trade in clothing and textiles is at present regulated by the Multifibre Arrangement, a detailed and very restrictive set of bilateral quotas for delivery of those products to the ICs. The European Community's Common Agricultural Policy provides protection to domestic producers through export and input subsidies, quotas and variable tariffs which are required to maintain domestic price floors. Further, the imposition of an array of tariff and NTBs (especially new ones like orderly marketing arrangements, voluntary export restrictions and restrictive 'quality' requirements and health regulations) has affected a range of DCs' semi-manufactured and manufactured goods.

Attempts are being made at present to liberalize world trade via the Uruguay Round of World Trade Negotiations. However, the likelihood of an outcome with major reforms in all areas under negotiation now appear remote. The lack of agreement in the contentious areas of agriculture, services and textiles has led to considerable delays in the negotiations and it is now being acknowledged that only a modest 'face-saving' outcome can be expected. These developments coupled with the emergence of regional blocs such as the European Single Market have fuelled fears concerning continued protectionism in the future. In such a situation the need for promoting trade within the South is of paramount importance.

Internal factors

Changes in the external economy indicate an urgent need to explore S–S trading opportunities, but it is factors which are internal to the South that provide the fundamental case for S–S trade. The main ones include forces

7

associated with supply side transformation as a result of shifting comparative advantage; likely demand side changes connected with rising incomes per head in DCs; the strong 'development promoting' properties of S–S trade; and the potential for DCs to increase their bargaining power in Northern markets.

Until the 1950s most countries in the South had low per capita incomes, limited capital and skills, undeveloped industrial bases and small and fragmented markets. The potential for expanding S–S trade was therefore extremely limited. Since that time however, countries have grown at divergent rates, achieved varying levels of industrialization and acquired comparative advantages in different areas. As a result, there now exists considerable potential for the expansion of trade among different subgroups of countries within the South and in various categories of both goods and services. Exploitation of this potential could lead to much higher levels of growth in the DCs and assist in creating a Southern 'engine of growth'.

Countries which have had high and sustained growth over the past two decades and achieved a high degree of industrial diversification appear to have the greatest potential for developing trade with other DCs. The East Asian NICs (Hong Kong, Taiwan, South Korea and Singapore) are undoubtedly among those. But others which are rapidly emerging as dynamic Southern exporters can also be included in this group. They include Mexico, Brazil, Argentina, Indonesia, the Philippines, Thailand and Malaysia. These countries have developed a strong competitive advantage in a range of semi-manufactured and manufactured goods (as evidenced by their ability to penetrate successfully Northern markets) which they are now able to export to other DCs. The NICs and a few other countries also have a demonstrated potential in the export of technology which they explore through, for example, the supply of technical, management and marketing services.

Other groups of DCs with strong agricultural bases and relatively smaller and less diversified manufacturing sectors also have potential for exporting to the South. They include middle income countries such as Jamaica, Costa Rica, Mauritius and Turkey; several least developed ones such as Bangladesh and Zimbabwe; and a few high income, oil exporting countries, principally those in the Middle East. Goods with export potential include a range of agricultural raw materials, agro-processed goods, traditional early stage manufactures such as textiles and footwear, chemicals and other oil derived products. In general then, the trade potential of a heterogeneous South is large and can be fruitfully explored to enhance its future growth and development.

The markets in the South for the range of products which the DCs now manufacture are small in relation to those in the ICs. However, according to Helleiner (1990), in the future Southern markets are likely to grow more rapidly than those in the North. Population growth is faster in the South and the income elasticity of demand for many Third World exports such as primary products and simple manufactures is higher in the South than in the North. The NICs and the high income, oil exporting countries are likely to be the major importers in the region although the latter group now has considerably

8

less import potential. However, China and India, two of the largest countries in the South, are potentially of great importance as importers. At present their levels of imports are quite low, but extensive opportunities for trade can be created within the South if they were to raise these.

Besides the above, S–S trade is expected to bring special gains to its participants and this perhaps constitutes one of the strongest arguments for its promotion. In addition to the range of benefits normally associated with the extension of international economic activity (production gains resulting from the inter-country substitution of trade, consumption gains associated with changes in relative prices, greater exploitation of scale economies, and diversification of risks) S–S trade is expected to generate benefits connected with technological learning and skill accumulation. Observations on the content of S–S and S–N trade reveal that whereas the former consists of a relatively larger proportion of skill and technology intensive items such as capital goods, the latter involves relatively more labour intensive goods such as textiles and clothing. By providing a larger market for the adapted products and technologies produced by DCs, S–S trade can promote skill accumulation and the growth of technological capabilities in those countries. Further, since the human resource variable is key to the development process and S–S trade allows the utilization of a country's human resources it will undoubtedly be of enormous developmental value to the South.

Finally, S–S trade could contribute to an improvement in the DCs' collective terms of trade position against the ICs. Assuming that trade among the DCs is at least to some extent a substitute for trade with the ICs, its effect will be an upward shift in the export supply curves from the DCs to the ICs. This will reduce the DC export volume and improve the overall terms of trade against the ICs. S–S trade therefore has an important role to play in achieving a more equitable distribution of the gains from trade.

Plan of the book

The study is divided into two parts. Part One (Chapters 2–4) analyzes the main theoretical, empirical and policy aspects of S–S trade; whereas Part Two (Chapters 5–6) presents the case study of S–S trade. Chapter 2 examines the theoretical bases for S–S trade by drawing upon the existing trade theory literature. The traditional Heckscher–Ohlin (H–O) theory is considered as well as the more 'modern' trade theories which emphasize variables such as technology, scale economies and similarity in taste patterns. Chapter 3 analyzes the changing structure and composition of S–S trade over time; examines the factor characteristics of trade among DCs; and discusses some quantitative estimates of the scope for S–S trade. Chapter 4 assesses the influence of a host of barriers to S–S trade and considers the types of policies required to overcome them. These barriers include tariffs and NTBs as well as those arising from the system of finance, shipping, marketing and distribution, the influence of North based transnational corporations (TNCs) and tied aid.

Several of the above issues are explored in the case study of Brazil–Trinidad and Tobago trade. Chapter 5 examines prospective trading linkages between Brazil and Trinidad and Tobago. In particular, it undertakes a detailed investigation of the structure and functioning of the petrochemical industries in the two countries, and outlines specific areas for the development of trade. Chapter 6 assesses the potential for trade in these areas through an evaluation of the trade competitiveness of selected products, their future demand and the likely constraints to trade. Chapter 7 provides a summary of the study and discusses its major conclusions.

Notes

1. See Lewis (1980).
2. For purposes of this study the South is regarded as the group of DCs, whereas the North is considered as the group of industrialized ones.
3. The term NICs is used extensively to describe DCs where there has been particularly rapid industrial growth.
4. The New International Economic Order (NIEO) was launched at the 1974 United Nations Sixth Special Session which adopted the Program of Action for the NIEO.
5. The 1979 UNCTAD Resolution on Economic Cooperation Among Developing Countries.
6. See Table A.1 for a list of major Third World regional economic integration groupings.
7. See, for example, Willmore (1976) on the Central American Common Market (CACM) and Bennett (1982) on the Caribbean Community (CARICOM). It must be pointed out however, that although the static effects of regional integration have been quite limited the dynamic ones have been extremely important for Third World countries. The dynamic effects refer to ways in which integration influences the growth rate of member countries through, for example, its impact on the volume and location of investment, the achievement of economies of scale and increases in economic efficiency and trade due to changes in competitive pressures. In general, these dynamic effects are quite difficult to measure, but one study which attempted to quantify them showed that they were very important in the case of the CACM. See Cline (1978).

2 South–South trade: theoretical issues

Introduction

Until the early 1970s little attention was given to directional issues in the trade theory literature, for it was generally held that the direction in which a country traded was not important. In the case of trade among DCs the discussion centred around customs union or integration theory. The latter, formulated by Viner (1950) and elaborated upon by Meade (1955) and Lipsey (1960), dealt with the trade creation and trade diversion effects of a customs union. This analysis was later applied to other forms of preferential trading arrangements such as free trade areas and economic communities. Indeed, customs union theory has been useful in explaining trade among DCs, for the creation of regional integration arrangements encouraged fairly rapid growth of intra-DC trade during the 1950s and 1960s. However, recent expansions in S–S trade include far more than intraregional trade and trade preferences now appear to be of less importance in stimulating trade among DCs. Further, the patterns of S–S trade have become much more complex over time and wider explanations are now needed to analyze them.

It must be stated at the outset that no attempt has been made to formulate a separate theory of S–S trade. Rather, to the extent that S–S trade is viewed as a subset of world trade, the approach has been to draw upon the existing trade theory literature to derive explanations. In this chapter some of the new theoretical insights into S–S trade are discussed. The most important works in this regard are by Krueger (1977), Deardorff (1979, 1985) and Stewart (1976, 1984). Krueger and Deardorff conduct their analyses within a Heckscher–Ohlin (H–O) framework and attempt to develop a formal theory which provides a normative explanation of multilateral specialization patterns. Stewart's work on the other hand, though less robust, gives more varied theoretical insights into S–S trade. It consists of an examination of the more 'modern' trade theories and their implications for S–S trade.

11

Since theorizing about S–S trade has drawn upon the general trade theory literature, the approach in this chapter is first to outline briefly the various trade theories and then discuss their implications for S–S trade. These theories include those on the supply side – factor endowment, neo-technology and scale economy theories, as well as those on the demand side – preference similarity theory and theories of monopolistic competition and product differentiation. The discussion is largely concerned with trade in manufactured goods for, according to Stewart (1976) 'there appears to be less choice about the direction of trade for primary products, since location of production is largely determined by natural factors and location of consumption depends upon income levels' (pp. 93–4).

Factor endowment theory

The simple H–O theory

Perhaps the most widely used theory to explain and predict international trade patterns is the H–O theory. It states that the basis for international trade lies in inter-country differences in factor endowments.[1] Countries are endowed with different factor supplies and so not only will relative factor prices differ between countries, but also domestic commodity price ratios and factor combinations. Since commodities require productive factors in different relative proportions, then a country with abundant labour supplies, for example, will have a comparative advantage in the production of commodities which are labour intensive. Likewise those countries which are relatively well endowed with capital will have a comparative advantage in capital intensive goods. More generally, the H–O theory predicts that countries will tend to produce and export commodities which require relatively intensive use of their relatively abundant factors. At the same time, they will import those goods in which they do not have a comparative advantage.

The exposition of the simplest form of the H–O theory is based upon a number of simplifying assumptions. These include a perfectly competitive world with two factors of production (capital and labour),[2] identical technologies and preferences, constant returns to scale, non-reversibility of factor intensities, free trade, no transport costs, and complete mobility of productive factors within countries. It is clear that these highly restrictive assumptions do not hold in the real world, and so this variant of the H–O theory has been strongly criticized on account of its patently unrealistic assumptions. Indeed, since in reality many of the basic assumptions of the theory are untenable the reliability of the theory's predictions may be uncertain. In addition to this and notwithstanding the difficulties associated with a full test of the H–O model, empirical testing has shown that factor proportions alone cannot explain the pattern of international trade.[3] For example, the H–O theory has been unable to explain trade between economies with similar factor endowments and the growing importance of international trade that is intra-industry in nature. Furthermore, the hypotheses generated from empirical studies that have proved useful require an increase in dimensionality of the model.

The simple H–O theory has also been criticized by Stewart (1976, 1984) because of its failure to deal directly with the direction of trade, and its implications that trade patterns would run in a N–S/S–N direction. According to Stewart, if it is assumed that countries in the North and South represent two homogeneous groups specializing in the export of capital and labour intensive goods respectively, then the North countries will export capital intensive goods to the South, and the latter, in turn, will export labour intensive products back to them. The pattern of trade implicit in the H–O model is therefore a N–S/S–N one. Stewart further claims that since the theory is essentially a static one with no allowances made for growth, the implications are that DCs cannot change their factor endowments and, hence their underdeveloped status as exporters of labour intensive goods.

However, it must be pointed out that the above line of criticism is based on the simplest version of the H–O theory. Over the past few years the theory has been refined and extended, and a dynamic version now exists. It is in the context of these new developments that the H–O theory yields insights into the potential for S–S trade.

The extended H–O theory

Many attempts have been made to extend the basic H–O model.[4] One important approach has been to expand the factors of production to include skilled labour or human capital. This emerged out of an attempt to explain the Leontief paradox which showed capital abundant USA to be exporting labour intensive goods and importing capital intensive ones (Leontief, 1954). The basic argument was that labour of different qualities could be distinguished on the basis of skill or educational levels; and education and training represented investments in human capital. Capital, then should be redefined to include not only physical capital but also human capital (Kenen, 1965; Bhagwati, 1964). The prediction which follows is that an economy which is relatively abundant in skilled labour can be expected to export skill intensive or, more generally, capital intensive goods.

Besides the above, attempts have been made to formulate a dynamic version of the theory (Stiglitz, 1970). By introducing a time dimension into the analysis, it has been shown that a country can progress up the commodity chain. That is, as it starts accumulating capital more rapidly relative to labour it can move from the specialization and export of labour intensive goods to more capital intensive ones. Empirical support for this process is provided by Balassa who refers to a country's movement through successive stages of comparative advantage as a movement up the 'ladder' of comparative advantage (Balassa, 1979a). The dynamic theory, then makes allowances for a growing country to change its factor endowment over time and thereby alter its comparative advantage.[5]

More recent attempts at extending the basic H–O model have particular significance for the study of S–S trade. They include the works of Krueger (1977) and Deardorff (1979, 1985) which investigate multilateral trade flows in manufactured goods, and explore directional issues. The view taken in these models is that a country's comparative advantage constitutes a range of goods determined by its factor endowments, and parts of this range of comparative advantage can be related to different geographical destinations of exports.

In both the Krueger and Deardorff formulations, all the standard H–O assumptions are retained, except that the models are extended to include m countries and n commodities. The n commodities are produced with two factors of production, capital (K) and labour (L), and the production functions display constant returns to scale, with diminishing marginal product to each factor of production. There are assumed to be no factor intensity reversals. This implies that the ordering of factor intensities is the same across industries and countries. Perfectly competitive conditions prevail in the market; there is perfect factor mobility among all producing industries but no factor mobility between countries. Further, the wage rate equals the value of the marginal product of labour, and the rental on capital equals the value of the marginal product of capital.

Each country has a specific capital labour (K-L) endowment, and countries are numbered so that a higher number is associated with a greater abundance of capital relative to labour. Similarly, commodities are numbered so that a higher number implies a higher K-L ratio in production. An important assumption in both models is that factor prices are not equalized across countries. This, argues Krueger, is a natural assumption for dealing with countries of vastly different levels of development. All geographic units with the same wage-rental (w-r) ratio are treated as a single country, so that countries can be ordered monotonically according to their relative K-L endowment. Finally, it is assumed that consumer preferences are identical in all countries, international prices are given, and there are no transport costs or other impediments to trade.

The Krueger and Deardorff models which yield similar conclusions are discussed below.

The Krueger model. With the set of assumptions stated above, Krueger investigated the trading patterns of nine commodities and eleven countries.[6] She ranked countries according to their relative factor endowments and commodities (produced in the manufacturing sector) according to their relative factor intensities. From the resulting pattern (shown in Figure 2.1), she drew some general conclusions as follows:

Country	Commodity								
	1	2	3	4	5	6	7	8	9
1	X	X							
2	X	X	X						
3				X					
4				X					
5				X	X				
6				X	X				
7					X	X			
8					X		X		
9						X	X		
10							X		
11								X	X

Figure 2.1   Production patterns for eleven countries and nine commodities

Source: Krueger (1977)

1   Production in the most labour abundant country will be concentrated on the most labour intensive commodity or commodities, and production in the most capital abundant country will include production of the most capital intensive good. Further, a relatively more capital abundant country will not produce a more labour intensive good than any less capital abundant country. The assumption of no factor price equalization ensures this.

2   If a country produces more than one commodity they will lie adjacent to each other in the factor intensity ordering. Whether the additional commodities produced are import substitutes or exports will depend on the country's factor endowment and on demand conditions. At least one produced commodity will be exported and all nonproduced commodities will be imported. Except for the most and the least capital abundant countries, import competing industries can lie on either or both sides of the factor intensity of export industries.

3   In the case where two countries produce a common commodity without factor rental equalization between them, the more capital abundant country will utilize a more capital intensive technique of production than the labour abundant country. The w-r ratio will also be higher than in the labour abundant country.

4   In general, the factor proportions explanation of trade will show up in the pattern of specialization of production rather than in the factor intensity of exports and import competing goods. Countries in the middle of the factor endowment ranking will tend to specialize in commodities in the middle of the factor intensity ranking. They will import labour intensive commodities

from more labour abundant countries and capital intensive commodities from countries with relatively higher K-L endowments.

The Deardorff model. Deardorff (1979) attempted to explain trade in many commodities by first ranking goods in order of factor intensity, and then showing that all of a country's exports must lie higher on this list than all of its imports. A three-country, two-factor, six-commodity version of Deardorff's model, as outlined by Khanna (1985), is discussed below. The basic analysis however, extends readily to many countries and many commodities.

Figure 2.2 shows three unit isocost lines which reflect equal cost combinations of K and L for the three countries. These are AA for country A, BB for country B, and CC for country C. Country A is depicted as having a higher w-r ratio than B, and B, in turn, as having a higher one than C. Isoquants are drawn for the six goods which are ranked unambiguously in terms of capital intensity, with X_1 being the most capital intensive and X_6 the least capital intensive. The prices of goods are $p_1 \dots p_6$ and these must be such as to place each product's unit value isoquant exactly tangent to the outermost of the three unit isocost lines. This is necessary for if a product's price were too low, causing the corresponding unit value isoquant to lie wholly outside the isocost lines, the good will not be produced in any country. On the other hand, if its price were too high, causing its unit value isoquant to lie anywhere inside either one of the isocost lines, then its production would yield a positive

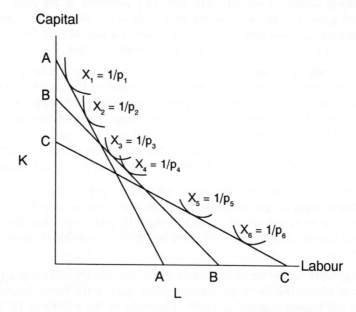

Figure 2.2 **Production patterns for three countries and six commodities**

Source: Khanna (1985)

profit in the corresponding country, thereby violating the assumption of perfect competition. Further, while it is possible for an isoquant to be tangent to two isocost lines, this need not happen for any good and, without factor intensity reversals, cannot happen for more than one between any pair of countries.

The pattern of trade that emerges in Figure 2.2 is interesting, since it is in line with the ranking of goods by factor intensity. The most capital intensive goods (1 and 2) can only be produced in the high wage country A, and must therefore be exported by that country. By contrast the least capital intensive or most labour intensive goods (5 and 6) are produced and exported by C. The goods produced and exported by country B (3 and 4) are in the middle range – they are less capital intensive than those by A, but more capital intensive than those by C. The chain of goods which are ranked by capital intensity is broken into segments, one for each country, and the segments are ordered in accordance with the relative capital abundance of the countries. Adjacent segments may contain one good in common if the isoquant for such a borderline good happens to touch two countries' isocost lines. Otherwise the division between segments of the chain occurs between goods. Each country must export all goods which appear only in its segment of the chain and import all goods which do not appear in its segment. Deardorff concludes from his analysis that each of a country's exports must be at least as capital intensive as each of the exports of all less capital abundant countries, and at least as labour intensive as each of the exports of all less labour abundant countries.

The extended version of the H–O theory developed by Krueger and Deardorff predicts that a country will trade in both N–S and S–S directions. Therefore, it is of direct relevance to DCs. However, a model which includes a finer breakdown of labour and resources is more useful for analyzing S–S trade, that is, one which includes physical as well as human capital. From a theoretical point of view this is difficult to work through, since the inclusion of three factors imposes two rankings each of countries and commodities and thus prevents clear-cut predictions of trade patterns. Notwithstanding this difficulty however, a verbal exposition of likely predictions of DCs' trade has been made, based on a three-factor model (Richards-Loup, 1984).

One line of reasoning leads to the prediction that the more industrialized DCs (that is, the NICs) will export to the South more skill and capital intensive products than they will to the North. At the same time they will also import from the North more skill and capital intensive products than they will import from the South. The products traded among themselves will cover a range of production techniques. The less industrialized countries, on the other hand, will export more labour intensive products to both the NICs and the North countries, and will import from them more skill intensive and capital intensive ones. They, too, will trade among themselves goods which cover different production techniques. Further, the dynamic aspects of the theory suggest that if a DC acquires technological and capital expertise at a faster pace than the rate of growth of its unskilled industrial labour force, its exports

17

will become more sophisticated in all directions, while the distinction between kinds of products exported North and South will narrow but remain.[7]

The interactive effects of S–S trade implied by the theory, and the potential gains have also been elaborated upon by Richards-Loup (1984). If it is assumed that the goods exported by the NICs to the South are more technology and skill intensive than to the North, then an increase in the production and export of these will allow benefits to be gained in terms of learning-by-doing and economies of scale which, in turn, will permit more rapid growth in the NICs. The LDCs, on the other hand, will also be able to achieve higher levels of growth by exploiting the expanded markets created by the NICs. Further, with the knowledge and experience gained by DCs from exporting more technologically sophisticated products to other DCs, this will improve the DCs' competitive position vis-à-vis the ICs and speed up the process of industrial diversification. This will take place across a wide range of goods and geographical markets.

From the above discussion it is clear that although the simple 2 x 2 x 2 version of the H–O theory does not have any direct relevance to S–S trade, in its extended form it assists greatly in understanding the dynamics of S–S trade.

Neo-technology theory

In the traditional factor endowment model, technology and skills are assumed to be widely available and identical across countries. The neo-technology theory challenges this assumption and emphasizes technological innovation as an important factor in influencing patterns of trade specialization. Although its explanations are confined to trade in manufactured goods, this theory has the important characteristic of being dynamic in nature. That is, it incorporates the time element into its analysis. There are two major models which embody the neo-technology theory: the technology gap model and the product cycle model.[8]

The technology gap model

The technology gap model was developed by Posner (1961) in order to explain trade in manufactures among ICs. He stated that 'trade may be caused by technical changes and developments that influence some industries and not others; because particular technical changes originate in one country, comparative cost differences may induce trade in particular goods during the lapse of time taken for the rest of the world to imitate one country's innovation'. In other words, Posner's proposition is that leads and lags in technological innovation among countries determine the pattern of their specialization and trade composition. This proposition is illustrated below.

18

Whenever a product is developed, it is usually first sold in the domestic market. As foreign demand grows, the product is exported and the early producer will enjoy a monopolistic advantage by virtue of its possession of the new technology. But other producers, both domestic and foreign, who may be threatened by the introduction of the new product are likely to take defensive action and try to imitate the innovating firm. However, there is usually a lag between innovation and imitation. When imitation eventually takes place, the monopolistic advantage of the innovating firm gradually becomes eroded, and the home country may become a net importer of that product. Therefore, according to this model, the capability to innovate technologically is considered to be an essential factor in a country's competitiveness. Countries with high innovative capacity will export a large share of new products which have not been imitated elsewhere.

The product cycle model

This model was initially developed by Vernon (1966) to explain trade in manufactured goods on the basis of stages in a product's life. The theory proceeds from the premise that products typically pass through three different stages during their life cycle – early, growth and mature. During the 'early' stage of the cycle when new products are introduced, production tends to be characterized by high skill intensity, the availability of which determines the location of manufacturing production. That is, countries which are well endowed with highly skilled labour are most likely to have an advantage in new products, and location is close to the main market as quick communication is required between producers, consumers and suppliers.

In the 'growth' stage as demand for the product grows and product information and know-how become more widely available, mass production and distribution become possible. Countries with less technical expertise begin to produce and market the products. This migration of industry is facilitated through some degree of standardization of the product. Economies of scale and production costs become more important while labour skills decrease in importance. Finally, in the 'mature' stage of the product cycle the product becomes completely standardized, technology and market information become internationally diffused and mass production takes place. The location of industry is more flexible, and the sources of competitiveness are determined by economies of scale and costs of production. In particular, as skills become less important, the relative share of labour costs increases.

The product cycle model has been subjected to several modifications over time in the light of changing conditions internationally. In recent years leading transnational corporations (TNCs) have developed international networks of subsidiaries and the choice of location of production may not be in accordance with the predictions of the theory. Vernon himself (1971, 1979) now places greater emphasis on oligopolistic behaviour and the desire of firms to maintain their oligopolistic lead by erecting barriers to entry. He argues, however, that the theory still continues to explain certain aspects of trade and direct foreign investment, especially in relation to small firms which have not yet acquired worldwide networks, and to DCs.

The technology gap/product cycle explanations of trade emerged primarily to explain N–N trade. Within the framework offered, the ICs are the ones which stimulate technological change and they exchange among themselves products which embody new technologies as well as those which are standardized. The DCs, on the other hand, do not fit into this schema, for they are viewed essentially as receivers of technological change. They import products from the North when they are at the 'new technology' stage, and engage in production and export only later on when the technologies become mature and standardized. This theory therefore rules out S–S trade in technology intensive goods, but maintains that trade may flow in a N–S/S–N direction with skill intensive goods from the ICs being exchanged for standardized commodities from the DCs.

Stewart (1984) states that this type of trade flow has implications both for the terms of trade and the direction of technological change. First of all, when new products are developed and marketed they command high prices, and innovators are able to earn quasi rents and pay high wages in the ICs. But when the technology becomes mature and standardized, and many producers enter the market, product prices fall. The fact that South countries are continuously in a position of importing the products of later and later innovations while exporting back those which embody mature technologies implies that the terms of trade are likely to have adverse consequences for the South. That is, Southern countries have to pay a form of 'Schumpeterian' profit to the ICs in the form of high product prices, but must accept low prices for the products they export to them.

A second implication of the neo-technology theory derives from the fact that the technologies imported from the North are developed to suit the factor characteristics and income levels of that environment, and these may be inappropriate to those of the South. Since the ICs tend to be relatively more capital abundant, both in terms of physical and human capital, the new technologies tend to be more capital and skill intensive and hence may not suit the factor endowments of the South. Further, to the extent that income levels in the ICs are much higher than in the South, the new products from the North will reflect increasingly high income characteristics. Both from a product and process point of view therefore, technologies imported from the North will be inappropriate to a Southern environment.

A third implication of the theory is that if DCs can become innovators themselves they will be able to reap the benefits of technical change in much the same way as the ICs have been able to in the past.

Scale economy theory

Whereas the traditional factor proportions explanation of international trade assumes a technology which exhibits constant returns to scale, in scale economy theory increasing returns to scale provide a basis for trade. In its simplest form the scale economy thesis states that the larger the home market the more likely is a country able to specialize in goods produced with increasing returns to scale. That is, it is expected that large countries will have large industries and therefore, other things being equal, will have relatively low autarky prices in those industries where economies of scale are most important. Economies of large scale production can lead to a reduction in unit costs and convey an international competitive advantage. It follows that large countries will have a comparative advantage in, and export from, industries with significant economies of scale. Drèze (1960) extended the scale economy thesis to include small nations. He argued that large countries will have an advantage in differentiated goods since a larger total market will be needed to allow producers in specific product lines to exhaust the benefits of economies of scale. Small countries can also benefit from economies of scale but they will have to specialize in more standardized goods.

The scale economy theory has direct implications for both large and small DCs. Large DCs such as South Korea, Brazil and China are likely to enjoy comparatively high productivity and cost advantages by producing for their large home markets. The benefits from large scale production can allow them to export to other DCs. Small DCs can also benefit from specialization, although the largest potential exists for standardized goods. Some specialization along these lines already takes place, but this is undertaken mainly by North based TNCs and through vertically integrated production. However, there still remains great scope for this type of trade.

Preference similarity theory

All the trade theories discussed so far are supply oriented, for they attribute patterns of trade to inter-country differences in supply conditions. However, the preference similarity theory formulated by Linder (1961) emphasizes the importance of demand conditions as determinants of trade. Demand side theories are very important since differences in the prices of goods among countries can be traced not only to differences in production costs but also to changes in demand. That is, demand responds to changes in tastes and income, prices reflect the demand shifts, and trade in turn follows international differences in product prices.

Linder hypothesized that similarities in taste between nations are important in explaining trade patterns. According to him, 'international trade is really nothing but an extension across national frontiers of a country's own web of economic activity' (Linder, 1961, p.88). That is, trade in manufactured goods is simply an outgrowth of internal markets. The notion is that goods are first produced in response to domestic demand, for in a world of imperfect knowledge entrepreneurs will respond to opportunities of which they are most aware – those in the domestic market. Since exports are viewed as an extension of the domestic market, then exporters will look towards countries with similar demand patterns with which to develop trading links. Linder posits then that the more similar the range of products demanded in the two countries, the more intensive is trade likely to be between these two countries. That is, if two countries have exactly the same demand structures, all their exportables and importables will be the same.

The question of what influences the demand structure of a country is important in Linder's theory, for this helps to determine the types of countries that are most likely to develop trade. Linder states that although influences such as language, culture, religion and climate are important, the single most important factor on the structure of demand is the level of average income. The hypothesis generated from this assertion is that the scope for trade is potentially greatest between countries with the same per capita income. The corollary to this is that per capita income differences are a potential obstacle to trade since the costs incurred in adapting products to meet foreign demand are likely to be high.

Linder's theory provides an explanation of international trade patterns that contradicts that provided by factor proportions theory. However, it is closely related to theories put forward to explain intra-industry trade since one of the major trade creating factors is product differentiation.[9] With respect to consumer goods, it is stated that 'even minor qualitative differences in goods serving the same basic needs may be sufficient to introduce into the demand structure of one country some significant differences compared with that of another country' (p. 95). Further, with respect to capital goods, that 'it is probable that the technical possibilities for qualitative variations in capital goods are at least as great as for consumer goods' (p. 96).

The preference similarity theory, like the neo-technology ones, emerged primarily to explain N–N trade but it also carries powerful implications for S–S trade. If, according to the theory, trade takes place because of similarity in tastes, then it is unlikely that S–N/N–S trade will develop. In general, the Northern and Southern countries have different income levels and their taste patterns differ markedly. The Southern countries, although they have substantially lower income levels, can encourage lucrative trade among themselves in products with low income characteristics. This type of trade, however, is inhibited on the demand side by the existence of a number of small, high income groups within the DCs which demand products from the North; and on the supply side by the unavailability of products from the South. If these two obstacles are removed, and the South is able to stimulate its own inventions and produce goods more appropriate to its environment, then it will be able to reap the benefits from preference similarity trade (Stewart, 1984).

Theories of monopolistic competition and product differentiation

Within recent years a number of models have emerged to explain the empirical phenomenon of intra-industry trade (IIT), or observed two-way trade in the same industry. In one of the early investigations by Grubel and Lloyd (1975) a number of explanations were offered to account for this growing phenomenon, which was observed among predominantly high income, developed countries. These included locational, time or other special factors that characterized particular goods; improper aggregation of trade data; differences in income distribution profiles and consumer tastes; and differences in the rate of technological adaptations for new products and processes. These factors have been important in explaining some IIT – for example, trade in perfectly homogeneous goods. But they cannot explain fully the recorded quantities of IIT, especially of trade in differentiated products.[10]

The search for an explanation of IIT has led to several attempts to formulate a theory of differentiated products. These include the works of Dixit and Norman (1980); Krugman (1979, 1980, 1981); Helpman (1981); Lancaster (1980, 1984). All the models offered by these writers make two basic assumptions. Firstly, it is assumed that consumers demand many varieties of a good and this variety comes from minor variations in the same basic good. Secondly, this demand for variety cannot be efficiently met locally because of economies of scale. The most efficient way of supplying the varieties demanded in a trading world is by specialization and subsequent two-way trade. There are differences in some of the models, either in terms of the specification of demand or in terms of the production structure. For example, in Krugman's models a consumer's utility is positively related to the number of varieties of manufactured goods and each variety is produced subject to increasing returns to scale. In Helpman's model however, each economy produces not only varieties of the manufactured good that are subject to increasing returns but also a commodity exhibiting constant returns to scale. In all the models product differentiation leads to imperfect competition, usually monopolistic competition where firms face downward sloping demand curves, and free entry to the industry competes profits down to normal levels.

In the models of differentiated goods there are additional gains to be made besides the usual benefits from exchange and specialization. They include those arising out of product diversity or those associated with dynamic benefits from scale economies. In the former case, these gains are important to the extent that consumers value variety, or because this allows production of more specialized intermediate inputs. In the latter, trade may lead to higher output levels of each variety, thereby reducing average resource use as well as prices. The theories of monopolistic competition and product differentiation imply that countries can benefit from international trade in several ways. Consumers are allowed a wider choice of products, greater productivity gains can be made as a result of specialization, and cost reductions realized through economies of scale.

Stewart (1984) states that the above benefits are, at present, being enjoyed mainly by Northern countries since they are the ones that engage in production on a large scale and manufacture differentiated goods. Given the particular features of the South however, these gains are not being realized by DCs although there exists potential for trade in differentiated goods. In many South countries, production is often undertaken on a small scale and characterized by high levels of X-inefficiency. Consumer variety is also quite limited. However, if resources are allocated more efficiently, producers can fully exploit economies of scale by expanding their size of plants and undertaking longer production runs. Consumers can also gain through increased access to a wider variety of goods, which are likely to be of a higher quality. In the long run, production and trade can be stimulated in goods that are more appropriate to Southern environments and income levels.

Summary

This chapter attempts to provide a theoretical basis for S–S trade by reviewing the main theories of international trade, and examining their implications for trade among DCs. It is found that with the exception of the simple version of the H–O theory, all existing theories provide useful insights into S–S trade. The Krueger–Deardorff extension of the H–O theory which investigates multilateral trade flows in manufactured goods and explores directional issues shows that differences in factor endowments among DCs could provide a strong basis for S–S trade. Although that model deals with only two factors of production, capital and labour, and makes no allowances for changes over time, the implications of the theory are far greater when viewed within a dynamic context and with a finer breakdown of capital. A DC that is relatively more endowed with human and physical capital for example could export human and physical capital intensive goods to another DC which is relatively less endowed with these factors. At the same time it could import more labour intensive goods from the latter DC which may be relatively more endowed with supplies of unskilled labour.

An analysis of the more 'modern' trade theories reveals that there exist several other bases for S–S trade. These include differences in technological advancement among DCs (neo-technology theory); scale economies and product differentiation (scale economy and monopolistic theories); and similarities in tastes (preference similarity theory). DCs which are more technologically advanced could export technology intensive goods to those which are not able to stimulate innovations, and the latter countries could export back to them goods which are fairly standardized. A basis also exists for trade where countries are able to enjoy scale economies, either as a result of their large market size or because of long production runs; and where consumers' demand for variety provide the incentive for the exchange of differentiated goods. Further, DCs with similar demand structures can engage in mutually beneficial trade by producing both capital and consumer goods which are appropriate to their income levels.

In terms of the potential gains from trade it is found that all countries could benefit from the types of trade suggested above. These gains include not only static ones such as access to wider markets and cost savings but also dynamic ones which are particularly important within a wider developmental context. These dynamic gains include skill accumulation and technological learning, scale economies, improvement in the terms of trade, the provision of goods which are more appropriate to Southern environments and income levels, and greater consumer variety.

Notes

1. See Ohlin (1933) for an exposition of the theory.
2. It must be pointed out that Ohlin's basic formulation included nine factors of production. Furthermore, it is logically expandable to a n factorial model. See Vanek (1968).
3. For a discussion of some of these tests and the methodological difficulties involved, see Stern (1975) and Deardorff (1982).
4. See Jones and Neary (1984) for a review of some of these approaches.
5. Ohlin himself, in his basic formulation, specifically mentions that factor quality and relative quantity can be and are altered over time. Implicitly this is a proto model for dynamic acquired comparative advantage.
6. Krueger (1977) states that the model can be applied to other numbers of countries and commodities.
7. Kiljunen's study (1985) on Finland (considered as a NIC) while not specifically testing the H–O theory does provide empirical evidence tending to confirm these hypotheses.
8. A third model which is essentially a simple version of the technology gap model is the North–South model developed by Krugman (1980).
9. See the later discussion in this chapter on the theories of monopolistic competition and product differentiation.
10. Recent evidence suggests that IIT is now becoming important in the trade of DCs. See Balassa (1979b) and Tharakhan (1984).

3 The growth, characteristics and scope for South–South trade

Introduction

Whereas trade among DCs constituted a relatively small portion of world trade until the mid-1960s, its growth has increased markedly in recent years. This development has prompted numerous enquiries into the growth, nature and composition of S–S trade. Further, the question as to whether the recent growth in S–S trade is temporary or whether there is scope for continuing expansions has been subject to discussion. All these issues are addressed in the present chapter. The trends and patterns of trade among DCs are first examined, including the commodity and geographical composition of trade. Throughout, comparisons are made with prevailing patterns of S–N/N–S trade. The types of goods traded among South countries are then examined in greater detail through an investigation of the factor content of S–S trade. This discussion is an important one since it raises some controversial issues regarding the differences between S–S and S–N trade, and the implications for the costs and benefits of trade. Finally, some quantitative estimates of the potential for S–S trade are examined and the main issues discussed in the chapter are summarized.

Trends and patterns of South–South trade

In analyzing the changes that have taken place in S–S trade over time, early trends in the trade of DCs are first discussed. Such a historical perspective is important in order to appreciate fully the magnitude and significance of changes that have occurred over time. Trends in the more recent period are subsequently analyzed, with detailed discussions on the commodity and geographic composition of S–S trade.

Early trends in the direction of DCs' trade

The pattern of DCs' trade prior to World War II and until the mid-1960s was very much influenced by the nature of existing colonial relationships. During the colonial period the trade of DCs was completely determined by the economic needs of the metropolitan countries. The *raison d'etre* of the colonies was to produce primary commodities and raw materials for export to the metropolitan countries. In turn the colonies obtained all their imports from the same source. This type of economic exchange gave rise to a strict N–S/S–N pattern of trade, and in general levels of trade among DCs remained very low.

The scanty data available on DCs' trade in the nineteenth century reveal that the ICs absorbed the bulk of DCs' exports throughout the period, and this increased over time although some countries/regions changed their relative shares. Figures presented by Hanson (1980) for these early years reveal that in 1840 some 73 per cent of exports from Asia, Africa and South America were directed to the ICs (Western Europe and North America). By the end of the century however, this proportion of S–N trade had decreased slightly to 70 per cent. Whereas the share of exports to North America and several Western European countries increased, that to the UK experienced a large decline – from 44 per cent in 1840 to 24 per cent in 1900. In fact, it was this latter development that contributed to the overall decline in DCs' exports to the ICs over the period.

Regarding trade among DCs, the fragmentary evidence available indicates that for most countries this element of trade was quite small. South America, for example, exported roughly eight per cent of its total exports to other DCs, while Africa and Central America directed even smaller proportions (Hanson, 1980). The Asian countries, however, recorded fairly high levels of intraregional trade. In 1840 Asia directed 32 per cent of its total exports to other DCs in the region, and although this figure declined to 30 per cent towards the middle of the century it rose to 37 per cent in 1900. The most important item in intra-Asian trade was opium, which was shipped mainly from British India to China. However, opium imports gradually came to a halt towards the end of the century[1] and were subsequently replaced by other export items, mainly cotton and rice. This led to a substantial decline in China's role as a major importer in the region. Singapore and other Strait Settlements countries quickly replaced it.

Intra-DC trade increased considerably in the post-World War II period, and this is reflected in Table 3.1 which provides data for the period 1938–65. The pre-1955 figures are not strictly comparable with those for subsequent years since they exclude the inter-territorial trade of East Africa, and include certain elements of trade which involve double counting such as petroleum re-exports and Singapore–Malaysian entrepôt trade. In the post-1955 figures appropriate adjustments have been made to the data. But besides the problems arising from the lack of strict comparability of data, the early 1950s cannot be

27

regarded as an appropriate base period from which to measure secular trends. For whereas the European countries' share of world trade declined sharply in the early 1950s as a consequence of World War II, the DCs' share of trade to the world and to other DCs rose accordingly.

Notwithstanding the above difficulties, some observations can be made on the overall features of DCs' trade over the period 1938–65. Measured as a percentage of world trade, trade among DCs declined from the peak attained in the early post-World War II years of 8.8 per cent to 4.1 per cent in 1965. The adjusted figures reveal an even greater decline to slightly less than three per cent. This trend is not surprising since the ICs' trade, and intra-European trade in particular, underwent large expansions from the late 1950s onwards. A more important observation from Table 3.1 is that the share of DCs' trade with respect to their own trade also showed a declining trend, although this decline was arrested somewhat in 1964. The adjusted share of DCs' intra-trade with respect to their overall exports fell from 16.7 per cent in 1955 to 15.8 per cent in 1965, and with respect to their total imports from 17.2 per cent to 15.3 per cent over the same period.[2] These developments are not surprising, for if the ICs' markets are growing faster than those of the DCs one would expect an increasingly larger share to be directed to the ICs' markets. By contrast, the share of intra-DC trade can be expected to decline.

It must be pointed out however, that whereas trade among DCs showed a general decline over the entire period, the decline in 1960–65 was less than in 1955–60. Whereas for example the unadjusted and adjusted shares of intra-DCs' exports in world exports fell by 1.4 per cent and 0.8 per cent respectively in 1955–60, the proportional declines in 1960–65 were 0.7 per cent and 0.2

Table 3.1
Trade among DCs: percentage share of world trade and of DCs' total trade, 1938–65[a]

Year	Share of world trade		Share of DCs' total exports		Share of world exports to DCs	
	Not adjusted	Adjusted	Not adjusted	Adjusted	Not adjusted	Adjusted
1938	5.5	..	21.7	..	25.2	..
1948	8.8	..	29.1	..	30.0	..
1955	6.2	3.9	24.3	16.7	25.6	17.2
1960	4.8	3.1	22.2	15.7	21.2	14.7
1964	4.3	3.0[b]	21.2	15.9[b]	20.8	15.6[b]
1965[b]	4.1	2.9	20.8	15.8	20.3	15.3

Source: UNCTAD (1972)

[a] Figures for the 1955–65 period include the inter-territorial trade of East Africa and are adjusted to eliminate double counting.
[b] estimated figures

per cent respectively. The relatively more favourable development in the later period may have been due to the rapid growth of Latin America's trade with other DCs during the 1960s. Latin America's exports to DCs faced a moderate decline over the 1955–60 period, but rose at an annual average rate of 9.7 per cent over 1960–65. This was the highest growth rate for all DC regions, including Western Asia which registered an annual growth rate of 8.2 per cent over the same period (UNCTAD, 1972).

Patterns of South–South/South–North trade: the post-1965 period

More comprehensive data are available on international trade flows for the post-1965 period and this permits a fairly detailed analysis of trade patterns. Over the period 1966–89 several important changes occurred in the world economy which led to shifts in the structure of world trade, including the direction of trade. One major development has been the rapid growth of the DCs and, in particular, the emergence of a small group of semi-industrial countries known as the NICs. A parallel development has been the increasing industrialization of many of the traditional, primary commodity exporting countries.

During the period 1950–70 the DCs as a group registered quite high annual growth rates, especially in terms of industrial production and compared with the ICs. In the 1965–70 period in particular, the DCs' annual growth rates of industrial production ranged between 6–10 per cent, while the ICs' record showed rates between 4–6 per cent.[3] Growth of industrialization in the Third World allowed the DCs to expand the volume of their exports greatly. But because the rate of growth of their exports was much slower than that of the ICs, this led to continuing decreases in their share of world exports. Table 3.2 shows that whereas Southern exports as a percentage of world exports was 21.05 per cent in 1966 this share dropped to 19.14 per cent in 1970. Declines were also registered in the proportion of DCs' exports to both the North and the South over the same period – from 16.4 per cent to 15.03 per cent and from 4.65 per cent to 4.11 per cent respectively.

From the early 1970s significant changes took place in respect of the relative importance of the various trade flows. The decline in the share of Southern exports in world trade was halted in 1973 as the price of oil, the major export commodity of the South, increased dramatically. This single important event gave S–S trade a strong stimulus, boosting exports from the oil-exporting DCs and also increasing the import capacity of this group. The ability of the South to absorb increasing amounts of exports was evidenced by an expansion in both N–S and S–S trade. Between 1973 and 1982 N–S exports as a proportion of world exports increased from 15.04 per cent to 18.62 per cent, whereas the share of S–S exports almost doubled, rising from 4.69 per cent to 8.79 per cent. In fact, throughout most of the period S–S trade was the most dynamic component of world trade.

Trends in the trade of ICs over the period 1966–82 differed markedly from those of the DCs. The share of Northern exports in world exports increased in the latter part of the 1960s and early 1970s (in contrast to the trend of Southern exports) and this increase was almost entirely attributable to a rapid expansion in N–N trade. The latter increased from 61.70 per cent in 1966 to 65.65 per cent in 1972. The N–S component, however, was systematically reduced over the period – from 17.25 per cent to 15.09 per cent. Increases in the share of Northern exports in world exports continued into the 1970s and early 1980s, although at a much slower rate. But N–N trade which was historically the most buoyant element of trade contracted in 1973–82. Its share declined from 64.03 per cent in 1973 to 51.99 per cent in 1982. N–S trade, on the other hand, fluctuated throughout the same period but its share moved upwards from 15.04 per cent in 1973 to 18.62 per cent in 1982.

Table 3.2
Direction of world exports, 1966–82 (current values/%)

Year	S–S	S–N	Total S	N–S	N–N	Total N
1966	4.65	16.40	21.05	17.25	61.70	78.95
1967	4.54	16.36	20.90	16.81	62.29	79.10
1968	4.43	15.98	20.41	16.56	63.03	79.59
1969	4.24	15.54	19.78	16.00	64.22	80.22
1970	4.11	15.03	19.14	15.64	65.22	80.86
1971	4.29	15.01	19.30	15.70	65.00	80.70
1972	4.32	14.94	19.26	15.09	65.65	80.74
1973	4.69	16.24	20.93	15.04	64.03	79.07
1974	6.56	22.83	29.38	15.61	55.01	70.62
1975	6.66	20.09	26.74	18.72	54.54	73.26
1976	6.86	21.49	28.36	17.42	54.22	71.64
1977	7.15	21.33	28.48	17.95	53.57	71.52
1978	6.40	19.32	25.72	18.66	55.62	74.28
1979	7.16	20.84	28.00	16.70	55.30	72.00
1980	8.06	22.84	30.91	17.07	52.02	69.09
1981	8.55	22.40	30.95	18.91	50.14	69.05
1982	8.79	20.60	29.39	18.62	51.99	70.61

Source: Ventura-Dias and Sorsa (1985)

In analyzing the structural changes in international trade over the period 1973–82, it is important to separate price and volume changes since the large increases in the price of oil may have obscured the underlying structural changes. An examination of the price and volume indices for intra-DC trade revealed that whereas the price index shot up by 576.3 points over the 1973–82 period the volume index increased by only 28.3 points.[4] These data indicate that a large part of the increase in S–S trade was on account of price rises. A more accurate picture can be obtained by considering trade shares in constant $US 1983 (Ventura-Dias, 1989). These data reveal that in real terms the share of S–S exports increased throughout most of the oil boom period. It rose from 6.66 per cent in 1973 to 7.12 per cent in 1980. By contrast, both the share of Southern exports in world exports and the share of S–N exports in world exports fell over the same period. The former fell from 37.82 per cent to 30.86 per cent, whereas the latter declined from 31.16 per cent to 23.74 per cent. Despite the fact that exports from the South represented a declining share of world trade during the period 1973–80, S–S exports continued to grow relative to S–N exports.

The rising trends in S–S trade during the 1970s gave rise to great optimism regarding the future growth of S–S trade, and the notion that such shifts in world trade may become permanent. However the 1980s witnessed a dramatic reversal of these trends. There have been sharp declines in the growth of world trade, and with these S–S trade has largely fallen, or at best stagnated. Its share in world trade declined from 7.4 per cent in 1983 to 5.4 per cent in 1988 (Table 3.3). The fall is less dramatic when fuels are excluded (from 4.7 per cent in 1983 to 4 per cent in 1987) but the general trend is the same. These figures are based on current prices and in the light of the general fall in commodity prices and depreciation of the dollar in the first half of the 1980s, they have to be interpreted with caution. However, according to UNCTAD (1989b) even when these factors are taken into account, the general trend of a fall in S–S trade is not altered significantly. The post-1985 figures show continuing declines in S–S trade.

The drastic fall in S–S trade must be analyzed within the context of developments in the world economy which have adversely affected the economic performance of the DCs, and hence their ability to trade with other DCs. Decreasing world demand and prices for many raw materials in the 1980s, coupled with increasing protectionism in the ICs, have led to a

Table 3.3
The relative importance of DC intra-trade, 1983–88 (%)

	Share of trade among DCs					
	Including fuels			Excluding fuels		
Year	World trade	Total exports of DCs	Total imports of DCs	World trade	Total exports of DCs	Total imports of DCs
1983	7.4	29.7	30.4	4.7	30.0	18.6
1984	7.0	28.3	30.3	4.6	28.2	19.6
1985	7.0	29.1	31.8	4.2	26.8	19.1
1986	5.7	27.6	28.8	4.0	25.4	19.2
1987	5.3	26.4	26.3	4.0	24.7	20.1
1988	5.4	27.4	26.2	-	-	-

Source: UNCTAD (1990a)

31

contraction of export earnings in the majority of DCs. Increases in world interest rates and contraction of commercial credits have imposed additional burdens on them. Whereas the volume of DCs' exports grew by 25.9 per cent in 1970–80, it grew by 0.7 per cent in 1980–89.

Despite the sluggish growth of the DCs in recent years however, and the decline in S–S export shares, the DCs have continued to increase their shares of DCs' import markets. The share of DCs' non-fuel exports in other DCs' import markets rose from 18.6 per cent in 1983 to 20.1 per cent in 1987. This trend illustrates the underlying potential for the growth of S–S trade.

The commodity composition of South–South trade

Fuel has always dominated S–S trade and although it continues to be the single largest traded item among DCs, its role has declined over time. In 1970 it accounted for roughly three-quarters of the real value of S–S trade, but in recent years it has fallen to one half (Ventura-Dias, 1989). By contrast, manufactured goods have accounted for a steadily increasing share of S–S trade and currently represent the most dynamic component of such trade. This latter trend can be best observed by considering the non-fuel exports of DCs.

Table 3.4 shows that there has been a large shift away from trade in primary products and a movement towards manufactures. Whereas in 1960 food and agricultural raw materials accounted for more than a half of S–S non-fuel exports, in 1986 this share fell to a little over one fourth. Consistent declines have been recorded in both categories over time. The share of trade in manufactures rose rapidly over the period, from 26.9 per cent to 62.6 per cent. Trade in machinery and transport equipment showed the largest gains, for its share more than quadrupled over time – it increased from 3.6 per cent in 1960 to 22.7 per cent in 1986. With the exception of non-ferrous metals, all categories of manufactured goods, including chemicals, iron and steel and other manufactures, experienced large increases.

The trend towards an increasing share of manufactured goods in S–S trade is a reflection of a more general one in the trade of DCs. The manufacturing share in S–S non-fuel exports rose from 26.9 per cent in 1960 to 62.6 per cent in 1986; and that in the DCs' non-fuel exports to all destinations from 12 per cent to 60.8 per cent over the same period (UNCTAD, 1989a). The fact that the increase has been less rapid for S–S trade than for trade to the world implies that the DCs have been exporting declining proportions of their manufactured products to the South. It has been estimated that whereas in 1960 some 43 per cent of the DCs' manufactured exports were to the South, by 1986 this proportion had fallen to 26 per cent (UNCTAD, 1989a). The decline in S–S manufacturing shares was most pronounced during the 1980s, reflecting the general stagnation and decline of the DCs' import markets. However, it must be pointed out that the increasingly large amounts of manufactured goods exported to the ICs is a reflection of the DCs' growing international competitiveness over time.

Table 3.4
The product structure of S–S trade, 1960–86
(non-fuel exports/%)

Product Group	1960	1965	1970	1975	1980	1985	1986
Food items	43.2	38.4	30.8	32.7	24.3	22.6	20.2
Agricultural raw materials	22.9	14.5	16.5	9.8	9.1	6.1	6.7
Crude fertilizers	..	2.2	2.9	2.3	2.4	2.4	2.7
Chemicals	..	4.3	5.8	7.4	7.2	8.4	9.6
Iron and steel	..	1.9	3.7	2.8	3.3	4.6	4.2
Non-ferrous metals	..	2.5	3.2	2.3	3.0	2.4	2.5
Machinery and transport equipment	3.6	5.0	8.9	15.3	19.9	22.7	22.7
Other manufactures	..	18.2	27.1	26.7	28.9	27.2	30.3
Total manufactures	*26.9*	*31.5*	*41.8*	*49.4*	*55.9*	*58.2*	*62.6*

Source: UNCTAD (1989a)

An important observation on the product composition of DCs' manufactured exports is that whereas goods exported to other DCs consists of a relatively large proportion of skill intensive items, those exported to the ICs are mainly labour intensive. GATT estimated that in 1988 roughly 42 per cent of the DCs' exports to the ICs consisted of labour intensive products such as textiles, clothing and other consumer items. These products accounted for only 28 per cent of intra-DC trade, while other skill intensive ones such as chemicals and other semi-manufactures accounted for roughly the same proportion (GATT, 1990). This pattern of trade implies that S–S trade has an important role to play in raising the level of human capital development in the DCs.

The geographic structure of South–South trade

Several features are usually emphasized in connection with the geographic structure of S–S trade: (a) the dominant position of the South and Southeast Asian countries; (b) the strong intraregional focus; (c) the rapid growth of interregional trade, especially during the 1970s; and (d) the concentration of trade among a small group of countries.

Table 3.5 shows that since 1965 the South and Southeast Asian countries have accounted for the largest proportion of S–S trade, their contribution ranging between 50–60 per cent of total non-fuel trade over the period 1965–86. They have been particularly important in manufactures trade (including machinery and transport equipment) as well as in trade in agricultural materials. In 1986 they accounted for roughly 70 per cent of non-fuel exports in each of these categories. By contrast, Africa, which has suffered large declines in all categories of its exports since 1970, accounted for the smallest share of S–S

33

Table 3.5
Shares of major geographical regions in S–S exports, major product groups, 1965–86 (%)

	Year	Total non fuels	Food	Agri--cultural materials	Manufactures Total	Machinery and transport equipment	Other Manufactures
Latin	1965	21.8	26.4	23.4	20.4	21.9	15.1
America	1970	26.2	31.5	20.4	22.7	26.1	17.4
	1975	28.7	36.1	18.6	25.1	30.7	18.2
	1980	26.3	35.1	15.5	22.7	25.8	17.4
	1986	20.1	33.4	17.0	14.0	14.1	9.3
Africa	1965	12.7	17.2	14.3	12.0	7.7	12.7
	1970	14.6	18.2	15.9	11.6	4.5	15.2
	1975	9.5	14.2	9.8	4.8	2.5	5.2
	1980	5.6	10.9	6.0	2.7	1.0	2.5
	1986	5.3	8.6	10.2	3.6	1.6	3.3
West Asia	1965	6.0	8.3	5.0	6.3	7.7	6.3
	1970	7.1	8.7	3.9	7.2	6.5	7.0
	1975	9.8	6.3	5.8	12.7	11.2	11.5
	1980	8.7	7.7	3.4	10.3	11.2	9.3
	1986	11.4	11.2	6.9	13.3	10.7	15.0
South and	1965	59.2	47.9	57.4	61.2	62.3	65.8
Southeast	1970	49.5	41.1	59.1	53.3	48.8	58.2
Asia	1975	48.8	42.7	64.0	52.0	45.2	62.4
	1980	59.1	45.6	74.7	64.3	61.9	70.7
	1986	60.5	44.2	70.6	68.2	69.7	75.0
Intra-	1965	76.2	75.0	74.0	72.7	89.2	65.1
regional	1970	69.4	69.7	66.6	69.7	69.3	67.6
	1975	63.3	54.9	70.0	67.2	68.9	64.6
	1980	65.4	58.9	75.2	66.2	71.2	60.3
	1986	66.4	59.1	75.0	70.3	73.5	67.1
Inter-	1965	23.8	25.0	26.0	27.3	10.8	34.9
regional	1970	30.6	30.3	33.4	30.4	30.8	32.4
	1975	36.7	45.1	30.0	32.8	31.1	36.2
	1980	34.6	41.2	24.8	33.8	28.8	39.7
	1986	33.6	40.9	25.0	29.7	26.5	32.9

Source: UNCTAD (1989a)

non-fuel exports in 1986 (5.3 per cent). The Latin American region also showed marked decreases in its exports to the South, especially in the manufactures category and in the post-1975 period. As a result, its share in S–S non-fuel exports dropped from 28.7 per cent in 1975 to 20.1 per cent in 1986. The West Asian countries accounted for 11.4 per cent of total non-fuel exports in 1986, but unlike the African and Latin American countries they increased their shares in all major categories over time. This was especially for manufactures, the share of which more than doubled over the 1965–86 period: from 6.3 per cent in 1965 to 15.0 per cent. A large part of this increase was due to expansions in chemical export shares which rose from 4.9 per cent in 1965 to 13.9 per cent in 1986 (UNCTAD, 1989a).

By far the major part of S–S trade is accounted for by trade within regions, that is, intraregional trade. In 1986 it accounted for 66.4 per cent of total non-fuel S–S trade, compared with 33.6 per cent for interregional trade or trade between regions. Despite the minor position of interregional trade in S–S trade however, this element of trade represented a dynamic component during the 1970s, rising from 30.6 per cent of non-fuel S–S exports in 1970 to 34.6 per cent in 1980. This is in contrast to intraregional trade which declined from 69.4 per cent to 65.4 per cent over the same period.

The importance of exporting to the South varies considerably from region to region. In 1987 the West Asian countries directed 46.8 per cent of their non-fuel exports to other DCs, the largest proportion recorded among all regions. The most dynamic DC exporters, those in the South and Southeast region, sent only 25.1 per cent of their non-fuel exports to other DCs; while corresponding shares for Latin America and Africa were 21.3 per cent and 18.4 per cent respectively (Table 3.6). In general, Southern markets appeared to be relatively more important to DCs during 1970–80 than in recent years. Undoubtedly, the buoyancy of regional integration schemes during the 1970s contributed to the rapid growth of S–S trade in the earlier years. However, the world recession in 1982 and debt and payment crises in the Third World led to a collapse of most of the regional integration groupings in the post-1982 period, and this in turn affected S–S trade considerably. It has been estimated that between 1981 and 1985 alone, the intra-trade of ALADI, the ANDEAN Group, CACM and CEAO fell by over 20 per cent, and that of ECOWAS and UDEAC by over 40 per cent. Consequently in 1982–87 the shares of S–S non-fuel exports fell in all regions – by roughly 18 per cent for West Asia, 8 per cent for South and Southeast Asia, 5 per cent for Africa and 3 per cent for Latin America.

Table 3.6
The relative importance of exports to DCs in total non-fuel exports of individual regions, 1970–87 (%)

Year	Latin America	Africa	West Asia	South and Southeast Asia
1970	14.8	12.5	31.3	27.8
1975	21.4	16.6	47.8	31.7
1980	26.5	15.9	47.2	33.4
1982	24.7	23.4	64.3	33.2
1985	21.3	21.3	55.0	28.1
1987	21.3	18.4	46.8	25.1

Source: UNCTAD (1990a)

Besides its concentration in particular regions, S–S trade is also concentrated among a handful of countries. Table 3.7 shows that in 1975–79, the period of buoyant growth in S–S trade, ten countries accounted for almost three-fifths of S–S non-fuel trade. The situation was much the same for trade in manufactures, although the concentration was more marked on the export side than on the import one. The ten major exporters of manufactures accounted for 68.6 per cent of total S–S manufactured exports, whereas the ten main importers accounted for 48.1 per cent of them. Many of the top importing countries were also major exporting ones. Five of them were from the South and Southeast Asian region (Singapore, Indonesia, Malaysia, South Korea and India); two from Latin America (Brazil and Argentina); and one from Europe (Yugoslavia).

Table 3.7
Major importers and exporters in S–S trade, 1975–79 (%)

Importer	Share of of all non-fuel products	Share of manufac- tures	Exporter	Share of all non-fuel products	Share of manufac- tures
1 Saudi Arabia	10.7	15.7	1 Brazil	11.4	11.9
2 Indonesia	9.7	2.9	2 Singapore	10.2	12.0
3 Singapore	8.8	5.7	3 South Korea	8.0	13.8
4 Brazil	7.0	7.0	4 Argentina	7.6	5.8
5 South Korea	4.2	1.6	5 India	7.1	8.0
6 Venezuela	3.9	4.8	6 Malaysia	6.8	3.1
7 Argentina	3.6	3.5	7 Thailand	4.3	1.5
8 Malaysia	3.4	3.1	8 Indonesia	4.0	1.2
9 India	3.3	2.6	9 Yugoslavia	3.8	5.9
10 Yugoslavia	3.1	1.2	10 Kuwait	3.2	5.4
Total	*57.7*	*48.1*	*Total*	*57.4*	*68.6*

Source: Thomas (1988)

Ventura-Dias (1989) has pointed out that the concentration in S–S trade has been no greater than in N–S trade. Whereas the share of the ten largest Southern exporters accounted for 65 per cent of the value of total S–S exports in 1979, the share of the ten largest exporters in N–S trade accounted for 90 per cent in the same year. The concentration of countries in N–S trade appears to be greater when one considers that there are roughly 25 countries in the ICs' group and more than 120 countries in the DCs' one. But whereas S–S trade is highly concentrated among a few countries, it should be noted that the number of DCs participating in this trade has grown considerably over time. Thomas (1988) found that between the periods 1965–69 and 1975–79, about three-quarters of all DCs had increased the number of DC destinations to which they exported, or the number from which they imported. Latin America had the largest proportion of countries with an increased number of DC export partners, while for non-fuel imports the corresponding proportion was highest in Asia.

The factor characteristics of South–South trade

In the above discussion on the composition of trade it was noted that not only do the goods traded among DCs cover a wide range, but they are different from those traded with the North. This latter observation has led to numerous enquiries regarding the characteristics of S–S versus S–N trade. Is S–S trade more capital intensive than S–N trade? Is it more technology intensive? Does it provide opportunities for reaping economies of scale, and is it characterized by product differentiation? These questions are very important because of their implications for the costs and benefits of trade, and for policy formulation. For example, if S–S trade is found to be more capital intensive than S–N trade this may have implications for employment generation in DCs. On the other hand, if it is more skill intensive there may be benefits in terms of learning and skill accumulation. In such a case Third World governments may wish to implement policies to encourage S–S trade, given the important role of technology in development.

A number of studies have explored the above issues, and although their results are not conclusive they provide interesting insights into the nature of S–S trade. These studies span a wide range and utilize different theoretical frameworks. Some are country-specific while others focus on large groups of countries; and some address the issue in an indirect way while others give specific attention to it. The majority of studies have utilized either a simple 2 x 2 H–O framework or relied upon the extended version of the H–O theory; while others have used frameworks incorporating more 'dynamic' factors such as scale economies, product differentiation or technology. These studies are all reviewed below according to the type of theoretical framework used. Throughout, the emphasis is on the method of investigation and on the general findings.

Studies conducted within a H–O framework

Many early studies which examined the characteristics of S–S trade used a simple 2 x 2 H–O framework, with capital and labour as the only factors of production. These include Diaz-Alejandro (1974), Krueger (1978) and Havrylyshyn and Wolf (1981). Several other works include a finer breakdown of capital: Tyler (1972), Richards-Loup (1984) and Havrylyshyn (1985). Each group of studies will be reviewed in turn.

The simple 2 x 2 H–O framework. Diaz-Alejandro's (1974) work on intra-Latin American trade was one of the earliest to investigate the characteristics of DC trade. Diaz-Alejandro observed that the bundle of goods exported from Latin America to the rest of the world appeared to include mainly 'simple' products such as cotton, leather and textiles; while exports to other Latin American countries consisted of more 'sophisticated' exports like pharmaceutical products and petrochemicals. He questioned the economic benefits to be derived from the latter type of trade on the grounds that it was highly capital and import intensive. In such a case S–S trade was considered to have adverse employment effects and lead to balance of payments problems.

In order to give support to his contention, Diaz-Alejandro tested the capital intensity of Colombian 'minor' exports to LAFTA countries. The analysis considered exports of 62 industries (excluding coffee and crude petroleum) for the year 1969. A simple regression equation was tested relating the share of Colombian exports to LAFTA countries to a measure of capital intensity. K-L ratios from the USA were used for the capital intensity variable, on the assumption that factor intensities did not differ significantly across countries. The results showed a strong, positive correlation between LAFTA shares and capital intensity. This finding therefore implied that S–S trade was highly capital intensive.

Diaz-Alejandro's study was quite limited in scope. Capital was the only variable considered and tests were conducted for S–S trade alone. Krueger's (1978) study represented an improvement over Diaz-Alejandro's since it compared the factor content of S–S trade with that of S–N trade. In this case however, labour was the only variable considered since Krueger was mainly concerned with evaluating the employment implications of alternative trade strategies. Krueger first computed the labour content of trade per unit of domestic value added in domestic production of tradables for 11 DCs, and compared the results for exports with those for import substitutes. The countries considered were Brazil, Chile, Colombia, Indonesia, Korea, Ivory Coast, Kenya, Pakistan, Thailand, Tunisia and Uruguay. Her findings were in line with the broad predictions of the H–O model. That is, exports were more labour intensive than import competing industries. The differential in labour requirements between export and import competing industries was quite marked – almost 2 : 1 in Thailand, Columbia and Indonesia.

The second step in Krueger's analysis was to examine the differentials in labour intensity between exports to ICs and those to other DCs. This was done for a subset of four countries – Thailand, Uruguay, Chile and Kenya. In each case it was found that the labour requirements for exports to ICs were higher than those for intra-DC trade. For example, it was estimated that Uruguay's exports to ICs required 84 per cent more labour per unit of domestic value added than exports to other DCs. In other words, S–N trade was found to be more labour intensive than S–S trade. Based on this finding Krueger concluded that there seemed to be few prospects for trade among DCs.

Whereas investigations into the characteristics of S–S trade were not a focal point of the above studies, Havrylyshyn and Wolf (H–W)'s (1981) study set out to examine specifically the factor intensity of S–S/S–N trade. Their research attempted to test the hypothesis that S–S exports are more capital intensive than S–N exports. H–W used a similar method to Krueger (1978) and calculated the direct K-L ratios for bundles of NIC exports to ICs and to other DCs. The study was confined to manufactured exports (SITC 5 to 8 minus 68) in 1977. NIC exports were subdivided into four categories: (a) principal IC markets (80 per cent or more of exports to the North); (b) secondary IC markets (60–80 per cent of exports to the North); (c) principal DC markets (50 per cent or more of exports to the South); and (d) secondary DC markets (30–50 per cent of exports to the South). The results of the investigation revealed that the K-L ratio of NIC exports to DCs was $45,347. This was substantially higher than for exports to ICs ($25,407) and for exports to all destinations ($30,664). Further, the disparity was even greater when comparisons were made for exports to principal DC markets ($53,589) and exports to principal IC markets ($15,075). From this analysis, H–W concluded that S–S trade was more capital intensive than S–N trade.

The extended H–O framework.   The studies in this group include an early one by Tyler (1972), and more comprehensive investigations by Richards-Loup (1984) and Havrylyshyn (1985).

In studying the pattern of Brazil's trade in manufactures, Tyler observed that despite the relative scarcity of skills in Brazil, its manufactured exports appeared to be highly skill intensive. It was in search for an explanation of this observed paradox that Tyler turned his attention towards an investigation of the destination of Brazil's manufactured exports. The specific enquiry was to determine whether Brazil's manufactured exports to members of LAFTA and to all DCs were more skill intensive than its exports to ICs. Tyler used an industrial cross-section of 1968 data, and employed regression analysis relating a measure of geographical export performance to indices of skill intensity. The dependent variable was each industry's share of manufactured exports to LAFTA countries, ICs and DCs respectively, expressed as percentages of the sum of Brazil's industrial exports to the particular market concerned. The independent variable was a measure of skill intensity as reflected by (a) a labour skill index calculated from US data, and (b) a labour skill index utilizing Brazilian data. The number of industries considered was 46 in the case of measure (a) and 21 in the case of measure (b).

Tyler's study showed that the export skill intensity index for Brazil's industrial exports to LAFTA was higher (0.406) than for its exports to the world (0.340) and to the ICs (0.283). Further, the regression equations dealing with exports to the ICs showed a negative correlation between exports and skill intensity, while the opposite results were obtained for exports to both LAFTA and the DCs. Tyler's analysis therefore implied that S–S trade was more skill intensive than S–N trade.

The greater skill intensity of S–S trade was also highlighted in more comprehensive studies undertaken by Richards-Loup (1984) and Havrylyshyn (1985). Richards-Loup undertook an empirical test of the extended H–O theory developed by Deardorff and Krueger which predicts that in a three-way classification of countries, middle level countries such as the NICs will tend to export their labour intensive manufactures upstream to the ICs, and their capital intensive manufactures downstream to the DCs. Richards-Loup analyzed the 1978 manufactures trade of ten NICs, considering three factors – human capital, physical capital and labour, comparing their trade with three groups of ICs and with five groups of DCs. The methodology consisted of a two step regression procedure, where the first step linked indexes by direction of export and import specialization and of export comparative advantage, respectively with product characteristics (factor intensities and industrial structure). At the second stage the coefficients obtained from the first step regression were correlated with the ratios of NIC-country group factor endowments. Japanese industrial coefficients were used on the assumption that the Japanese industrial structure closely resembled that of the NICs.

Richards-Loup's study showed that not only did the NICs' exports to other DCs contain more physical capital than their exports to the ICs, but they were also more human capital intensive. According to her, 'the results which most clearly substantiated the extended theory were obtained from the export and import specialization regressions including estimators of human capital'. In other words, not only was S–S trade more capital-intensive than N–S trade, but it was also more skill intensive.

Among all the studies on the factor characteristics of S–S trade, the Havrylyshyn (1985) study covered the largest number of countries – 45 DCs. Working within a three-factor framework of human capital, physical capital and unskilled labour, Havrylyshyn first of all demonstrated that the basic factor endowment theory adequately explained the DCs' trade patterns. This was done by applying a test of the H–O model (the factor content version) to the sample of 45 DCs for selected years: 1963, 1968, 1973 and 1978. He then examined the relative factor content of trade to different destinations. A summary of his findings for exports is presented in Table 3.8.

One major finding was that exports to the DCs contained more physical and human capital than exports to the ICs. For example, in 1963 and 1978 the physical capital to labour ratios for exports to ICs were 3.75 and 4.08 respectively, whereas the corresponding ratios for exports to DCs were 4.34 and 5.14. Similarly, the human capital to labour ratios for exports to ICs in 1963 and 1978 were 1.98 and 2.62 respectively, compared with 2.62 and 3.17 for exports to DCs. This pattern was observed for the majority of countries studied, with reversals occurring in only 19 per cent of the cases for physical capital and 15 per cent for human capital. The broad conclusion of Havrylyshyn's study was that S–S trade was both more physical and human capital intensive than S–N trade.

Table 3.8
Relative factor content of selected DCs' exports, by
destination: 1963, 1968, 1973 and 1978

Year		DCs	ICs	ICs/DCs
1963				
	PKL	4.34	3.75	1.15
	HKL	2.62	1.98	1.32
1968				
	PKL	4.78	4.13	1.15
	HKL	2.83	2.29	1.24
1973				
	PKL	5.14	4.08	1.26
	HKL	3.17	2.62	1.21
1978				
	PKL	5.14	4.08	1.26
	HKL	3.17	2.62	1.21

Source: Havrylyshyn (1985)

Note: PKL – physical capital to labour ratio
HKL – human capital to labour ratio

Studies utilizing other frameworks

Whereas the above studies focused on the factor intensity of trade, the works of Amsden (1980), Lall (1985b), Havrylyshyn and Civan (1985) and Lall, Ray and Ghosh (1989) considered some of the more dynamic factors in S–S trade such as technology, scale economies and product differentiation.

Amsden (1980) examined the trading patterns of ten DCs whose exports of manufactures in 1973 accounted for 70 per cent of S–S trade. They included four LAFTA members (Argentina, Brazil, Colombia and Mexico) and six Asian countries (Hong Kong, Singapore, Republic of Korea, India, Pakistan and Thailand). The study was restricted to trade in manufactures (SITC 5 to 8 minus 68), and data were collected for 93 industries. A cross-section regression equation was estimated, with the dependent variable as the ratio of S–S exports by product category to the ratio of S–N exports. The explanatory variables included physical capital intensity (stock and flow measures), two measures of skill (average wage and ratio of technical, scientific and professional employees), a measure of natural resource intensity and one of scale economies. The results of the equation revealed that, for most of the ten countries considered, only skill intensity was statistically significant. The natural resource and scale economy variables performed poorly and physical

41

capital intensity, though positively related, failed to show statistical significance. There were few differences in the export behaviour between the Asian and Latin American countries. Amsden concluded from her study that whereas capital intensity was not all that different in S–N and S–S exports, skill intensity was more important in S–S exports than S–N ones.

Lall's study (1985b) on the pattern of Indian manufactured exports investigated the importance of specific kinds of skills in exports to different destinations. The previous studies regarded skills as a factor input in its aggregate form, but Lall suggested that different types of skills should be regarded as different factor inputs, for S–S trade may embody different kinds of skills compared to S–N trade. Eight skill categories were constructed for the analysis: (a) engineers, architects and surveyors; (b) all technical workers; (c) all administrative, executive and managerial workers; (d) all sales workers; (e) all metal workers; (f) all chemical workers; (g) testers and packers; and (h) all skilled and unskilled production workers. In addition to the above, several other explanatory variables were used – two measures of capital (stock and flow measures), one to capture overall skill differences (average wage) and one for scale (value added per factory). The dependent variables measuring export performance were: (a) total exports of each industry as a percentage of total industrial exports, (b) exports of each industry to ICs as a percentage of total industrial exports to that destination, and (c) exports of each industry to DCs as a percentage of total industrial exports to DCs. The export performance variables were calculated for two periods, 1973–74 and 1977–78, each covering two years in order to reduce the impact of erratic fluctuations in exports.

The results of Lall's study are interesting. The capital intensity variable (stock measure) in all instances had negative signs and were almost always significant.[5] This implied that India had a comparative advantage in labour intensive industries. But the results did not differ much according to destination, except in the earlier period exports to DCs were slightly more capital intensive than exports to ICs, and in the latter period, slightly less capital intensive. The general skill variable on the other hand had a positive, significant effect on exports to ICs, and none on exports to DCs in 1973–74, although in 1977–78 the situation was reversed. The scale factor was significant and positive in the first period for exports to DCs only, but did not achieve statistical significance in any of the equations for the latter period. The variables capturing different types of skills did not perform very well. In fact, only metal working skills showed a strong, positive statistical effect in respect of DC exports, and for only 1977–78. Lall's broad conclusion, based on 1977–1978 data, was that exports to the South were more skill and labour intensive than to the North, and metal working skills in particular, appeared to be more important in exports to the South.

The study by Lall, Ray and Ghosh (1989) is the most comprehensive in terms of the range of variables considered. Four measures of export performance were regressed upon various indexes of industry characteristics. The dependent variables included three RCA measures (for manufactured exports to the world, to the North and to the South) and a variable reflecting the propensity of each country to export to the South (PS). The independent variables were capital intensity (flow measure), skill (wages per production worker and the proportion of non-production workers in the total work force), technology (R & D per unit of sales), scale (value added per establishment), product differentiation (the ratio of advertising to total sales), concentration (concentration levels in each sector), natural resources and non-traditional exports. The analysis was undertaken for 14 DCs – Argentina, Brazil, Colombia, Egypt, Hong Kong, India, Malaysia, Mexico, Pakistan, Philippines, Singapore, South Korea, Taiwan and Yugoslavia. Data were collected for 100 manufactured products for 1963, 1970 and 1980.

The results obtained by Lall, Ray and Ghosh were generally quite poor, since almost all the variables failed to show any statistical significance. For example, the technology variable did not exert much influence on the sample's export performance index in the expected, negative direction – and where it did, it had a positive sign even in exports to the North. This result was also obtained for the PS regression. Aside from the non-traditional exports variable which in many respects overlapped with other industry variables, the only other variable which performed well was skills. In this case the PS analysis confirmed that exports to the South were more skill intensive than to the North.

One final study should be mentioned which attempted to measure the extent of intra-industry trade (IIT) in S–S and S–N trade (Havrylyshyn and Civan, 1985). IIT essentially reflects similarity of factor endowments between trading partners, a greater diversity of production and greater differentiation in consumer demand and supply. Therefore, one would expect IIT to be lower in the total trade of DCs as opposed to the ICs' trade, but higher in S–S trade compared with S–N trade. Some of these expectations were confirmed in the study by Havrylyshyn and Civan which examined the non-fuel manufactured trade of 44 DCs, including 13 NICs and 18 ICs, for the years 1968 and 1978. A summary of the results of the study is provided in Table 3.9.

As expected, IIT for ICs in general, is much higher (58.9 per cent) than for DCs as a whole (22.6 per cent), and the latter is lower than IIT between DCs (26.4 per cent). When the trade of DCs is disaggregated, it is seen that IIT between the non-NICs and the DC group (21.5 per cent) is higher than the non-NICs' trade with the world (14.5 per cent). This pattern reflects the fact that DCs tend to be more similar to each other than to ICs, and their intra-trade therefore contains more IIT compared with their trade with the ICs.

The case of NIC trade appeared to be somewhat paradoxical. Contrary to expectations, IIT for intra-NIC trade was low (30.5 per cent), compared to IIT for the NIC-DC group (38.0 per cent) and for NIC-world trade (42 per cent). However, it was higher than non-NIC IIT with the DCs. Further, a closer examination of NIC trade revealed that whereas the East Asian NICs had high levels of IIT with the world, the Latin American NICs had high levels of IIT among themselves, and quite low levels with the rest of the world. This led to the implication that more inward looking countries and those which are members of regional integration agreements tend to have higher levels of IIT. Such simple correlations cannot be made however, for, as pointed out by the authors, because of the complexity of factors that impact upon trading patterns it is difficult to separate the influences of trade agreements and trade regimes.

Table 3.9
Intra-industry trade of ICs and DCs, 1978 (%)

Country groupings	Total trade	Trade with DCs only	Trade with NICs only
ICs	58.9	-	-
DCs	22.6	26.4	-
NICs	42.0	38.0	30.5
Non-NIC DCs	14.5	21.5	-

Source: Havrylyshyn and Civan (1985)

It is difficult to draw firm conclusions from the range of studies discussed above, given the varying frameworks used and scope of analyses undertaken in terms of countries, variables and time periods. The early studies, for example, were far too limited to enable generalizations. Tyler's study tested for skill intensity alone, while the framework used by Krueger and Diaz-Alejandro in which capital and labour were the only determinants of trade was far too simple. The later studies which incorporated more variables into their analyses also had their shortcomings. In particular, the study by Amsden (1980) contained numerous statistical problems which affected the validity of their findings. With reference to Amsden's study, Sabolo (1983) noted:

> From our point of view, the mediocrity of the results is mainly caused by a technological weakness in the analysis (poor quality statistics, poor statistical identification of the independent economic variables, too many variables compared with the degrees of freedom of the equation, inter-correlation between the variables) on which we shall not dwell (p. 603).

Lall's study also faced similar problems, especially high levels of multicollinearity among the occupational skill variables. On the whole, attempts to incorporate dynamic factors into the analysis did not yield good results.

There is one important point that emerged from the above studies however, which must be stressed in view of its implications for policy formulation. This is that although many of the studies produced conflicting results on the physical capital intensity variable, there seemed to be general agreement on the human capital variable. That is, *all of the studies that tested for skill intensity found that S–S trade was more skill intensive than S–N trade.* This finding implies that S–S trade has special development promoting properties for it can assist in developing the human resource potential of the DCs.

44

Scope for South–South trade

Given the important role of S–S trade in DCs' growth, and in the context of trade liberalization in general, what potential exists for such trade? More specifically, what types of trade can be fruitfully explored, what categories of goods traded and which countries can stimulate such trade? These questions can be answered by drawing upon our earlier theoretical discussion, taking into consideration the special features of the South, and by examining the results of one study which attempted to quantify the potential for S–S trade.

The DCs which constitute the South are a diverse group of countries at different levels of development. On the one hand there are the NICs which are regarded as semi-industrial countries. Being the most developed of the group, they are capable of producing a wide variety of manufactured goods, including capital goods, and they have substantial technological and managerial expertise. On the other hand, there is the group of oil rich countries which in relative terms are capital rich and have considerable purchasing power, but generally lack skilled and unskilled labour. There is a third group of countries which are among the least developed in the South. These countries are mainly primary product exporters with small domestic markets and limited industrial experience. It is often held that the heterogeneous nature of the South poses problems for the South in so far as the coordination of their long term interests are concerned. But it is precisely this heterogeneity which can create and expand the possibilities for S–S trade.

Our theoretical discussion suggested that DCs can stimulate and benefit from all types of trade in the same way as the North countries. Hence the more industrialized countries which are at similar levels of development such as the NICs can engage in an intra-industry type of trade. These countries with their well developed manufacturing sectors can explore trade in a variety of areas. For example, countries can use their resources more efficiently by specializing in differentiated final goods and exchanging them, thereby raising levels of productivity and exploiting economies of scale. There is also scope for intra-industry trade between the NICs and other DCs in the South. The manufacture of a product could be vertically integrated in such a way that the labour abundant countries can undertake the labour intensive part of production, whereas the NICs can specialize in the skill intensive end of the process. Third World TNCs have an important role in the organization of this type of trade.

Possibilities also exist for H–O type trade between countries which have different factor endowments and are at different levels of development. Some of the NICs (e.g. Singapore) are resource poor and require major raw materials and primary products. The oil rich and other DCs could supply these products to them. Lall (1985a) suggests that S–S trade can also encourage the latter countries to participate in the processing of their own raw materials, and facilitate trade in resource based manufactures. Further, as the NICs move up the ladder of comparative advantage and begin to export more sophisticated

45

manufactured goods, there will appear potential for the import of simple, labour intensive manufactures. The less developed countries of the group with abundant supplies of labour can then move towards export of these products.

In exchange for primary products, labour intensive and resource based manufactures, the NICs can supply capital goods and technology to other DCs. Substantial evidence now exists that confirm the growing technological competence of the NICs in both industrial and non-industrial technologies, and their ability to export increasing amounts of capital goods (Lall, 1984b). The NICs have recorded above average growth rates in the three most important capital goods categories: electrical machinery, non-electrical machinery and transport equipment.

Having mapped out the broad areas in which there is scope for S–S trade, the results of one study which attempted to quantify the potential for S–S trade are examined (UNIDO, 1985a). In estimating trade potential the South was first of all divided into five regions: Latin America, Tropical Africa, the Near East, the Indian Subcontinent and East Asia. Then a number of industrial branches were selected which were considered to have potential for increased production and trade within the South. Each region was paired with another, so there were 25 pairings to consider. Finally, pairs of regions were matched according to their potential to become trading partners in each industrial product group, given the prevailing demand and supply conditions in the importing and exporting countries respectively.

A number of criteria were set up for choosing products and for matching trade partners. The products chosen were those which (a) were imported on a large scale from the North, (b) made intensive use of the resources in the South as a whole, (c) were not constrained by technological dependence on Northern suppliers, and (d) could assist the South in reaping dynamic benefits in terms of learning-by-doing. The regions were chosen in accordance with possibilities for dynamic complementarity and flexibility in productive capability. On the demand side, a region was considered as having great potential as an importer in a particular product area if (a) it depended on the North for more than 50 per cent of its imports, (b) imports had been partially supplied by the South in the past, and (c) its reliance on Southern imports had been increasing over time. On the supply side, a region was considered as having great potential as an exporter in a product category if (a) it had demonstrated a strong export performance in that area, (b) the particular product had experienced rapid growth, (c) it had established a good base in the importing region, and (d) its market share in the Southern importing region was less than the share achieved in world markets. Further, in determining the extent to which Southern countries could increase their market shares in other Southern countries, consideration was given to the rates of expansion in production and export in the past, as well as receptiveness shown by the importing region.

The results of the partnership identification process and the potential increases in the value of S–S trade are shown in Tables B.1 and 3.10. The base year used was 1979 and the projections extended to 1990. Although these projections are somewhat dated, they do illustrate the underlying potential for S–S trade. Two scenarios are presented – a moderate S–S cooperation scenario (MSSC scenario) which extends recent trends towards greater exchange, and an intensified S–S cooperation scenario (ISSC) scenario which accords especially favourable treatment for the lower income regions. Table B.1 shows that Latin America and East Asia have the greatest potential for exporting to other Southern regions, particularly to Tropical Africa. This is expected since these regions produce and export a wide variety of products. In the case of Latin America, possibilities for export to Tropical Africa exist in 13 of the 15 product areas identified. These range from food products and textiles to electrical and non-electrical machinery.[6] East Asian export potential exists in similar product areas. Regions with the least number of products for export potential are Tropical Africa and the Near East. In the former case, export potential exists in only two areas – rubber products and non-ferrous metals; while in the latter six product categories have export potential, including electrical and non-electrical machinery, food products, industrial chemicals, metal products and iron and steel products. Besides interregional trade, intraregional trade also offered substantial trade potential. This was the case for all regions except Tropical Africa and the Near East.

Table 3.10 gives quantitative assessments of potential S–S trade in seven major groups – agricultural products, raw materials, energy, intermediate products, consumer non-durables, equipment and consumer durables. Over the period the volume of S–S imports rises from roughly $89 billion to $112 billion in the MSSC scenario and to $168 billion in the ISSC one. Manufactures trade in particular rises from $51 billion to $66 billion (MSSC) and $100 billion (ISSC), or from 18.2 per cent of total South imports to 20.4 per cent in the moderate scenario and 26.1 per cent in the intensified one. In terms of specific categories, consumer durables show the sharpest increase as the value of S–S trade nearly doubles in the moderate scenario and more than trebles in the intensified one. The smallest increase is for energy, the exports of which are already well developed within the South.

Agricultural products and raw materials also show large increases, and these are most pronounced in the intensified scenario where their potential increases twice as fast as in the moderate one. This is expected since the intensified version is designed to help the less industrialized countries in the South. In general however, substantial growth was projected for all categories of goods, including the equipment category which registered the third largest increase, after consumer durables and raw materials.

Table 3.10
South's imports from the South: before and after increased S-S cooperation

Item	1979			1990 MSSC Scenario			1990 ISSC Scenario		
	$bn	Index No.	%	$bn	Index No.	%	$bn	Index No.	%
Agricultural products									
Total imports by the South	54.25	100		58.31	134		78.18	144	
S-S imports	20.06	100		26.04	139		37.54	187	
Share of S-S imports in total imports of the South			37.0			46.2			48.0
Raw materials									
Total imports by the South	3.75	100		4.00	155		6.18	165	
S-S imports	1.26	100		1.81	185		3.36	266	
Share of S-S imports in total imports of the South			33.6			45.4			54.3
Energy									
Total imports by the South	39.14	100		42.35	127		53.95	138	
S-S imports	33.00	100		34.39	133		45.62	138	
Share of S-S imports in total imports of the South			84.3			81.2			84.5
Intermediate products									
Total imports by the South	90.89	100		94.36	111		117.72	129	
S-S imports	17.61	100		23.61	125		35.91	204	
Share of S-S imports in total imports of the South			19.4			25.0			35.5
Consumer non-durables									
Total imports by the South	16.54	100		17.55	133		23.25	140	
S-S imports	4.16	100		5.54	154		8.53	205	
Share of S-S imports in total imports of the South			25.1			31.60			36.7

Item	1979			1990 MSSC Scenario			1990 ISSC Scenario		
	$bn	Index No.	%	$bn	Index No.	%	$bn	Index No.	%
Equipment									
Total imports by the South	123.85	100		131.01	126		164.42	133	
S-S imports	8.67	100		12.51	181		22.61	261	
Share of S-S imports in total imports of the South			7.0			9.5			13.7
Consumer durables									
Total imports by the South	29.21	100		32.02	141		45.10	154	
S-S imports	4.48	100		8.08	174		14.07	314	
Share of S-S imports in total imports of the South			15.4			25.22			31.2
Total manufactures imports									
Total imports by the South	281.28	100		324.50	115		386.76	138	
S-S imports	51.13	100		66.30	130		100.80	197	
Share of S-S imports in total imports of the South			18.2			20.4			26.1
Total imports									
Total imports by the South	357.63	100		379.59	129		488.80	137	
S-S imports	89.24	100		112.0	150		167.64	188	
Share of S-S imports in total imports of the South			25.0			29.5			34.3

Source: UNIDO (1985a)

Note: MSSC: Moderate S-S Cooperation;   ISSC: Intensified S-S Cooperation

49

Table 3.11 shows the potential contributions of the five major regions to increased S–S trade. In terms of the moderate scenario, the East Asian and Latin American countries show the largest increases on the export side (48 per cent and 43 per cent respectively), but the smallest on the import side (24 per cent and 30 per cent respectively). In the intensified version Tropical Africa registers the largest increases – 245 per cent for exports and 164 per cent for imports. Both the Near Eastern countries and the Indian Subcontinent appear to have limited trade potential under the moderate scenario, but they fare well in the intensified version on the import side where imports are projected to increase by 104 per cent and 103 per cent respectively.

Table 3.11
Regional sources of increase in South–South trade

Region	Percentage increase in trade			
	Exports		Imports	
	MSSC	ISSC	MSSC	ISSC
Latin America	43	102	30	80
Tropical Africa	36	245	60	164
Near East	12	49	34	104
Indian Subcontinent	28	101	33	103
East Asia	48	103	24	69

Source: UNIDO (1985a)

Summary

This chapter examines the patterns of S–S trade over the 50-year period 1938–88, investigates the factor characteristics of such trade and the scope for future expansions. The scanty data available for the early years show that, except for intra-Asian trade, levels of S–S trade were very low. The growth of regional integration groupings in the 1960s encouraged some increases, but it was not until the mid-1970s with the emergence of the oil boom that S–S trade began to expand rapidly. The import capacity of the oil exporting DCs rose substantially and rapid export expansions took place in the NICs. The share of S–S trade in world trade expanded from roughly five per cent in 1973 to nine per cent in 1982. Manufactures trade, the largest proportion of S–S trade, experienced the most rapid growth while oil and agriculture declined. Further, although both intraregional and interregional trade expanded, growth was faster for interregional trade. Since 1982 the growth of S–S trade has slowed down considerably in the light of world economic recession, falling commodity prices and escalations in interest rates. However, despite recessionary conditions Southern countries continue to increase their import shares in other Southern markets. This illustrates the underlying potential for S–S trade.

Existing studies on the factor content of S–S and S–N trade are reviewed. It is quite difficult to arrive at general conclusions however, since varying frameworks were used and the scope of analyses varied in terms of countries, variables and time periods. Despite these complexities it is found that whereas many of the studies produced conflicting results on the physical capital intensity variable, there is general agreement on the human capital variable. That is, all of the studies which tested for skill intensity find that S–S trade is more skill intensive than S–N trade. This implies that S–S trade has special development promoting properties and therefore has an important role to play in exploiting and developing the South's human resource potential.

Given the prevailing demand and supply conditions in DCs, the scope for expansions in S–S trade is considered to be great. Future projections show that a more effective exploitation of trading opportunities within the South could actually lead to a doubling of S–S trade. There is potential for trade among all groups and in a variety of products, although some countries or regions are better placed to engage in and benefit from such trade. For example, Latin America and East Asia have the greatest potential for exporting to other DCs goods ranging from food products and textiles to electrical and non-electrical machinery. Tropical Africa and the Near East have the least potential for expanding trade with other DC regions. However, if especially favourable treatment were accorded these countries their import potential would be considerable.

Notes

1. Whereas China absorbed 72 percent of the region's exports in 1860, this share fell to 33 per cent in 1900 (Hanson, 1980, p. 61).
2. World exports to the DCs are taken as a proxy for their imports.
3. See UNESCO, *Statistical Yearbook*, (1965–70 issues).
4. These changes contrast sharply with those in the previous period 1966–72 when the price index rose by 18.5 points while the volume index increased by 81.5 points (Ventura-Dias, 1988).
5. The results of the flow measure were not stated since this variable did not perform very well.
6. The exceptions are wood products and transport equipment.

4 Obstacles to South–South trade and measures to overcome them

Introduction

While from a theoretical point of view there appears to be considerable potential for increasing trade among DCs, and empirical estimates suggest that there is scope for its development, S–S trade has been and continues to form a small part of world trade. One of the major reasons cited for this 'low' level of trade is the existence of numerous barriers to trade. They include those erected by DCs themselves such as trade policy barriers, and those arising from the established system of finance, transport, marketing and distribution, as well as tied aid and the dominance of North based TNCs. The main objectives of this chapter are to (a) examine the extent to which these policy induced and institutional barriers have prohibited S–S trade, and (b) recommend policies to remove them, taking into consideration the successes/ problems of past arrangements. The latter discussion is a very important one, since in attempting to remove existing barriers DCs have pursued a number of second-best policies and these have been the subject of great debate.

Two points should be made at the outset regarding the difficulties involved in analyzing the above issues. First of all, trade policy barriers such as tariffs are easy to identify and they lend themselves easily to quantification. The negative influence which they exert on S–S trade is widely accepted. However, the significance and impact of NTBs and institutional obstacles are far more difficult to assess. Institutional variables in particular, are hard to measure and isolating their influence from all others is problematic. Secondly, it is difficult to evaluate the performance of special arrangements devised to facilitate S–S trade because of the complexity of factors which have influenced their successes and failures. Without being able to assess the impact of individual factors it is hard to establish linkages between causes and effects.

Policy induced obstacles

Among the set of economic policies which influence the flow of goods internationally, trade policy is the one which has the most direct effect. It comprises both exchange rate policy and commercial policy. In this discussion the emphasis is on commercial policy and specifically, on the extent to which tariffs and NTBs adversely affect the intra-trade of DCs. A brief examination is first undertaken of the types of trade policies followed by DCs in the past and the main reasons for their implementation. A profile of protection in DCs is then provided, and the ways in which high tariff and NTBs affect their intra-trade are discussed. Finally, the efforts made by DCs to remove trade policy obstacles are examined, and the policies required to facilitate their intra-trade are outlined.

Although some DCs such as Singapore, Hong Kong and Taiwan have relatively liberal trade regimes and others are in the process of liberalizing their trade, the majority of DCs maintain highly protective trade regimes. A number of factors are responsible for this, the three most important of which are the type of industrialization strategy pursued in the past, the need to generate revenues and to reduce deficits in their balance of payments.

During the 1950s and 1960s the majority of DCs erected a range of protective barriers around their domestic markets to establish manufacturing industries. The protection of industry, based on the infant industry argument, was central to the import substituting strategy of industrialization (ISI) adopted at that time. Studies undertaken by Balassa (1971) and Krueger (1978) reveal that protection rates in DCs were very high during the years when the ISI strategy was most vigorously pursued. The nominal and effective rates of protection for the Brazilian and Chilean manufacturing sectors during the 1960s were 86 per cent and 127 per cent, and 89 per cent and 158 per cent respectively. High protection rates were also recorded for countries in other regions. In the early 1970s effective protection rates for the manufacturing sectors in Tunisia, Pakistan and Indonesia were 250 per cent, 200 per cent and 119 per cent respectively.

Since the mid-1970s the majority of DCs, especially the small ones, have shifted to an export oriented industrialization strategy. Despite this policy change however, the system of protection established in the early post-war period remains largely unchanged in many countries. In some it has become more extensive and prohibitive, while in others the policy shift has been partial. For example, industries producing for the domestic market may still continue to produce under import substitution conditions, while the discrimination against exports is reduced by means of subsidies and duty free import of intermediates and capital goods (Verbruggen, 1989).

Another major argument for protection which has gained increasing prominence since the mid-1970s, and especially in light of the debt crisis, is the need to rectify balance of payments problems. DCs with huge balance of payments deficits have adopted stringent import controls in an attempt to save

53

foreign exchange. These controls have included mainly quantitative restrictions such as quotas, import licensing and import prohibitions, and the major categories of products targeted for such protection have been non-essential and luxury items.

In addition to the above, governments also impose tariffs for revenue purposes. In many DCs import taxes have a similar function to that of internal 'value added' type sales and purchase taxes. They are considered to be an easy and inexpensive way of collecting taxes and are levied on a range of goods which are not produced locally. In such cases therefore, tariffs do not have a protective function but rather constitute an important source of public revenue. Some countries, particularly many of the least industrialized ones, rely heavily on import taxes as a source of revenue. Farhadian-Lorie and Katz (1988) reported that over the 1978–84 period, import duties as a percentage of total tax revenues for Swaziland, Burkina Faso, Nepal and Dominican Republic were 64.2 per cent, 41.3 per cent, 34.1 per cent and 29.9 per cent respectively.

DCs protect their domestic industries for a host of other reasons including political, ideological and strategic ones. For example, the need to reduce dependence on the external economy, encourage the development of more indigenous technologies or create self sufficiency in certain sectors have been considered powerful arguments for protection.

Tariff barriers

The existing levels and structure of tariffs in DCs act as powerful constraints to the growth of S–S trade. High tariffs reduce the ability of DCs to compete in Third World markets, while industries in which DCs have their greatest comparative advantage are often the most highly protected. These features of protection are illustrated below through a detailed examination of the levels and structure of tariffs in DCs.

Table 4.1 provides data on average tariff rates for a sample of 50 DCs in 1985. Unfortunately they do not reflect the full extent of protection since they are based on nominal tariffs only. Effective protection rates which take into consideration protection on both inputs and outputs would have been more appropriate, but these are not available. Table 4.1 shows that the unweighted average tariff rate for all products was 26 per cent and the weighted average, based on country imports was 24 per cent. These tariff levels are roughly five times greater than those in the OECD countries (Kelly et al, 1988). In terms of regional variations, West Asia had the lowest average tariff rate – seven per cent for unweighted, and four per cent for weighted; while the African countries (excluding North Africa) and those in South America had the highest ones – 35 per cent and 38 per cent for weighted averages and 32 per cent and 34 per cent for unweighted averages respectively.

In addition to tariffs, Table 4.1 provides data on para-tariffs. The latter consists of import charges such as customs surcharges and surtaxes, stamp taxes and other fiscal charges, and taxes on foreign exchange. Since tariffs and para-tariffs are usually levied together on imports and their economic effects are the same, they can be treated as a single import charge. When both tariffs and para-tariffs are considered jointly, unweighted and weighted averages for all products rise by six and eight points respectively above the rates for tariffs. The increases were particularly large for the Central and South American regions, as well as for the North African one where para-tariffs are extensively employed. In these cases the weighted average tariff rates rose by 42, 13 and 9 percentage points respectively.

Table 4.1
Average tariffs and para-tariffs in DCs by region (%)

	Carib-bean	Central America	South America	North Africa	Other Africa	West Asia	Other Asia	All regions
Tariffs								
Countries unweighted	16	23	34	29	32	7	36	26
Countries weighted	17	24	38	30	35	4	22	24
Tariffs plus para-tariffs								
Countries unweighted	18	65	46	36	34	9	42	34
Countries weighted	17	66	51	39	36	5	25	30

Source: Erzan et al (1987)

An important observation made by Erzan et al (1987) was that DCs' import charges appeared to differ according to income levels. They found that countries at the lowest income levels (GDP per capita less than $500) had the highest tariff rates, and those at the highest income levels (GDP per capita more than $5,000) had the lowest. For the former group the weighted average rate for tariffs plus para-tariffs was 66 per cent, while for the latter (which included mainly West Asian oil exporting countries), the rate was three per cent. The major reason offered to explain the higher duties in low income countries was the need for revenue generation. In addition to this however, is the need to protect existing industries which are very small and weak, and to give encouragement to new industries which can only be started under the protective shield of tariffs.

Turning to the structure of protection in DCs, Table 4.2 shows that manufactures had the highest level of protection, and food items the second largest. For these two sectors the weighted average total import charges were

32 per cent and 30 per cent respectively. Corresponding rates for other sectors were 21 per cent for agricultural raw materials; 19 per cent for ores and metals; and 16 per cent for mineral fuels. This general pattern of high import charges for manufacturing and low ones for mineral fuels was the same for all regions. However, average import charges in specific sectors and regions were much higher than the average for all regions. The weighted average import charges for manufactures in Central and South America were 39 and 23 per cent respectively higher than all regions.

Table 4.2
Sectoral average tariffs and para-tariffs by region* (%)

	Carib-bean	Central America	South America	North Africa	Other Africa	West Asia	Other Asia	All regions
Food	19	64	50	38	41	4	28	30
Agricultural raw materials	4	49	41	19	30	4	18	21
Mineral fuels	11	58	28	12	23	5	13	16
Ores and metals	7	49	34	17	28	3	16	19
Manufactures	20	71	55	45	37	6	27	32
Chemicals	8	39	40	22	25	5	20	22
Other manufactures	28	102	68	65	47	8	34	41
Machinery and equipment	15	40	44	27	29	5	21	24
All sectors	*17*	*66*	*51*	*39*	*36*	*5*	*25*	*30*

Source: Erzan et al (1987)

*Countries in each region import weighted.

The above structure of import charges which is weighted heavily against manufacturing particularly affects S–S trade, since manufactured exports is the fastest growing component of S–S trade. Further, within the manufacturing sector import charges were comparatively higher in labour intensive and resource based products, areas in which a vast number of DCs have their strongest comparative advantage. For example, the 'other manufactures' grouping had a weighted average import charge of 41 per cent, nearly double that for chemicals and machinery and equipment. This category consisted of mainly labour intensive products such as textiles and clothing, leather goods, plastic products and paper and paperboard. A recent UNCTAD study also noted that in a number of DCs the import charges on agro-based products were higher than the average for all products (UNCTAD, 1990a).

Finally, the weighted average import charge on machinery and equipment was 24 per cent, six percentage points lower than the average for all sectors. This protective structure provides little incentive for the domestic production of capital goods in DCs and, in fact, encourages the import of these items from the ICs which have a quasi-monopoly in the production of them. The lower tariffs on capital goods in the DCs therefore favour N–S trade rather than S–S trade.

Non-tariff barriers

Besides tariffs, the existence of numerous NTBs also serves as an obstacle to S–S trade. NTBs are defined to include any trade barrier other than tariffs which impede the access of foreign goods to domestic markets. They therefore include a wide variety of measures, ranging from quotas, subsidies, import licensing and prohibitions, to customs valuation, state trading monopolies and health and safety regulations.[1] Given the varied nature of NTBs and the fact that many of them are subtle and therefore hard to identify, it is difficult to assess their impact. Some NTBs work through the price mechanism such as subsidies, others operate through import quantities such as quotas, while some prohibit trade such as health regulations and import licensing. But whether they work through quantitative restrictions on foreign supply or influence foreign price margins, NTBs artificially raise the domestic price of the restricted good.

In spite of the problems associated with the measurement of NTBs, several attempts have been made to evaluate their importance in DC trade (Erzan et al, 1987; Verbruggen, 1989; UNCTAD, 1990a). The study by Erzan et al revealed that most NTBs were product specific rather than applied across-the-board; and quantitative restrictions were the most frequently used, particularly licensing. Measures such as foreign exchange authorization were important in selected regions (e.g. Central America), but on average affected only six per cent of the tariff lines. Others such as minimum price regulations and state monopolies affected an even smaller proportion of tariff lines.

Table 4.3 shows that the weighted average ratio of tariff lines for the sample of 50 DCs affected by some form of NTB was 40 per cent. When NTBs applied across the board for all imports are excluded, this ratio was 27 per cent. An important feature of NTBs in DCs is that they are stacked, that is, a given product is subject to several restrictions. When the stack total is considered, the average ratio of tariff lines affected was 55 per cent. Tariff lines affected by NTBs did not exhibit major differences across sectors. Foodstuffs appeared to be the most seriously affected, with 48 per cent of all tariff positions covered by one or other NTB. In general however, the structure of NTBs was found to be similar to that of tariffs. That is, they were most frequently applied to products such as textiles, clothing and footwear – areas in which DCs have strong comparative advantages.

NTBs in DCs affect S–S trade far more than NTBs in ICs affect S–N trade. UNCTAD (1990a) noted that the average frequency rate of NTBs in DCs is 61 per cent, compared to 14 per cent in ICs. In addition, whereas there is increasing resort to discriminatory measures by ICs, NTBs in DCs are normally applied on a nondiscriminatory basis.

Table 4.3
Frequency of non-tariff measures:
percentage of tariff positions affected

Sectors	Quantitative restrictions	Advanced import deposits	Other	Stack total	Non–stack total	Non–stack excluding general measures
Food	33	21	13	67	48	38
Agricultural raw materials	19	21	10	50	37	21
Mineral fuels	18	19	20	57	42	29
Ores and metals	18	21	12	50	38	21
Manufactures	23	21	11	55	39	26
Chemicals	21	21	10	53	39	24
Other manufactures	26	21	12	59	41	30
Machinery and equipment	20	22	10	51	36	22
Other	37	21	18	76	58	47
All sectors	*24*	*21*	*12*	*56*	*40*	*27*

Source: Erzan et al (1987)

The removal of trade policy barriers

DCs have recognized the need to dismantle their trade policy barriers in order to encourage trade among themselves, and several attempts have been made in this direction. These have mainly involved the establishment of trade preferences along regional lines such as through the formation of regional integration groupings. Although these arrangements have been very important in fostering trading linkages between sub-groups of DCs during the 1960s and 1970s, their record in recent years has been generally poor. The lack of complementary production structures among member countries, the resort to NTBs in times of economic hardships, and the lack of formal mechanisms to redistribute the gains from trade have been identified as key problems in these arrangements. Governments have taken steps in recent years to revive some of these ailing arrangements, but it is increasingly being recognized that this form of policy intervention may not be the most appropriate to allow the generation of full benefits from trade among DCs.

Since the early 1980s some DCs have begun unilaterally to dismantle their trading barriers, largely as part of structural adjustment programmes administered by the World Bank and the IMF. The World Bank reported that during 1979–87 alone an estimated 81 adjustment loans to 41 countries contained substantial proposals for trade policy reform (World Bank, 1990). For example, several countries in Latin America such as Mexico, Venezuela and Chile have simplified their tariff structures, reduced rates and bound their full tariff schedules in GATT. Many others (e.g. Morocco, Republic of Korea and the Philippines) have reduced or even discontinued most of their NTBs.

The adoption of non-discriminatory trade liberalization is indeed preferable to discriminatory trade liberalization. DCs recognize however, that in a less than 'first best' world some form of discriminatory trade liberalization will be required to expand S–S trade. To this end a Global System of Trade Preferences (GSTP) was established in April 1988 among member countries of the Group of 77, aimed at the mutual reduction of all trade control measures (tariffs, para-tariffs and NTBs) affecting trade among member countries.[2] At present over 30 DCs have ratified the agreement and become full participants. All major DCs are included except China, Hong Kong, Taiwan, Saudi Arabia and Kuwait. The first round of negotiations which was completed in 1988 involved the exchange of bilateral concessions on tariff and non-tariff restrictions, and the starting point was a linear tariff reduction of 10–20 per cent. These concessions were subsequently multilateralized on a most-favoured-nation basis for all participants.

Estimates of the impact of a GSTP on the level of trade among South countries have been made by Erzan, Laird and Yeats (1988) and Linnemann and Verbruggen (1991), and these authors question the magnitude of benefits expected from such an arrangement. Erzan, Laird and Yeats analyzed the effects of a linear tariff reduction on the mutual trade of 23 major DCs and found, assuming a 50 per cent tariff cut, an expansion of mutual trade of 8.5 per cent. For manufactured products only, assuming the same tariff cut and infinitely elastic supply, the projected trade expansion was roughly 39 per cent. The study by Linnemann and Verbruggen involved a sample of 39 DCs and was confined to trade in manufactures. It revealed that a lowering of tariffs for intra-DC trade by 20 per cent would lead to an expansion of trade in the short run by 5.5 per cent and in the long run by 14 per cent. Larger tariff cuts by 50 per cent would lead to a trade expansion of 15 per cent in the short run and 42 per cent in the long run.

In general, the above studies indicate fairly modest results from a GSTP in the short run but substantial ones in the long run. Unfortunately, they do not take into consideration the dynamic effects of a liberalization of trade among DCs, effects which are particularly important for the South and which are likely to be much larger than the static ones. As the authors themselves point out:

> the trade expansion estimates do not reflect the value of increased economic activity in domestic sectors that are linked to the export industries, neither do they reflect additional gains from scale economies that may result from higher production and export volumes. In addition, the 'comparative statics' nature of our analysis will also fail to reflect any dynamic comparative advantage gains that developing countries may achieve under the GSTP. Such gains would be particularly important in sectors where the GSTP enables 'infant' industries in developing

countries to become fully competitive internationally [Erzan, Laird and Yeats (1988), p. 1442].

Institutional obstacles

As noted above, whereas policy induced barriers like tariffs are easy to identify and can be quantified, the identification and assessment of institutional obstacles are far more difficult. Nevertheless an attempt is made to examine the nature of such obstacles and to suggest measures for their removal. First, the historical origins of such constraints and the results of one study which attempted to quantify them are briefly discussed. Then the main issues relating to specific constraints are examined.

The significance of institutional obstacles to S–S trade must be viewed within a historical context (Stewart, 1976; Nayyar, 1979; Ul Haq, 1980). This is largely because many of the obstacles which confront S–S trade today have their origins in the framework which evolved to support a specific pattern of trade during the period of colonialism. This pattern was determined by the nature of existing colonial relationships and followed, in the strictest sense, a N–S/S–N one. The colonies produced primary commodities and raw materials for export to the metropolitan countries, and obtained all their imports from the same source. In line with the above pattern of trade, the basic trading infrastructure such as transportation networks, financing, marketing and distribution systems were constructed to channel trade between colonies and the countries which governed them. It was not in the interest of the colonial powers to develop trade among DCs, and the infrastructure to support their trade was never developed. For example, there were no direct shipping links between African countries and intra-African trade could only be facilitated by transhipping through ports in Western Europe.

In the post-Independence years substantial efforts were made to build the required infrastructure to facilitate S–S trade. For example, new shipping routes were organized and special payments and credit arrangements established in order to finance the intra-trade of DCs. However, in spite of these developments the obstacles to S–S trade still persist. Two major factors account for this. First of all, the institutional framework which supported N–S trade has become so firmly embedded in the DCs' economic structures that it has become difficult to re-orient trade along S–S lines. Secondly, at present there are other forces at work which serve to reinforce and maintain N–S trade. These include *inter alia* the presence of North based TNCs, the tying of aid and the purchase of technology from the ICs.

Although there are difficulties in assessing the influence of institutional obstacles to trade, one study which explored such issues deserves mention. Roemer (1977) investigated the patterns of manufactured exports for five countries in 1971 – the UK, USA, Japan, Canada and West Germany – and found that countries tended to market their weakest sectors of manufactures disproportionately[3] in their strongest areas of influence and vice versa. Using regression analysis he attempted to relate this disproportionality in trade to distance, a proxy for transportation costs, and market share, a proxy for sphere of influence factors. The latter included 'historical and cultural ties between traders, the tying of aid, the setting up of multinational subsidiaries, and preferential treatment of one country's exports for other reasons' (p. 318). The results showed that for four of the countries investigated (West Germany was the exception), transportation costs alone could not explain the observed disproportionality in trade. Sphere of influence factors were considered to have an important role. The results were strongest for the UK and a separate test was undertaken for that country, defining the British sphere of influence as its former colonies. Once more the results confirmed the finding that sphere of influence factors were absolutely more important than transportation costs.

Financial constraints

Given the important role of international finance in world trade, constraints in this area are some of the most severe. There are two major issues to consider. The first relates to the heavy reliance on the use of convertible currencies and the second to the lack of adequate export credit facilities.

Reliance on the use of convertible currencies. DCs have historically relied upon the currencies and financial network of the North to finance their intra-trade. This has rendered them vulnerable to changes in the financial policies of the main reserve currency countries, such as those that occurred in the 1980s. The period 1973–78 was characterized by more or less easy monetary policies, and the financial system to some extent absorbed the inflationary shock from the oil price increases. In 1979–85 however, there was a reversal in policy and the major ICs adopted highly restrictive monetary and fiscal policies. This led to a soaring of interest rates in the major financial centres and exerted a strong influence on international capital markets. In turn, the cost of borrowing finance escalated, debts began to accumulate, investment was reduced and there was a slowdown in the expansion of world trade.

In general DCs face considerable structural foreign exchange constraints, and the monetary developments in the ICs during the early 1980s worsened these constraints, and hence their ability to finance their intra-trade. The liquidity strain on the DCs was reflected in the reduction of their reserve-to-import ratios from 39.4 per cent in 1979 to 24.5 per cent in 1982.[4] The Latin American countries were most severely affected, for their reserve-to-import ratios declined from 41.3 per cent to 23.1 per cent over that period. The severity of the situation was also reflected in the rapid escalation of the DCs' external debt which rose from $424.8 billion in 1978 to $846.6 billion in 1982. For the 15 most heavily indebted countries, the debt servicing to export ratio rose from 33.7 per cent to 48.9 per cent over the same period, and their debt to export ratio increased from 204.3 per cent to 267.6 per cent.[5]

It is not easy to assess the influence of changes in the ICs' financial policies on S–S trade since there are many factors which influence such trade. However, for the period 1978–82 Tran-Nguyen (1989) has made some interesting observations on changes in the DCs' growth of net financial inflows and foreign exchange reserves on the one hand, and on the growth of their trade on the other. She noted that during the period 1973–78 financial inflows and foreign exchange reserves in the DCs grew on average by 27 per cent per annum (Table 4.4). Their intraregional trade also grew rapidly – by 28 per cent annually in 1973–79. However, in 1979–82 there was a drastic decline in all these flows. The average annual growth rate of net financial inflows into DCs declined from 27 per cent in the first period to one per cent in the second, and foreign exchange reserves fell from 27 per cent to minus four per cent. Intraregional trade also fell dramatically, from 28 per cent in 1973–79 to minus one per cent in 1980–83. The Asian countries were least affected by financial problems, but their growth in foreign exchange reserves and in trade were nevertheless reduced considerably. In view of the DCs' heavy reliance on convertible currencies, their structural foreign exchange constraints and monetary developments in the early 1980s, these trends indicate that financial factors had an important impact on the volume of DCs' trade.

Table 4.4
Average annual rate of growth of net financial inflows to DCs, their foreign exchange reserves and intraregional trade, 1973–82 (%)

	Financial inflows		Foreign exchange		Intraregional trade	
	1973–78	1979–82	1973–78	1979–82	1973–79	1980–83
Africa	32	3	16	–8	18	–7
Latin America	21	7	22	–14	25	–4
LAIA	21	13	20	–16	25	–9
Middle East	59	–11	40	–2	31	8
Other Asia	10	13	23	6	23	6
All DCs	27	*1*	27	*–4*	28	*–1*

Source: Tran-Nguyen (1989)

International financial markets have been extremely volatile in recent years. Several factors have contributed to this: the increasing liberalization and deregulation of financial activity; the change in the conduct of monetary policy, away from targeting interest rates; and the lack of coordination in macroeconomic policies, especially fiscal policies (UNCTAD, 1990b). As a result interest rates have become much more variable, the cost of external debt in DCs has increased considerably, and many DCs have experienced breakdowns in their external financing from capital markets, as well as large scale capital flight. Real interest rates in the USA rose on average from 3.3 per cent annually in 1980–82 to 4 per cent in 1983–89, and from –0.3 per cent to 5.2 per cent in the UK over the same period (UNCTAD, 1990b). The vulnerability of the DCs to changes in the financial policies of the main reserve currency countries continues, with its adverse consequences for the intra-trade of DCs.

The lack of adequate export credit finance. The ability to offer deferred and liberal terms of payment for traded goods is an important factor in determining trade flows. This is especially for intermediate and capital goods which often require substantial amounts of finance. In the North, governments have elaborated highly developed export credit schemes which typically involve credit for activities before or after shipment, and insurance for export credit against commercial or political risks. These schemes contain implicit subsidies, and ICs' exporters are therefore able to increase their advantage over the trade position of other countries. It has been estimated that the annual credit subsidies granted by the US Export-Import Bank during the 1970s and 1980s ranged from $500 million to $1 billion, and those by the UK's Export Credits Guarantee Department in the early 1980s ranged between £300–500 million (Boyd, 1982; Baron, 1983; Byatt, 1984; Fleisig and Hill, 1984).

Given the general lack of financial resources in DCs the provision of credit to buyers, especially on a medium or long term basis is severely restricted. DCs frequently cannot match the volume or attractive terms of payment offered by the North. The levels of interest rates in DCs are usually higher than in ICs, which means that a large amount of interest subsidies are required to enable suppliers from the South to compete with those from the North. Securing finance for traditional exports is generally easier than for non-traditional exports. The former generally requires short term finance and benefit from well established channels of financing, such as transnational producing companies. Non-traditional exports, however, face particular difficulties. The commercial banks which are usually geared towards short term loans may not be able or willing to finance these new ventures, especially those earmarked for new developing country markets. In general, Southern countries suffer considerably from the lack of financial resources, for not only is the financial infrastructure in place to finance N–N trade, but also S–N trade is more readily financed through Northern importers obtaining import financing even where the DC exporter cannot obtain export financing, whereas in S–S trade there is difficulty of financing at both ends of the transaction.

The ability of DCs to extend credit to exporters has weakened considerably since the mid-1970s, given their mounting debts and debt servicing difficulties. At the same time the need for credit by importing DCs has become more pressing. Large, debt ridden countries like Brazil and Argentina which are major exporters of capital goods to the Third World have suffered greatly.

Tran-Nguyen (1989) has noted that whereas the annual average rate of growth of Brazilian goods to DCs covered by export credits of one year or more was 45 per cent in 1973–78, this dropped to zero per cent in 1979–83. In the case of Argentina the corresponding decline was from 16 per cent to –0.22 per cent.

In general, DCs find themselves in a vicious circle. In order to solve their foreign exchange problems they must be able to compete in foreign markets. But in order to do this they must liberalize their terms of payment for export credits. Maturities have to be lengthened and interest rates subsidized. But this liberalization would only result in a strain on the balance of payments and further foreign exchange problems.

Measures to overcome the problems of finance

DCs have attempted to overcome the problems noted above in a number of ways. They have formed special payments arrangements, introduced export credit schemes and entered into non-traditional forms of payments such as countertrade. Despite these efforts however, the problem of financing still looms large in S–S trade. Indeed, as long as there are no moves towards reform of the international financial system the DCs will continue to be vulnerable to changes in the financial policies of the North. Therefore in the future DCs will have to strengthen their special financing arrangements in order to boost their intra-trade.

Payments arrangements among developing countries. In order to alleviate the problems associated with the use of convertible currencies, DCs have set up various types of payments arrangements to strengthen financial cooperation among themselves. The most advanced form of these arrangements is the monetary union which involves complete monetary policy harmonization among members, pooling of exchange reserves and adoption of a common currency.[6] Two simpler types which are used extensively in the South are multilateral clearing arrangements and credit arrangements. A clearing arrangement is the simplest form of a payments arrangement. Its objective is to allow for the clearing of current transactions among members in local currencies without resort to the use of convertible currencies, except for the settlement of net balances at agreed intervals. These intervals are usually short and do not exceed three months. Clearing arrangements do not normally extend credit to member countries, except in selected cases where small amounts of interim short term credit are required to permit periodic settlements.

The main advantage of a clearing arrangement is that it allows members to secure foreign exchange savings. The extent of these savings however, depends upon the proportion of intra-member trade to members' total trade. If this is high, substantial savings can be acquired which can then be used to finance trade with countries external to the union. Other advantages from clearing arrangements include: 'more rapid settlement of transactions; savings on commissions; the establishment of correspondent relationships between participating commercial banks, thereby strengthening cooperation in the banking field; a diminution of correspondent relationships with commercial banks in Europe and North America for intra-subregional trade, consequently reducing working balances maintained abroad; and the availability of credit for subregional trade' (UNCTAD, 1986).

Credit arrangements generally build upon clearing arrangements and they function to provide balance of payments support for member countries. Countries belonging to a credit arrangement agree to provide short or medium term credit to finance imbalances in their mutual trade. This provides an economical method of payment for mutual trade transactions and allows each country more time to make the necessary balance of payments adjustments. Credit arrangements also assist countries in avoiding stringent exchange controls and other trade restrictions which may have been imposed for balance of payments purposes. There are numerous operational differences among existing credit arrangements. Credit may be automatic or discretionary; borrowing may be unconditional or have stringent conditions attached; there may be varying amounts and maturities of credit extended; and repayments may be financed in various proportions of hard and national currencies.

At the end of 1989 there were seven recorded clearing and payments arrangements (UNCTAD, 1990c). They included the ALADI Payments and Reciprocal Credit System (CAIA, 1960); the Central American Clearing House (CACH, 1961); the Asian Clearing Union (ACU, 1974); the West African Clearing House (WACH, 1975); the CARICOM Multilateral Clearing Facility (CMCF, 1977); the Central African Clearing House (CAFCH, 1979); and the Preferential Trade Area Clearing Arrangement (PTA, 1982). In addition there were five multilateral credit arrangements: the ASEAN Swap Arrangement (1967); the Central American Monetary Stabilization Fund (1969); the Arab Monetary Fund (1977); the Andean Reserve Fund (1978); and the Latin American Reserve Fund (1988). Since the early 1980s and in the light of the debt crisis, several of the above payment and credit arrangements have encountered tremendous difficulties and some countries have withdrawn from existing schemes, while others have ceased operations. In 1984 the CMCF reached its credit ceilings and eventually ceased operations in that year; in 1986–87 Guatemala and Costa Rica abandoned the use of the CACH;[7] and the Santo Domingo Agreement which provided lines of credit to participating countries up to a total of US$650 million was effectively brought to an end in 1987 when a decision was taken to have no further recourse to financing under its provisions (UNCTAD, 1990c). Despite these setbacks however, governments are taking steps to revive these arrangements.

It is difficult to evaluate the impact of the above arrangements, since most of them are associated with other attempts to promote intraregional trade, particularly with agreements on tariff liberalization. Further, since the early 1980s there has been a marked deterioration in the general financial and trading environment for most countries. Nevertheless some observations can be made on the workings of these arrangements and the trading patterns of the groups with which they have been associated. First of all, during the 1960s and 1970s when the world financial and trading environment was fairly stable, the schemes appeared to have worked quite successfully. Stewart (1987) noted two aspects to this success: (a) membership and functions of the schemes grew over time, and (b) the combined effect of specific monetary and trade agreements showed that, in general, intra-regional trade rose as a proportion of the total trade of the region in areas with agreements. For example, between 1960 and 1980 the share of intra-grouping trade in the total group trade of LAFTA increased from 7.7 per cent to 13.5 per cent; in the Andean group from 0.7 per cent to 3.5 per cent; in CACM from 7.5 per cent to 22 per cent; in CARICOM from 4.5 per cent to 6.4 per cent; and in ASEAN, which launched its preferential trading agreement in 1976, from 13.9 per cent in that year to 17.8 per cent in 1980 (UNCTAD, 1990c).

Secondly, there were large declines in intraregional trade in the 1980s, especially during the crisis period of 1981–86, and in the volume of transactions channelled through the clearing arrangements. UNCTAD (1990c) reported that over the period 1981–86 the share of intra-group trade in the total trade of ECOWAS declined from 4.6 per cent to 3.2 per cent; in PTA from 9.0 per cent to 6.9 per cent; in ALADI from 12.6 per cent to 11.5 per cent; in the CACM from 20.7 per cent to 17.7 per cent; in CARICOM from 7.4 per cent to 5.4 per cent; and in ASEAN from 18.9 per cent to 16.7 per cent. Large declines were also recorded in the volume of transactions channelled through clearing arrangements.

Table 4.5 shows that over the period 1981–89 the ALADI system declined by 36.1 per cent and the WACH by 77.5 per cent; the PTA by 8.9 per cent over 1986–89 and the CACM by 78.5 per cent over 1981–87. The ACU, the only facility which generated large increases up to the mid-1980s, declined by roughly one half between 1987–89. The liquidity crisis in the early 1980s is considered to have been the single most important factor influencing the poor performance of the clearing arrangements. As member countries struggled with mounting debt problems, it became increasingly difficult for them to settle outstanding balances in convertible currencies. This, in turn, led to chronic accumulation of arrears at the end of clearing periods and, in some cases, to unsustainable operations.

Despite the poor performance of the clearing arrangements in the 1980s however, two important observations indicate that they achieved some measure of success. One is that whereas the group's trade with non-member countries during the prosperous 1970s were better than for intra-group trade, the latter was far more resilient than trade with non-member countries during the turbulent period 1980–83. Tran-Nguyen (1989) pointed out that in the case of only three of 11 existing clearing and payments arrangements were the declines in intragroup trade greater than those among other groups of countries. They included the CACH, the Arab Monetary Fund and the Santo Domingo Agreement. This indicated that payments arrangements did, to a large extent,

Table 4.5
Multilateral clearing arrangements of DCs:
transactions settled in foreign exchange, 1981–89*

Facilities/Years	Volume of transactions ($USmn)	Transactions settled in foreign exchange as a percentage of total transactions
Central American Clearing House (CACH)		
1981	979.5	28.0
1983	644.0	23.0
1986	189.0	27.1
1987	210.5	21.6
1988	98.0	34.6
1989	40.0	32.5
ALADI Payments and Reciprocal Credit System		
1981	9 331.4	27.0
1983	6 005.3	25.0
1986	6 268.0	15.6
1987	5 360.0	14.3
1988	6 115.0	15.0
1989	5 960.0	15.0
Asian Clearing Union (ACU)		
1981	233.3	38.0
1983	475.8	63.0
1986	651.5	31.0
1987	580.0	20.6
1988	217.0	23.9
1989	290.0	17.3
West African Clearing House (WACH)		
1981	171.0	82.0
1983	171.5	91.0
1986	109.3	85.9
1987	56.5	98.8
1988	26.2	76.7
1989	38.5	68.8
PTA Clearing Arrangement		
1981	..	..
1983	..	..
1986	79.0	82.0
1987	65.2	18.4
1988	64.0	51.5
1989	72.0	35.8

Source: Tran-Nguyen (1989), UNCTAD (1990c).

* Figures for 1989 are preliminary.

67

serve a useful role in protecting trade between member countries from external financial disturbances.

A second observation relates to the reduction in the use of convertible currencies in the settlement of intra-member trade. Table 4.5 shows that although the proportion of transactions settled in foreign exchange was large for many groupings, in all of the arrangements this share declined over time. In ALADI it fell from 27 per cent in 1981 to 15 per cent in 1989; in ACU, from 38 per cent to 17.3 per cent; in PTA, from 82 per cent in 1986 to 35.8 per cent in 1989; and in CACH, from 28 per cent in 1981 to 21.6 per cent in 1987. Since one of the primary aims of clearing arrangements is to reduce the use of convertible currencies in the settlement of intra-member trade, these trends suggest that clearing arrangements have played a useful role in stimulating intra-DC trade.

In the absence of international financial reform and continued reliance of the DCs on the currencies of the North, payments and credit arrangements will continue to be important methods of financing the intra-trade of DCs. In recognition of their potentially useful role countries in almost every region are taking steps to revive and strengthen clearing arrangements (UNCTAD, 1990c). These include the establishment of a new clearing house to replace the existing CAFCH; the construction of a credit facility with a capital base of $50 million to support the activities of WACH and the introduction of currency and swap arrangements by the ACU. Various proposals are also being studied for the revival of CACH and the CMCF, and for the strengthening of other arrangements. One proposal which has already been effected in Central America is the use of aid monies to settle outstanding arrears.[8]

Two final points should be made with respect to the efficacy of clearing arrangements. First of all, if they are to protect intraregional trade at times of general foreign exchange crisis, it is essential that the imbalances within the region are not financed by hard currencies but by credit from the payments union, or a non-convertible DC currency. Secondly, the fundamental problem which currently face clearing arrangements, that is, the lack of complementarity in production structures, will have to be given priority. For as long as deficit countries continue to produce goods that are not demanded by creditor countries, structural imbalances will remain. In order to overcome this problem member states will need to undertake joint actions and programmes to expand and diversify production regionally.

Export credit finance institutions. Since the mid-1970s a number of DCs have taken steps to establish export credit financing schemes, either at the national or regional level. Unfortunately these schemes are few, and the resources they provide are limited. In 1986 only 17 DCs had nationally supported export credit facilities: Argentina, Brazil, Chile, Colombia, Indonesia, Iran, Jamaica, Malaysia, Mexico, Pakistan, the Philippines, South Korea, Singapore and Thailand (UNCTAD, 1986). In addition, there are five regional trade financing institutions which provide credit to DCs, three in Latin America and two in the Middle East. They include the Inter-American Development Bank (IDB) Trade Financing Facility; the Latin American Export Bank (BLADEX); the Andean Trade Financing System (SAFICO); the Islamic Development Bank (IsDB) and the Arab Monetary Fund (AMF) Trade Financing Facility. The IDB scheme is geared towards the financing of intra-Latin American trade, especially capital goods and other non-traditional goods and services. It provides refinancing facilities at preferential rates to DCs, especially those with limited access to capital markets. BLADEX is a private multinational bank which functions as a link between participating international banks (such as the IDB) and local banks in member countries. It specializes in the promotion of exports from Latin America, mainly non-traditional exports.

SAFICO, which was formed by members of the Andean Development Corporation, also finances mainly non-traditional exports but is geared towards the financing of intra-member trade. The two Middle Eastern regional export credit schemes include those operated by the Islamic Development Bank and the Inter-Arab Investment Guarantee Corporation. The former finances mainly essential goods imported by member countries with balance of payments difficulties; while the latter extends export credits to all intra-member trade, and provides insurance coverage for Arab investments undertaken in member countries against losses resulting from political risks.

The resources provided by the regional trade financing institutions are quite limited in relation to the size of trade among DCs. Table 4.6 shows that in 1989 the lending capacity of all five institutions for trade related credits was approximately $2.9 billion. This is indeed a modest amount, compared with the value of trade among DCs which in that year exceeded $150.0 billion (UNCTAD, 1990a). Further, the two largest schemes, the IDB Trade Financing Facility and BLADEX, are not geared exclusively to financing trade between DCs, but also include the ICs.

In general, efforts should be made in the future to increase the resources of these institutions in order to enable them to play a more useful role in the financing of DCs' intra-trade.

Table 4.6
Trade-related credits extended by regional institutions, 1983–89 ($mn)

Trade financing scheme	1983	1984	1985	1986	1989
BLADEX	292.3	295.5	394.4	489.9	600.0
IDB Trade Financing Facility	62.0	65.1	72.1	85.3	79.1
IsDB	519.5	704.4	659.4	647.3	79.0
SAFICO	15.1	14.3	19.1	24.8	30.0
AMF Trade Financing Facility	-	43.1	46.5	34.8	37.0

Source: UNCTAD (1990c)

Countertrade. Countertrade, and barter in particular, is considered to be an important way of saving foreign exchange. Indeed, the dominant force behind the recent upsurge in countertrade has been the balance of payments difficulties which countries faced during the late 1970s and early 1980s. Countertrade is also considered to generate additional foreign exchange by helping to overcome entry barriers in export markets since the import is made contingent on the export of the countertrading country. Precise information is not available on the extent of countertrade among DCs, but estimates indicate that it is higher than world countertrade which is currently considered to be about 15 per cent of world trade (UNCTC, 1988). Countertrade takes many forms, but the most widely used ones are barter, counterpurchase and buy-back. Barter is a spot transaction which requires no involvement of foreign exchange, whereas counterpurchase and buy-back involve long term contracts for the exchange of goods and/or services which are paid for in hard currency. In addition, buy-back agreements usually entail the export of a plant or technology and the repurchase of some portion of the output produced by that plant.

A recent study by Jones and Jagoe (1988) which analyzed 1,350 countertrade deals involving DCs in 1980–87 sheds light on the nature of countertrade in DCs. It reported that roughly one half of all transactions consisted of barter and counterpurchase arrangements, followed by others such as bilateral inter-state trade treaties establishing payments mechanisms, agreements for debt repayment through goods and repurchase agreements. Both commodities and manufactured goods are traded, the most important of which are oil, cereals, cotton, timber and iron and steel in the first category, and textiles and clothing, fertilizers, vehicles and spare parts, paper and chemical products in the second. Brazil, Indonesia, Iran, Mexico and Zimbabwe were found to be the largest countertraders, but scores of other DCs participate in this trade. In fact, a few countries have enacted legislation to encourage this form of trade. They include the Dominican Republic, Ecuador, Guatemala, Honduras and Peru (UNCTC, 1988).

Despite its alleged advantages and growing importance there are numerous objections to countertrade. It is often considered to involve relatively high transaction costs, encourage the promotion of expensive goods which may be hard to sell in third markets, and to have distortional effects on resource allocation. More generally, countertrade is associated with a return to bilateralism and reciprocity, and therefore viewed as a threat to the multilateral trading system.

It is indeed true that in some cases countertrade has led to higher costs in comparison with those of conventional methods of financing and payments. But according to UNCTAD (1989b) the experience of the 1980s has made possible a learning process for DCs and they now adopt a more discriminatory approach to countertrade. Some forms of countertrade which involve high costs are being avoided, for example, the use of counterpurchase for certain categories of trade. It is recognized however, that under certain circumstances countertrade can stimulate important efficiency gains.

70

Marin (1990) has outlined two sets of conditions under which countertrade can be beneficial to DCs. First, where there are widespread distortions in the form of imperfect competition and collusive agreements, countertrade can be used to change the terms of trade and to utilize excess supplies of exportable goods. A price discriminating monopolist in a NIC who wishes to sell to a LDC at a lower price than its customers in the North can use barter to discriminate in a hidden way. In such a case, countertrade provides a way for the LDC to extract monopoly rents from the NIC firm. Countertrade can also be used by DCs which have excess supplies but are constrained in their ability to export them because of their membership in international pricing agreements. A DC can offer their excess supplies at the official price to another DC and take some overpriced goods in exchange, thereby circumventing the collusive agreement. In the presence of market distortions then, countertrade can assist DCs in changing the terms of trade and in restoring price flexibility.

Countertrade can also benefit DCs in cases where large, irreversible investments are being planned, and countries wish to be guaranteed that their investments will generate foreign exchange earnings in the future. A LDC firm can negotiate with a NIC firm for a forward contract in which the latter firm commits itself to purchase at a future date the products that the LDC will produce. If such a contract is concluded, countertrade serves as an insurance against future price fluctuations and a firm indication of future demand for the product. These types of arrangements are especially beneficial to DCs since even though they may have a strong comparative advantage in particular goods, they often face a 'reputational' barrier in other DCs' markets. That is, consumers in DCs may consider goods manufactured in other DCs to be of an inferior quality.

Overall then, there are powerful arguments for countertrade in the presence of market distortions and where there is a need for insurance against fluctuations in future foreign exchange earnings.

Recent proposals. Two proposals have been put forward in recent years to strengthen financial and monetary cooperation among DCs: the establishment of a South Bank and the creation of a Third World currency. The former proposal, which was introduced in 1976 at the Non-Aligned Meeting in Colombo and subsequently revised by UNCTAD and others, envisaged the creation of a special banking facility to serve the needs of the DCs.[9] Its wide ranging functions were expected to include the mobilization of financial resources and promotion of capital markets within the South; encouragement of better resource utilization and diversification of production; provision of balance of payments support and advice on debt management and investment activities; the coordination of regional financial and monetary policies; and a strengthening of the bargaining position of DCs vis-à-vis transnational enterprises. Unfortunately, the proposal for the establishment of a South Bank has never materialized in view of the shortage of financial resources in the

South and the fact that some countries have not been convinced of the viability of such a venture.[10]

The second proposal, that of the creation of a Third World currency, has also proven to be unattractive to policy makers. The basic idea is that DCs would issue their own international currency for use in the financing of their intra-trade, and its acceptability will be determined by the Central Banks in participating countries. Its value will be defined in terms of some external unit, and a central authority will be responsible for allocating the currency to countries in accordance with some agreed formula. Such a scheme should provide an incentive for DCs to import from others, since it will cost less in terms of convertible currency. It should also stimulate an expansion in exports, especially if sales are limited to the ICs because of lack of markets or the existence of trade barriers. Despite these potential advantages however, little support has been given to the scheme because of the perceived difficulties associated with its implementation. These relate to fundamental questions regarding the initial amount and distribution of money, as well as how to ensure the acceptability of the new currency.

Transport constraints

The role of transport in international trade is very important, although it receives far less attention than other areas such as tariffs. The lack of adequate transport facilities constrains the free movement of goods, and high transportation costs can reduce a country's trade competitiveness considerably. This discussion examines the ways in which transport constraints serve as impediments to S–S trade and the attempts to remove them. It recognizes the importance of air transport, especially for landlocked countries, but focuses on ocean transport since the bulk of DCs' trade is seaborne. In order to understand fully the problems that confront S–S shipping two major issues must be elaborated upon: the pattern of world fleet ownership and the functioning of the world liner conference system.

Although the DCs have increased their share of the world fleet over the past two decades, they still depend heavily on foreign owned ships and it is this dependency which is central to their shipping problems. The DCs accounted for 36.2 per cent of total world cargo turnover in 1989, but owned 21.2 per cent of the total world fleet. By comparison the ICs and open registry countries[11] together generated 56.7 per cent of the world's international seaborne trade and owned 67.5 per cent of the world's fleet (Table 4.7 and UNCTAD, 1990d). The dominance of the ICs is evident in practically every type of vessel group. In the oil tanker category, which is the largest in terms of tonnage, ICs' ownership was 78.9 per cent and the DCs' share was 21.1 per cent. In most other categories, including ore and bulk/combined carriers and container ships, the ICs own roughly two-thirds of the world fleet. The exceptions are in the general cargo and ore and bulk/combined carrier groupings, where the DCs account for 25.2 per cent and 25.9 per cent

72

respectively of the world total. Overall, the ownership of vessels in DCs is concentrated mainly in the Asian region, and particularly in Singapore, South Korea, Philippines, Hong Kong and India. Some countries in Latin America, notably Brazil and Argentina, have also expanded their fleets tremendously.

Table 4.7
World seaborne trade by type of vessel and country groups,
1970 and 1989 (% deadweight tons)[a]

Country group	Year	% of world total	Oil tankers	Ore and bulk/combined carriers	General cargo ships	Container ships	Other ships
World total	*1970*	*100.0*	*39.4*	*20.2*	*30.2*	*0.9*	*9.3*
	1989	*100.0*	*37.2*	*35.6*	*15.8*	*3.9*	*7.5*
ICs, including	1970	83.9	90.3	93.3	73.2	100.0	72.7
open registry	1989	67.5	78.9	63.5	49.9	68.9	66.7
countries							
Eastern Europe/	1970	8.9	4.7	2.1	13.1	-	29.1
Socialist countries	1989	10.2	4.5	9.7	23.6	6.9	14.0
of Asia							
DCs	1970	6.7	4.7	4.3	12.6	-	5.9
	1989	21.1	16.2	25.2	25.9	15.3	19.2
of which in:							
Asia	1970	3.4	1.7	2.9	6.9	-	2.6
	1989	13.9	10.9	18.1	13.9	12.8	10.0

Source: UNCTAD (1970, 1990d)

[a] The 1970 data are expressed in gross registered tons.

The pattern of world fleet ownership has had serious consequences for DCs, since it implied that DCs have little control over their seaborne trade. The ICs indirectly govern the direction of their trade and the types of goods transported, and they also influence the level and structure of shipping rates. The latter issue relates closely to the role of liner conferences in world trade. Liners are ships which serve a given trade route in accordance with a fixed time schedule. Sailing times and routes are predetermined by the liner companies, and little flexibility is allowed except with respect to volume of goods being shipped. When two or more liner companies service a particular trade route, they normally do so under basic agreements which cover freight rates or other aspects relating to the provision of liner services such as cargo sharing. These agreements are known as liner conferences.

Liners are the most widely used shipping services by DCs, although their role has declined somewhat over the past 10–15 years, on account of the development of national fleets. They are regular and reliable, take varying quantities of goods and are more suitable for carrying a range of goods, including 'sensitive' goods such as butter, cocoa and coffee. They operate within an oligopolistic market structure and therefore have considerable power in key areas such as price setting, provision of services and route structure. DCs have long complained about the functioning of the liner conference system and the negative impact which they exert on their trade and development. They claim that freight rates do not generally reflect cost and efficiency factors, but are often based on 'what the traffic will bear'. They allege that conference lines deliberately favour their own countries' trade, or that of other industrial countries; discriminate in favour of given ports and routes; against incoming trade, against primary goods and against small shippers (Bennathan and Walters, 1969; Yeats, 1981b). While conferences have consistently denied these charges, their unwillingness to reveal information on pricing and costs has contributed to the feeling that rate discrimination is, in fact, practised.

Given this brief background on the shipping problems of DCs, two major issues which relate to S–S shipping can now be addressed. One concerns the adequacy of shipping services while the other pertains to the structure of freight costs and the competitiveness of Southern countries in DCs' markets. With respect to the former it is stated that the route structure of international shipping favours N–S trade, and this adversely affects the availability of shipping services to facilitate S–S trade. During the colonial period the shipping routes were established by the ICs to support N–S trade and this route structure remains intact until today, thereby impeding the development of trade among DCs. The established routes do not allow many DCs to engage in direct trade contacts and they therefore act as an impediment to the development of S–S trade. According to Yeats (1981b) whereas DCs often find it relatively easy to contract liner services linking them to one or a few ICs, they encounter many difficulties in shipping goods to other DCs. In many cases this may only be possible by transhipping goods through an IC port – an undertaking which may lead to considerably higher freight rates due to increased distance and handling charges. DCs which have small consignments or are located in remote areas are at a particular disadvantage since shipping services to these countries may be infrequent or non-existent.

The severity of the problem was noted by Sidney Dell (1966) in respect to neighbouring countries. He reported freight rates for lumber shipped from Mexico to Venezuela at $24 per ton compared with $11 per ton from Finland to Venezuela. The distance from Finland to Venezuela was three times greater than from Mexico to Venezuela, but the freight rate was roughly one-half. Further, goods shipped from Porto Alegre in Brazil to Montivideo in Argentina actually reached their destination more quickly if sent via Hamburg, West Germany. Other evidence provided by Prewo (1978) gives an indication of the high transport costs involved in intra-Latin American trade. Prewo estimated that freight rates for Colombian exports to Argentina were more than 70 per cent, whereas Venezuela's exports to other countries within the region involved rates between 100–200 per cent.

Concerning the structure of freight costs and the competitiveness of Southern countries, it is claimed that DCs are often at a disadvantage in competing against ICs in Third World markets since they are made to bear relatively higher transport costs. The small volumes of merchandise exported by the DCs, their lack of ownership of fleets and in general the weak bargaining position of DCs in the liner market all contribute to these relatively higher transport costs. The competitiveness of the DCs is further reduced if one considers the interaction of these adverse freight differentials with tariffs. Tariffs are generally levied on the basis of c.i.f. values. Therefore, a country which bears a relatively higher freight rate will also be faced with relatively higher tariff charges. Yeats (1981b) estimated that a freight rate differential of 18 per cent in connection with a 60 per cent tariff rate would produce an adverse tariff margin of over 10 percentage points.

In practice it is difficult to substantiate a claim of a bias against S–S shipping since there are many factors which influence the level of freight rates besides distance. These include size of consignment, quality of vessels, differences in loading costs, duration of run and degree of competition and countervailing power on the part of shippers (Fashbender and Wagner, 1973). One study which sought to investigate the claim of a bias found no clear evidence in favour of or against the hypothesis of a S–S freight rate disadvantage (Langhammer, 1983). Using Brazil as a case study, Langhammer compared 1978 freight rates for Brazilian imports from DCs (S–S trade) against those from the USA (N–S trade). His sample consisted of 235 items at the three-digit ISIC level which covered imports from seven developing areas: North Africa, West Africa, East Africa, India/Middle East, ASEAN, Hong Kong/Taiwan and Israel. Sectoral average ratios were computed between Brazilian imports measured c.i.f. and f.o.b. from the various developing areas and from the USA in the same item. A ratio exceeding unity indicates a S–S freight rate disadvantage against competing products from the North.

The results showed that in only three of eight cases was there evidence of a significant S–S freight rate disadvantage: Hong Kong/Taiwan (1.081); intra-ASEAN (1.135) and India/Middle East (1.235). Further, the disadvantage appeared to be more pronounced for manufactured products than for primary ones. The clearest bias was against Brazilian imports from Southeast Asian countries in metal products, electrical and non-electrical machinery, transport equipment and professional goods. These findings have to be interpreted with caution, however. Brazil cannot be considered representative of DCs since its size as a trading partner and the large national fleet it possesses would undoubtedly have allowed it to acquire greater transport cost savings than other DCs. In addition, if the freight rate comparisons were made on the basis of c.i.f./f.a.s. differentials rather than c.i.f./f.o.b. ones, then the N–S/S–S differentials would have been much larger. The f.o.b. figures exclude the costs of loading cargo on board, whereas the f.a.s. data include them. These loading charges average around 50 per cent of the costs of using ports in an IC and are likely to be much higher in a DC. There is every likelihood therefore, that a

75

c.i.f./f.o.b. comparison would have underestimated the real transport costs and narrowed the differential between N–S and S–S shipping costs.

Measures to remove transport constraints

Tremendous efforts have been made in the past, both by national governments and international agencies, to deal with the shipping problems of DCs. But whereas some degree of success has been achieved, many of the fundamental problems still remain. One policy initiative has centred on the establishment of national shipping fleets. During the past two decades a number of DCs, notably Philippines, South Korea, Singapore, Hong Kong, India and Brazil expanded their shipping fleets considerably, and together they now account for a little over one half of the DCs' fleet[12] (UNCTAD, 1990d). Other countries, such as those in Africa, Central America and the Caribbean, also increased their fleets, but their expansions were on a much smaller scale.

DCs have gained from increased national ownership of vessels in a number of ways: through greater control over freight rates, increased availability of services, and expanded trade in new products and to new DC destinations.[13] They also earned the right to participate in liner conferences (and therefore to influence decisions regarding transport policy); and have been able to minimize the risks involved in relying on foreign ships, such as having their services disrupted during hostilities or their trade stopped if they were considered no longer commercially viable.

Unfortunately however, the establishment of national fleets is not an option which all DCs can explore. Many poor countries cannot afford the huge investments required for the purchase of vessels, and small countries may not find it economically feasible to establish national fleets. These problems are expected to become increasingly severe in the future in the light of technological changes taking place in the industry. The present trend is towards containerized shipping which is highly capital intensive and the development of multimodal transport which is organizationally complex. Multimodal transport ensures carriage of goods from the shipper's to the consignee's platform under a single operator.

One of the most effective ways to overcome the above problems is for countries to strengthen ties among themselves, through the establishment of joint shipping lines and harmonization of transport policies. Investments can be spread over several countries and unit costs reduced by pooling small consignments for transport by the shipload. Countries can also benefit from a joint approach to port activities such as the harmonization of tariffs and the development of transhipment ports (UNCTAD, 1987). Several cooperative ventures have been formed along these lines, and these have played an important role in expanding S–S trade.[14] Existing arrangements include joint shipping lines such as the West Indian Shipping Corporation, regional port organizations such as the Port Management Association of West/Central

Africa, and the creation of bodies to harmonize national maritime transport policies such as the Latin American Shipping Commission.

Despite the above however, a recent survey of shipping companies in DCs reveal that cooperation among DCs is still quite limited (UNCTAD, 1987). There is substantial scope for joint activities relating to shipping, ports and multimodal transport, and in special areas such as joint training of shipboard personnel, equipment exchange and joint insurance coverage. Concerted efforts are required in this direction, for increased cooperation could lead to lower freight costs (including port charges) and an improvement in the economic viability and long term competitiveness of companies.

At the international level, UNCTAD's role has been instrumental in reducing the stronghold of liner conferences and controlling their anticompetitive practices. In 1974 the UN adopted a Code of Conduct for Liner Conferences which provided an internationally accepted regulatory framework for the operation of liner conferences and the attainment of a greater participation in shipping by DCs. As of May 1991, 75 states had acceded to or ratified the Convention (UNCTAD, 1991). The main objectives of the Code are to (a) ensure the rights of participation of national lines in trade so that they are entitled to carry a substantial share of their countries' foreign trade; (b) balance the interests of shippers and shipowners; and (c) facilitate the orderly expansion of liner trade. This has resulted *inter alia* in the sharing of cargoes and growth of non-conference liners, and brought into the open the levels of conference freight rates and the processes of conference decision-making. The growth of non-conference liners, in particular, has provided strong competition to the established conferences and therefore indirectly led to a reduction in freight rates.[15]

UNCTAD has also encouraged the formation of shippers' councils in DCs to coordinate shippers' interests. These have played an important role in negotiations with conferences and/or shipping lines regarding freight rates and the scheduling and conditions of shipping services. Continued work by UNCTAD and other international agencies is important for the promotion of maritime transport in DCs. In the future the Code of Conduct will have to be adapted to incorporate technological changes in containerization and multimodal transport; and the liner conferences which are now imposing special surcharges on particular routes will have to be monitored (UNCTAD, 1990d, 1991).

Finally, Erzan and Yeats (1991) have recommended that DCs shift their valuation base for tariff assessment from a c.i.f. to a f.o.b. one in order to remove the bias against S–S trade. This shift would remove the discriminatory interactive effect of tariff and freight costs and allow the competitiveness of countries to be influenced only by their relative freight costs.

TNCS and technology barriers

TNCs occupy a dominant role in DCs' exports, although the forms and nature of their involvement have changed over time. Until the 1970s foreign direct investment (FDI), that is, 100 per cent foreign ownership, was the principal mode of their involvement, and primary products dominated production and exports. Within recent years however, 'new forms'[16] of foreign investment have emerged and increasing emphasis is now being placed on manufactured goods and services. These new forms include joint ventures, licensing agreements, franchising, management contracts, turnkey contracts, production sharing contracts and international subcontracting (Oman, 1984). This section investigates the extent to which North based TNCs have influenced the direction of DCs' trade, particularly in manufactured goods. The discussion is confined to FDI and joint ventures involving majority ownership by foreign corporations, since comprehensive data are not available on the entire range of transnational corporate activity.

A recent UNCTC publication reported that the majority of transnational corporate investments in DCs are concentrated in particular regions and countries. In 1985 Latin America and the Caribbean accounted for 40 per cent of all FDI in DCs, while Asia (excluding West Asia), which has increased its share over the past decade, accounted for 39 per cent. Africa accounted for a small share of 15 per cent. The bulk of FDI however is concentrated in only a few countries in these regions: Argentina, Brazil, Mexico, Chile, Colombia, Trinidad and Tobago and Venezuela in Latin America and the Caribbean; China, Hong Kong, Singapore, Malaysia, Thailand, Indonesia and Taiwan in South and Southeast Asia; Oman in Western Asia; and Egypt, Nigeria and Tunisia in Africa. In 1980–85 these 17 countries accounted for some 86 per cent of all FDI flows into the DCs. In terms of major investors US corporations are the dominant ones, although Japanese firms are emerging as important investors, especially in the Asian region (UNCTC, 1988).

Manufactured goods now represent a far greater proportion of investments, compared with previous years. Recent data provided by Blomstrom (1990) show that US majority owned manufacturing affiliates increased their shares in DCs' manufactured exports from 3.9 per cent in 1966 to 7.2 per cent in 1986. For Japanese affiliates increases were from 3.4 per cent in 1974 to 5.2 per cent in 1983. Within the manufactures category, chemicals and machinery and transport equipment hold the largest shares. These two industries are characterized by labour intensive processes and component specialization within vertically integrated industries such as automobile parts, electrical appliances and machine tools and parts. TNCs now find it advantageous to relocate these industries to countries where abundant supplies of skilled, low cost labour are available.

Turning to the direction of TNCs' trade, it has been alleged that North based TNCs reinforce traditional trading links with the North in at least two ways: (a) by sourcing the majority of their imports from that region, and (b) by directing the bulk of their exports to it. On the import side, TNC subsidiaries are likely to source machinery and other intermediate inputs as well as technology from their home countries or from other ICs. This pattern may be due to at least three factors. Firstly, certain goods and services, for example, specialized pieces of equipment or advanced technologies, may be only available from the ICs. Secondly, TNCs may have a greater familiarity with ICs' suppliers and consider goods and services produced by them to be more reliable in terms of quality, speed of delivery and spare parts availability. Thirdly, certain goods and services purchased from within the TNCs' global network may be cheaper than if obtained from external sources.

The majority of TNCs which direct the bulk of their exports to the ICs do so because of the higher profits which they could realize in those markets based on the gains associated with locating subsidiaries in the DCs. TNCs typically produce low value products in DCs, utilizing cheap natural resources or low cost, skilled or unskilled labour. These products are then exported to the ICs for further processing into high value products, or vertically integrated with the home country's operations. With respect to the latter, TNCs are increasingly shifting the production of parts or components of manufactured items to DCs which are then later exported to the home countries for assembly into finished manufactures. High tariffs and NTBs in the ICs' markets do not constrain the development of those exports since North based TNCs are able to jump such entry barriers. By exploiting the comparative advantages of the DCs then, North based TNCs are able to compete effectively in the more profitable home country markets.

Empirical evidence on the direction of TNCs' trade is not extensive. Most studies involve patterns of trade in particular industries or countries in Latin America during the 1960s and 1970s. This poses problems for making generalizations, especially since the tendency in Latin America has been for TNCs to locate local market-oriented subsidiaries there. Table 4.8 shows that in 1977 the share of exports in total sales of US majority owned manufacturing affiliates was roughly ten per cent in Latin America, compared with over 80 per cent in the Asian NICs. A more general point however relates to the difficulties in isolating the various influences on the geographic distribution of affiliates' exports. For example, observed trading patterns may be attributable to the type of industrialization strategy or to the nature of products rather than to foreign ownership *per se*.

In surveying the evidence on Latin America for the pre-1980 period, del Castillo (1989) concluded that:

1   TNCs sourced the bulk of their imports from the North, mainly parent countries. At the same time they sold most of their exports to other DCs, mainly those in Latin America. This pattern implied a reinforcement of traditional S–N flows, but an orientation towards S–S exports.

79

2   When the trade patterns of TNCs were compared with those of local firms, it was found that both on the export and import sides, TNCs traded more heavily with the ICs than did local firms.

A recent study by Blomstrom (1990) contains more comprehensive data on TNCs' exports which contradict the findings of earlier studies. The data which relate to US majority owned manufacturing affiliates located in DCs revealed several interesting features (Table 4.8).

Table 4.8
Export shares of US majority owned manufacturing affiliates
in relation to their total sales and exports to the US
as a percentage of their total exports

Region/ Country	Exports as a % of total sales				Exports to the US as a % of total exports			
	1966	1977	1982	1986	1966	1977	1982	1986
All Countries	18.6	30.8	33.9	38.3	30.4	29.4	28.6	34.6
ICs	20.4	33.1	36.6	39.2	29.9	27.3	24.9	30.8
DCs	8.4	18.1	22.0	32.6	37.9	50.2	55.0	63.6
Latin America	6.2	9.7	11.9	20.2	35.6	37.3	39.5	58.2
Brazil	3.0	8.7	12.4	17.4	87.2	26.3	22.5	46.5
Mexico	3.2	10.4	10.8	34.4	46.9	62.5	70.0	83.0
Asian NICs[a]	..	81.2	76.2	76.0	..	61.0	73.6	70.3

Source: Blomstrom (1990)

[a] Includes Singapore, Hong Kong, Taiwan and Province of China.

Firstly, there has been a significant increase in the export propensity of US TNCs in DCs. Over the 20-year period 1966–86, TNCs' affiliates increased their proportion of exports in total sales almost four-fold. From 1982–86 growth was most pronounced for Latin America whose share rose from 11.9 per cent to 20.2 per cent. Secondly, the proportion of exports to the US, that is, S–N trade, has grown consistently over time. For Latin America, export shares to the US increased from 35.6 per cent in 1966 to 58.2 per cent in 1986. The bulk of this increase took place in 1982–86, the period of rapid export expansion by TNCs. Thirdly, although affiliates in the Asian NICs showed a much higher propensity to export (roughly three-quarters of their sales were directed to exports in 1986), their exports as a proportion of total sales fell over time, and their exports to the US as a percentage of total exports declined in the 1982–86 period. These data do not, however, capture the full extent of TNC involvement in Asia, since the trend in this region is towards non-equity forms of ownership such as licensing, management sub-contracting and franchising. Overall the data in Table 4.8 show a reinforcement of S–N trade in the exports of TNCs.

Besides objections relating to the direction of trade, North based TNCs have been criticized for failing to transfer technology to DCs. This is an area which has stimulated great debate and in which available empirical evidence is not wholly conclusive. Nevertheless, a number of studies conducted in DCs lend support to the following:

1   North based TNCs do train some proportion of the workers they employ, but skills are not generally transferred in the critical high level management and engineering functions.

2   With few exceptions, North based TNCs do little research and development work in host DCs.

3   In many cases the impact on the technological level is negligible, since backward and forward linkages with the rest of the economy are weak or non-existent.

4   North based TNCs export technologies to DCs which are not 'appropriate' to their environments, both in terms of their production and consumption characteristics. These include the export of highly capital intensive technologies to labour abundant countries and the manufacture of products in low income countries which are suited to high income markets .

5   The costs of technology transfer are very high, as evidenced by the large royalty payments which subsidiaries pay to their parent companies.

In the mid-1970s a number of policy initiatives were taken by national governments to regulate the operations of North based TNCs, especially in the area of technology transfer. Many countries in Asia and Latin America, and a few in Africa, instituted regulations aimed at *inter alia* placing controls on royalty payments and removing restrictive clauses imposed by TNCs on transfer of technology recipients. The entry and operations of TNCs were therefore bound by rules regarding the maximum royalty payments and fees, the prohibition of certain tying requirements, export restrictions and the use of technology after the expiration of agreements. According to UNCTAD (1986) these measures managed to achieve some degree of success to the extent that they led to a reduction of payments abroad and to a revision of technology contracts. However, in recent years several countries have adopted a more liberal approach to foreign investment and relaxed many of the rules set up earlier to regulate foreign investment. Several factors have prompted such changes: slow economic growth and low levels of capital accumulation, mounting foreign debts and their declining attractiveness as locations for TNCs. Within such a context DCs have little bargaining power, and it is therefore unlikely that they would be able to exert control over the direction of their trade or encourage a more effective transfer of technology from North based TNCs.

81

In view of the dissatisfaction with North based TNCs, Southern countries are being urged to encourage the promotion of Third World Transnational Corporations (TWTNCs).[17] This recommendation has sparked off considerable debate for it is argued that transnationals from the South are not significantly different from those from the North. Several studies have found that their motives for investing abroad are basically the same, that is, to gain access to cheap natural resources and/or low cost labour, to increase market shares or diversify market risks (Sagafi-nejad, 1986; Khan, 1986; Lall, 1983). In addition, like TNCs from the ICs, many TWTNCs are large, they are involved in large scale, highly capital intensive activities and rely on product differentiation by the use of trademarks and advertising. Some 17 of the largest TWTNCs have sales of $1 billion or more, the majority of which are located in South Korea, Brazil and Mexico and are involved in mineral processing and extractive activities (UNCTC, 1988). For example, the giant Brazilian firm Petrobrás is involved in the exploration, production and marketing of oil in some 14 DCs (Villela, 1983). Indian investments abroad include the largest paper and pulp mill in Africa, the largest carbon black plant in South east Asia and the world's largest palm oil plant in Malaysia (Lall, 1984a, 1984b, 1984c). Further, roughly one half of South Korea's investments in DCs are in resource development industries (UNCTC, 1988).

However, not all TWTNCs exhibit the above features. A recent UNCTAD study has noted that most TNCs based in DCs are small. The majority of transnational firms from countries such as Hong Kong, India, Taiwan, Argentina and Venezuela have annual sales which run in the millions. These small firms have generated important trade and technology transfers, and because of their special advantages they are considered to have an important role in enhancing technical and economic cooperation among DCs. These advantages arise from the kinds of products manufactured, type of technologies used, the willingness of firms to transfer these technologies and the low cost nature of their operations (Wells, 1983).

Most small TWTNCs undertake investments in the manufacturing sector and they utilize small scale, mature, relatively labour intensive technologies. These are usually based on the adaptation of foreign technologies to the local conditions of the host countries. Such technologies may be better suited to the factor endowments of the host countries, and therefore enable a greater utilization of resources. For example, South Korea's manufacturing investments in neighbouring countries like Indonesia, Malaysia and Pakistan are found in standardized, labour intensive products such as textiles and unsophisticated product lines such as electric and electronic appliances. They have also set up a plant in Thailand to manufacture and assemble semi-automatic tools originally copied from Japanese and European models (UNCTC, 1988). The exporting countries benefit from the opportunities acquired to stimulate minor innovations. Besides advantages in production technologies, TWTNCs also appear to have an edge in terms of organizational and marketing expertise. Chen (1983) noted that the main competitive advantage of Hong Kong TNCs lie in their better management and marketing skills, and Lall (1984b) observed a similar pattern for Indian investors.

One of the most striking observations of TWTNCs is their willingness to transfer technologies to host countries. This was noted by Collins (1985) in his study of Brazil's trade with African countries, and by Villela (1983) who pointed out that Petrobras' policy has been to transfer more technology than its competitors, primarily through the training of personnel in Brazil. The more labour intensive technologies employed by TWTNCs and cheaper inputs in terms of managerial and technical personnel have contributed to lower costs of production. Therefore, TWTNCs tend to provide strong competition to other suppliers in terms of price (Wells, 1983). Overall, TWTNCs can make a substantial contribution to DCs through their trade creating abilities and stimulation of technological change.

The lack of adequate marketing, distribution and information networks in the South

There are two other sets of constraints which impede the development of S–S trade, although empirical data on their existence are scanty. One group relates to the lack of adequate marketing, distribution and information networks in the South, and the other to the tying of aid by the ICs.

In most DCs the marketing and distribution systems are not well developed, and firms do not have access to channels of information regarding goods and services available in other Southern countries. This presents a serious handicap to S–S trade, for if DC importers are not aware of the goods and services produced by other Southern countries nor suppliers aware of potential markets, trading opportunities will remain unexploited. Individual suppliers, especially small ones, do not generally have the finance nor organizational skills to erect elaborate marketing and distribution systems to penetrate other Southern markets. In addition, there are often few large retailers, specialized importers and wholesalers to assist in the development of marketing networks on the importing side.

The lack of marketing experience in DCs is due in part to two main factors: the type of industrialization strategy pursued and the dominance of foreign corporations in DCs' trade. The import substitution policy pursued by many countries in the past emphasized the promotion of industries for the local markets, and firms therefore had few opportunities to acquire the necessary experience and knowledge of export markets. The prominent role occupied by TNCs in the trade of DCs also served to limit the opportunities of DCs to accumulate marketing experience. In the case of wholly owned or majority owned affiliates, foreign corporations undertook the entire range of marketing functions. For primary products this did not amount to much since a large part of marketing simply involved linking local production to parent company operations. The 'new forms' of investment also involve substantial involvement by TNCs, although this is often more subtle and indirect. For example, in joint

83

ventures where TNCs have 'minority' holdings the marketing of output may be undertaken by the foreign partner through special management and operating arrangements or marketing contracts. Further, licensing arrangements made with TNCs may include clauses restricting production to the local market.

Given the recent emphasis on production for export in DCs, a number of measures have been taken, both at the national and international levels, to strengthen the marketing, distribution and information systems in those countries. At the national level this has involved the establishment of State Trading Organizations (STOs). According to Suarez (1986) state trading occurs when a government or government supported agency defines the terms (including quantities and/or price) by which exports and/or imports take place. The principal economic activity of STOs is to compensate for 'market imperfections' in world trade, that is, traders' inability to respond to market conditions due to a lack of or incorrect information; tariffs or other barriers to trade and the inability of producers to take full advantage of their position due to lack of resources to market their products. STOs, however, are of particular importance to DCs since they pursue not only economic objectives, but also social and political ones. Their wide ranging functions include domestic price stabilization, improvement in the terms of trade, the transfer of import or retail trade to nationals, export expansion (especially of non-traditional products), implementation of bilateral trading and geographical diversification of foreign trade.

A recent survey revealed that the number of STOs operating in DCs is in excess of 500, and they are involved in the marketing of primary and manufactured products as well as in international turnkey jobs and investments (UNCTAD, 1989c). It is not known what percentage of world trade is channelled through these enterprises, but estimates for the 1970s suggest a share of around 10–15 per cent of world trade (Kostecki, 1982). Individual country estimates vary in terms of exports, from 97 per cent in Venezuela to 0.5 per cent in Panama, and in terms of imports from 39.3 per cent in Brazil to 0.6 per cent in Panama (Sauliners, 1981).

International efforts to strengthen the marketing capabilities of DCs have involved initiatives to increase cooperation among STOs. In 1984 an International Association of State Trading Organizations (ASTRO) was formed under the auspices of UNCTAD, charged with the responsibility of expanding the trade of DCs, especially trade among DCs. Cooperation is currently being fostered in areas such as trade information, training, joint purchases, market studies and export promotion. Participating countries are expected to gain from these initiatives in a number of ways. Joint purchases, for example, can lead to cheaper imports; cooperation in transport and storage can lead to cost savings and increased competitiveness in foreign markets; and greater access to trade information can lead to the exploitation of wider markets. Further, enhanced cooperation can lead to strengthening the bargaining power of DCs in international markets, as for example, in negotiations with TNCs.

Finally, mention should be made of the UNCTAD/GATT Trade Information System (TIS) which consists of a computerized stock of data covering trade control measures (both tariffs and NTBs) in DCs. Such an information system has been extremely important for DCs: it has assisted in the evaluation of trading opportunities, market prospects, selection of trading partners, and in bilateral and global trade negotiations.

Tied aid

The practice by ICs of tying their aid to procurement of goods and services in the donor country serves as another obstacle to S–S trade. If procurement is not restricted and DCs allowed to choose their suppliers freely, this can permit an expansion of imports from other DCs. If, in addition, these imports involve goods and services in which DCs have a strong comparative advantage this could lead to lower prices for the aid recipients. Gains could also be achieved through the provision of goods and services that are more appropriate to their needs.

Aid-tying takes several forms (Bhagwati, 1967). Some proportion involves formal agreements which restrict the procurement of goods and services to the donor country or region. For example, recipients of French aid may be required to make procurement in France, or EC aid may be tied to procurement in the EC region. But a major part of aid is tied informally. Donors influence procurement in their countries through their choice of projects and programmes, and by tying aid to particular goods and services. There has been an observable trend towards the granting of project aid, especially those involving capital development projects where the scope for tying is great, rather than programme aid such as the provision of balance of payments support where fewer opportunities exist for the tying of aid. A recent OECD report revealed that in 1989 one half of the 18 Development Assistance Committee (DAC) members allocated less than five per cent of their aid to programme assistance. For most countries emphasis was placed on the financing of economic infrastructural projects. In Austria and Japan the shares of total aid devoted to these types of projects were 55.2 per cent and 31.7 per cent respectively (OECD, 1990).

In terms of aid tied to specific commodities or sectors, it has been observed that donors typically finance projects in areas where they have a strong comparative advantage, thereby increasing the chances of procurement in their countries. A study by Jepma (1988) on the aid policies of the EC countries noted that the UK gave strong support to the mining and energy sectors; West Germany to heavy metal and engineering industries; France to the transport sector and the Netherlands and Denmark to agricultural projects and several kinds of public services. Aid is tied in numerous other ways, although many of them are hard to identify. They include agreement through 'silent understanding' or as a result of 'mutual interests' or tradition; through initiatives taken by experts who may be involved with the aid donor's policies; or simply as a result of convenience (Jepma, 1991).

Given the complex nature of tied aid, it has been difficult to estimate its size accurately. Calculations based mainly on formal tying indicate that levels are high, both for bilateral and multilateral aid. Grundmann (1978) estimated that during the 1960s and 1970s roughly 77 per cent of West German aid was tied to procurement in that country, and the Overseas Development Administration (1984) obtained a similar estimate of 74 per cent for the UK in 1984. A more comprehensive study by Jepma (1991) revealed that in 1987 the average level of formal tying of total official development aid (ODA) for 17 DAC countries was 40 per cent. This figure rose to 50 per cent when partially untied aid was excluded, that is, aid involving procurement from the donor country and all DCs. Bilateral aid-tying was found to be particularly high – for individual EC countries it was estimated that some 70 per cent of bilateral aid led directly to procurement in the donor country. Further, of the $11.3 billion of technical cooperation expenditures committed in 1988, roughly 60 per cent was tied (OECD, 1991).

An issue of central concern to DCs is the cost of tied aid, for it is alleged that the tying of aid results in the delivery of goods and services to recipient countries at much higher prices than could be obtained when aid is untied. This proposition is a plausible one, for when restrictions are placed on the number of potential suppliers of a commodity there is greater scope for monopolistic pricing. As is well known, prices under monopolistic competition are normally higher than under conditions of perfect competition. It is difficult in practice, however, to assess the actual costs of aid-tying since data are not normally available to enable comparisons of aid financed deliveries with those not based on aid. A range of studies have examined this issue and they reveal that on average tying costs to recipients are about 20 per cent, although much higher tying costs have been recorded in individual cases.[18]

Details of selected cases are outlined below which illustrate the savings that could be derived from sourcing imports from DCs instead of from donor countries.

1   Imports of passenger carriages into Bangladesh based on tied aid from Denmark during the 1970s, were three times the value of those under international tender from South Korea and Pakistan (Huque, 1985).

2   The price of urea shipped from DAC countries to India in 1968–69 ranged between $72 to $87 per ton. If supplies were obtained from the Persian Gulf, the approximate price would have been $48 per ton (Kahnert, Germidis and Stier, 1971).

3   Tenders on the installation of a steam unit for Pakistan in 1985 led to a Japanese bid which was 225 per cent higher than the one submitted to the People's Republic of China (Jepma, 1991).

4   An evaluation of nine shipments of fertilizers sent to Pakistan from three aid donors in 1987–88 indicated an average price differential of 30 per cent due to tying (Jepma, 1991).

From a theoretical point of view, the untying of aid should lead to lower prices for DCs and hence to an increase in the real value of aid. In recognition of this, DAC members have made efforts to partially untie bilateral aid and to remove regional restrictions on multilateral aid completely. At present only a small percentage of multilateral aid is formally tied. But in spite of this donors still indirectly tie their aid to multilateral programmes through, for example, stipulating that part of their special contributions to regional development banks be tied to procurement in their countries. The record on the partial untying of bilateral aid is poor. In 1988 only eight of the 18 DAC members had partially untied some proportion of their aid, the percentages ranging from 0.9 per cent for Denmark, 2.8 per cent for Sweden, 3.2 per cent for France and 3.5 per cent for Canada to 10.2 per cent for New Zealand, 12.9 per cent for Japan, 13.7 per cent for the USA, and 33.1 per cent for the Netherlands (OECD, 1990).

In the light of the gains to be derived from the untying of aid, DCs have a strong case for continuing their demands for the partial untying of bilateral aid and complete untying of multilateral aid. Co-financing schemes which involve cooperation between bilateral donors and multilateral institutions should be promoted since they encourage untying of aid. For example, some multilateral agencies now request individual donors to untie part of their contributions to co-financing schemes and assume less responsibility for the administration of these programmes.

However, the untying of aid could well result in a reduction of the total volume of aid which donors are willing to give. Southern countries will therefore have to give serious consideration to a trade-off between the receipt of more tied aid as opposed to reduced amounts of untied aid.

Summary

This chapter examines the main barriers to S–S trade and suggests policy measures for their removal. It is found that, in general, trade policy and financial constraints are the most serious constraints. High tariffs and NTBs such as quotas and import licensing imposed by DCs impede the competitiveness of Southern countries' exports. This is compounded by the fact that the structure of protection discriminates against products in which DCs have their strongest comparative advantage such as labour intensive products and other simple unprocessed manufactures. At the same time little protection is given to the capital goods sector, an area which has great potential for S–S trade and holds special benefits for DCs in terms of learning and skill accumulation.

The financial constraints stem largely from the DCs' reliance on the currencies of the ICs to finance their intra-trade. This renders them vulnerable to changes in the monetary policies of those countries. It is observed that when the ICs pursue more or less easy monetary policies and finance is widely available at low cost, S–S trade flourishes. However, when highly restrictive monetary and fiscal policies are adopted this induces large net financial outflows from DCs and huge balance of payments deficits. This, in turn, has a severe negative impact on S–S trade. The lack of adequate export credit facilities in DCs also constitute a major financial constraint to S–S trade. Whereas ICs' firms benefit from government supported export credit schemes which contain implicit subsidies, exporters from the South are at a severe disadvantage since such facilities are only available to them on a highly restricted basis. Capital goods exports are particularly affected since they often require medium and long term financing.

The lack of adequate shipping services and high transportation costs also serve as obstacles to S–S trade. Existing shipping routes favour S–N trade, a legacy of the colonial structures, and the ICs which dominate world shipping do not encourage the transport of goods between DCs. Indeed, intra-DC trade often involves costly transhipment through ICs' ports. DCs which have small consignments or are located in remote areas are at a particular disadvantage since shipping services to these countries may be infrequent or non-existent. DCs claim that they are made to bear high transportation costs in relation to those borne by the ICs and this reduces their competitiveness in Third World markets. This is largely because freight rates which are normally fixed by North based liner conferences do not generally reflect cost-and-efficiency factors, but are often based on 'what the traffic will bear'. This claim is difficult to verify empirically, but indirect evidence suggests that such a bias does exist.

A range of other barriers inhibit the development of S–S trade, although their influences are far more difficult to assess. North based TNCs with subsidiaries in DCs, for example, source their main inputs from their parent companies or other firms in the ICs and direct the bulk of their exports to them. This pattern is being reinforced at present, through the production of parts or components of manufactured items in DCs and their subsequent export to the ICs where they are assembled into finished items. Other barriers to S–S trade include the lack of well developed marketing and distribution networks in the DCs and the practice by ICs of tying their aid to their home countries or other ICs.

In the light of existing barriers to trade, a number of policy measures are suggested to accelerate the development of S–S trade. They include the dismantling of trade policy barriers; strengthening of payments and credit arrangements; greater establishment of export credit facilities (both on a national and regional basis); selective use of countertrade; development of national fleets and/or joint shipping lines; and improvement in port management and more extensive training of shipping personnel. Further, it is suggested that greater attention be given to the promotion of TWTNCs and formation of STOs, as well as to the partial untying of bilateral aid and complete untying of multilateral aid.

Notes

1. UNCTAD's Trade Control Measures Information System classifies NTBs in several categories: licenses and quantitative restrictions; money and finance measures; control of price level; single channel for imports; special entry procedures; and additional fiscal charges.
2. The agreement was signed in Belgrade, Yugoslavia on 13 April, 1989.
3. Roemer explained the meaning of 'disproportionately' by the following hypothetical example. If it is assumed that for the USA textiles is a weak sector, aircraft is a strong sector, and Canada is a strong area, then the USA's share of the Canadian aircraft market should not be too different from its share of the aircraft market worldwide. However, since textiles is a weak sector for the USA, its share would vary greatly across areas and occupy a relatively large share in Canada since Canada is a strong area for the USA. Textiles, the weak sector, would be marketed disproportionately in Canada.
4. IMF, *International Financial Statistics* (1978–82 issues) and UN, *Monthly Bulletin of Statistics* (1978–82 issues).
5. OECD, *World Economic Outlook* (1978–82 issues).
6. Two examples of monetary unions in the Third World are the West African Monetary Union (1973) and the Central African Monetary Union (1972).
7. At present only the central banks of El Salvador and Honduras are using the CACH.
8. The United Nations Special Plan of Economic Cooperation for Central America has made provisions for funds to restore the liquidity of the CACH (UNCTAD, 1990c).
9. See *Technical Documentation for the Study of the Feasibility of a Bank for Developing Countries* (1983), UNCTAD Secretariat, Geneva.
10. Criticisms of the South Bank proposal are contained in Abbott (1986).
11. Open registry countries are those which allow foreign shipowners (usually from the ICs) to register vessels in their territories and sail under their flags. The major open registry countries are Panama, Liberia, Cyprus and Bahamas, but other countries such as Antigua and Barbuda, Bermuda, Cayman Islands, Malta, St Vincent and Vanuatu also permit open registration of vessels.
12. Individual shares are 12 per cent, 9 per cent, 8.8 per cent, 7.7 per cent, 7.6 per cent and 7.5 per cent respectively (UNCTAD, 1990d).
13. The expansion of Brazil–Africa trade is one of the clearest examples of the latter. Prior to the 1970s there were no direct shipping links between Latin America and Africa, and trade between the two regions was limited. However, during the 1970s Brazil constructed a direct shipping route to Nigeria and this facilitated a tremendous expansion in trade with a number of African countries, including Nigeria, Angola, Mozambique and Ghana.
14. Unfortunately several of these arrangements have sustained losses in recent years as a result of the depressed state of freight markets (UNCTAD, 1987).
15. An ESCAP study reported that the '... expansion in non-conference services resulted in restraint in liner conference pricing policy leading to a comparatively low rate of increase of freight charges in the period 1983–84'. (UN, ESCAP, 1985.)
16. This terminology was introduced by Oman (1984).
17. See the series of studies in Khan (1986).
18. See Jepma (1991) for a review of these studies.

89

Part Two
South–South Trade in Practice: A Sectoral Study of NIC–LDC Trade

5 Prospective trade linkages between Trinidad and Tobago and Brazil

Introduction

This part of the book presents a case study of S–S trade involving two countries which are at different levels of development – Brazil and Trinidad and Tobago; and within this bilateral framework opportunities for trade are explored in the petrochemicals industry. The case is interesting from both a country and an industry point of view, for whereas most studies focus on trade between the NICs, the present one investigates a case of NIC–LDC trade. Brazil belongs to the group of NICs and is one of the more developed countries in the South, whereas Trinidad and Tobago is one of the LDCs.

The detailed, industry study of S–S trade presented in this book has not been attempted before. Yet it is of great significance since it permits an in-depth examination of the major issues regarding the problems and prospects for S–S trade. The specific case of petrochemicals allows us to examine trade creation and trade diversion issues, and others such as the influence of trade policy barriers. Over the past two decades many oil rich DCs have developed a strong comparative advantage in petrochemicals and this has allowed them to compete effectively in both ICs' markets where petrochemicals production is extremely high cost, and in Southern countries where demand for these products is increasing rapidly. In fact, it has been projected that over the next 15–20 years, the most rapid growth in the consumption of petrochemicals will take place in the DCs (UNIDO, 1983a). These developments imply that the potential for S–S trade is likely to be greater than S–N trade and, far from being trade diversionary, is likely to lead to fruitful trade creating opportunities. Further, whereas in the past Southern countries have imposed high tariff and NTBs on petrochemical imports, recent trade liberalization efforts indicate that there will be expanded potential for S–S trade in the future.

This chapter introduces the case study on potential trade between Brazil and Trinidad and Tobago. It outlines a basis for trade between the two countries, and investigates the organization and functioning of their petrochemical industries with a view of selecting specific areas for the future development of trade.

Trinidad and Tobago and Brazil: a basis for trade

The features of the economies of Brazil and Trinidad and Tobago are different, and the two countries are at varying levels of development. Yet it is precisely these dissimilarities that create a basis for trade. There are two trade theories which suggest that countries at different levels of development can fruitfully engage in trade: factor endowment theory and neo-technology theory. The former states that differences in resource endowments provide a basis for trade, while the latter stresses the importance of differences in technological advancement. These theories provide the main guide for our study on potential trade between Trinidad and Tobago and Brazil. Empirical observations on differences in the trading structures as well as locational features also lend support for the development of trade between the two countries.

Differences in resource endowments

It is difficult to make comparisons of resource endowments across countries. This is largely because the empirical assessment of a country's relative abundance or scarcity of resources poses problems of measurement. Physical capital is normally counted among the primary factors of production, land and labour; and strict separation of human and physical capital is difficult because part of a country's human capital is the technology incorporated in its physical capital. The measurement of natural resources is also fraught with numerous problems.[1]

Notwithstanding the above problems, an attempt is made to compare differences in resource endowments by first of all providing a brief sketch of resource profiles in each country. Then, assuming that a country's relative factor endowment is reflected in its pattern of trade, the areas in which the two countries have a comparative advantage or disadvantage are examined by comparing revealed comparative advantage (RCA) indices. This latter investigation will assist in identifying a specific area in which trade can be developed between the two countries.

Sketch of resource profiles.   Brazil's natural resources are vast and its mineral wealth in particular is enormous. The country has 11 per cent of the world's iron ore and bauxite reserves; 3 per cent and 1.3 per cent of the world's gold and nickel reserves respectively; substantial nuclear mineral deposits as well as other minerals such as manganese, platinum, tin and zinc.[2] In addition it has a huge arable land mass of 66.5 million km^2 with a varied range of agricultural products and timber resources. It is the world's leading producer of coffee, oranges and sugar cane and the second largest producer of soya beans and cocoa. Further, its timber resources are second only to those of the USSR (Petrobrás, 1986).

There is one major deficiency in Brazil's natural resource base however, and this is oil. Over the period 1974–83 Brazil imported roughly 85 per cent of its requirements of oil (Wirth, 1985). But in 1984 large discoveries of oil and natural gas were made in the states of Bahia and Rio de Janeiro, and further oil finds have continued since that time. As a result, over the period 1983–89 crude oil and gas production increased by 80 per cent and 45 per cent respectively and oil reserves rose by 37 per cent. By contrast, Brazil's imports of oil as a proportion of total consumption have declined substantially to around 20 per cent. But despite these favourable developments Brazil still remains a large importer of oil. In 1988 its imports of oil amounted to 31.5 million tons, the largest in South America. The growing needs of Brazil's rapidly expanding industrial sector, increasing demand for fuel by the transport sector and by households for domestic heating have contributed towards this situation (APEC, 1990).

Trinidad and Tobago has a range of natural resources, which include oil and natural gas, agricultural land, marine resources, forestry, and minerals such as iron, gypsum, limestone and clay (Cooper and Bacon, 1983). However, except for the first two, many of these resources exist in small quantities and are largely underdeveloped. The country's proven oil reserves have been estimated at 536 million barrels and its probable reserves at 448 million barrels. Although the proven reserves are equivalent to only 0.05 per cent of the world's total, they are large in relation to the size of the country. Natural gas reserves are larger than for oil, and have been estimated at 462 billion cubic metres or 0.36 per cent of the world total.[3]

Another area in which resource bases differ widely is human capital. A country's human resources are often measured by the amount and types of education and training obtained by its population. Literacy rates provide an indication of the overall quality of the work force, and proportional shares of secondary and tertiary educational levels indicate the existing levels of higher skills. Data on these indicators show that Brazil has increased its stock of human resources substantially over the past three decades, largely because of expansions undertaken in its educational and training systems. Literacy rates rose from 61 per cent in 1960 to 78 per cent in 1985; the gross secondary school enrolment ratio increased from 16 per cent in 1965 to 38 per cent in 1986–88 and at the tertiary level the corresponding increase has been from 2 per cent to 11 per cent. Trinidad and Tobago has also increased its education and training facilities, but this has been mainly at the lower levels. Its literacy rate of 96 per cent is one of the highest in the Third World, and its secondary school enrolment ratio which was estimated at 82 per cent in 1988 was more than double that in Brazil. However, its enrolment in education at the tertiary level is only four per cent (UNDP, 1990).

Another valuable indicator of human resources is the number of scientists and technicians per thousand of population. This ratio reflects the approximate levels and pools of more specialized skills available in a country. In 1980–88 this ratio was 29.5 for Brazil and 8.5 for Trinidad and Tobago. The Brazilian ratio compares quite favourably with that for India (30.0) and Singapore (23.8), and is indicative of a fairly high level of human resource development (UNDP, 1990).

Both Brazil and Trinidad and Tobago are critically short of financial resources, and this is reflected in their large external debts. Brazil is currently the world's largest debtor nation. In 1989 its total external debt reached $111.3 billion, the ratio of debt outstanding to GNP was 24.1 per cent, and the debt service to export ratio was 31.3 per cent. Brazil's large scale borrowing during the 1960s coupled with the escalation in interest rates in the post-1973 period were major contributory factors to its massive foreign debt. As far as Trinidad and Tobago is concerned, the accumulation of a large foreign debt in that country is a fairly recent phenomenon. In 1980 its total external debt stood at $828 million and its debt service to export ratio at 6.8 per cent. But during the 1980s its external debt rose sharply as the need for borrowing increased in the light of falling oil prices and subsequent declines in export earnings. The country's external debt reached $2.0 billion in 1989 and the debt service to export ratio, 12.3 per cent. But whereas the external debt of Trinidad and Tobago appears small in comparison with that of Brazil, when viewed in relation to the national product, its debt burden is perhaps more onerous. Its ratio of debt outstanding to GNP in 1989 was 55.4 per cent which was more than double that for Brazil.

Trinidad and Tobago and Brazil: RCA indices. The brief comparisons of resource profiles in Brazil and Trinidad and Tobago indicate that these countries have different resource endowments. Trinidad and Tobago is an oil rich country, is scarce in physical capital and has a narrow human resource base. Brazil, on the other hand, is an oil deficient country, also lacks physical capital but has a large and growing human resource base. These features suggest that the two countries are likely to have different areas of comparative advantage, and hence complementary trading structures. The following examination of indicators of comparative advantage confirms this.

The data in Table 5.1 are based on Balassa's index of revealed comparative advantage. The basic RCA concept assumes that a country will export those products in which it has a comparative advantage, and import those in which it has a comparative disadvantage.[4] It is based on post-trade data and therefore incorporates all the influences on the pattern of international trade, including the influence of trade barriers.[5] If the RCA index assumes a value of less than one, this implies that the country has a revealed comparative disadvantage in the product. If however, it exceeds one this implies that the country has a revealed comparative advantage in the product. In view of data limitations, the RCA indices shown are for the manufacturing sector only. This does not limit our analysis however, since a wide range of resource based products are included among the indices for manufacturing.

The seven strongest and weakest areas of comparative advantage in each country are shown in Table 5.1. Brazil's strongest areas of comparative advantage are in agro-based products: coffee preparations, feeding stuff and fruit preparations. By contrast, the strongest areas of comparative advantage in Trinidad and Tobago are all petroleum based: refined petroleum products, inorganic chemicals and mineral tar oils. Two categories of petroleum based products, manufactured fertilizers and inorganic chemicals, are among Brazil's weakest areas of comparative advantage. Others include capital intensive goods such as rails and railway track materials and electronic equipment. Most areas of comparative disadvantage in Trinidad and Tobago also consist of capital intensive goods.

Table 5.1
Indicators of comparative advantage in Brazil and
Trinidad and Tobago, 1981–83

	Brazil			*Trinidad and Tobago*	
	Category	RCA index		Category	RCA index
	Areas of comparative advantage				
1	Coffee extracts, essences, preparations	27.10	1	Refined petroleum products	16.02
2	Animal feeding stuff	19.29	2	Inorganic chemicals	14.55
3	Preserved fruit, preparations	15.51	3	Mineral tar oils	6.64
4	Fixed vegetable oils and fats	9.43	4	Perfumery, cosmetics and soaps	3.54
5	Sugar preparations, honey	8.93	5	Sugar, honey and confectionery	2.02
6	Pig iron, sponge iron	8.71	6	Ships and boats	1.80
7	Wool and other animal hair	5.32	7	Iron and steel bars, rods	1.60
	Areas of comparative disadvantage				
1	Manufactured fertilizers	−4.50	1	Mechanical handling equipment	−0.91
2	Copper	−2.84	2	Misc. metal manufactures	−0.89
3	Rails and railway track materials	−2.56	3	Civil engineering plant and equipment	−0.84
4	Cereal preparations and starch	−2.28	4	Cereal preparations	−0.81
5	Electric power machinery	−2.08	5	Edible products and preparations	−0.71
6	Other inorganic chemicals	−2.00	6	Preserved fruit and fruit preparations	−0.64
7	Misc. non-ferrous metals	−1.68	7	Aircraft	−0.45

Source: UNIDO (1983a); Parsan (1988)

Differences in levels of technological development

The discussion above on human capital endowment gives an indication of the levels of technological development in both Brazil and Trinidad and Tobago. Since Brazil has a higher ratio of tertiary education enrolment than Trinidad and Tobago and a much larger number of scientists and technicians, it is clearly at a higher level of technological development. In fact, Brazil is known to be one of the most technologically advanced countries in the Third World. This is evidenced by its growing ability to produce and export a wide variety of technology intensive goods and services. A study by Sercovich (1984) concluded that 'technology exports by Brazilian firms reveal a general phenomenon of upgrading of technical skills, knowledge and experience for the Brazilian economy as a whole' (p. 575).

Table 5.2 shows the various ways in which Brazil exports technology – through the supply of technical services; sale of capital goods abroad; export of construction projects and foreign direct investment. Of these four categories, technology associated with construction projects is the largest. It includes mainly hydroelectric projects, highways and urban construction. The second largest category, disembodied technology, includes mainly technical services in the mining and oil sectors.

Table 5.2
Technology exports from Brazil, 1976–81 ($mn)

Concept	No. of operations	Value of operations	Imputed value of disembodied technology exports
Disembodied	112	357.4	357.4
Capital goods supply related Made-to-order capital goods	..	1 257.1	125.7
Complete plant exports	49	285.2	42.8
Construction project export related	147	4 283.5	856.7
Direct foreign investment related	232	252.0	..
Total			*1 382.6*

Source: Sercovich (1984)

Locational features

In addition to differences in resource endowments and technological levels of development, another factor which favours trade between Brazil and Trinidad and Tobago is location. Assuming that distance is indicative of transportation costs, trade between Trinidad and Tobago and Brazil is likely to benefit from relatively low transport costs since these countries are geographically close to each other. Transport costs are determined not only by geographic distance however, but by marine distance. The latter takes into account the structure of shipping routes. As discussed before, many DCs do not have direct shipping links with each other and this poses constraints on the development of trade. In the present case however, the shipping routes are fairly well developed between the two countries. The marine distance between Port of Spain (Trinidad) and Rio de Janeiro (Brazil) is 3,240 nautical miles. This is a relatively short one when compared with that between Rio de Janeiro and other major ports such as New York (4,780) or London (5,200).

Current trading patterns: Brazil and Trinidad and Tobago

To a large extent, the trading patterns of Brazil and Trinidad and Tobago reflect their underlying resource endowments. At present roughly 36 per cent of Brazil's exports consists of primary products, chiefly iron ore, soyabeans, coffee, meat and orange juice. Manufactured goods, which account for 64 per cent of total exports, consists of a wide variety of human and physical capital intensive goods such as metallurgical products (18 per cent), transport equipment and components (11 per cent), chemical products (6 per cent) and machines and mechanical instruments (5 per cent). On the import side capital goods account for the largest proportion of the total (27 per cent), but oil and chemicals also account for large import shares (20 per cent and 18 per cent respectively).[6] By contrast, Trinidad and Tobago's exports are dominated by oil and chemical products (roughly 80 per cent of the total). Their imports, however, are more varied and consist mainly of machinery and transport equipment (27 per cent of the total). In terms of the direction of trade, both Trinidad and Tobago and Brazil import roughly 60–70 per cent of their goods from the ICs (mainly the USA) and direct about 30 per cent of their exports to them.[7]

Trade between Trinidad and Tobago and Brazil did not develop on a large scale until the mid 1970s, despite their proximity to each other. The recent development in trade has been largely because of the growth in Trinidad and Tobago's import markets during the oil boom years, increased availability of both primary and manufactured goods in Brazil, and the latter country's drive towards trade with the South. Trade between the two countries however, is skewed in favour of Brazil's exports to Trinidad and Tobago. Table 5.3 shows that whereas in 1988 Trinidad and Tobago's imports from Brazil amounted to $TT 120.8 million or 3.2 per cent of its total, its exports to that country were

99

only $TT 3.1 million or 0.2 per cent of its non-oil exports.[8] Brazilian exports to Trinidad and Tobago are fairly diversified: its primary goods exports (which consist mainly of iron ore) account for roughly 58 per cent of total exports, and manufactured goods for 42 per cent. A large proportion of manufactured goods (70 per cent) consists of basic manufactures such as paper and paperboards, iron and steel products and wood manufactures. Machinery equipment such as compressors and pumps, heating and cooling equipment and textile and leather machinery also account for a substantial share of total manufactured goods (25 per cent). By contrast, Trinidad and Tobago's exports to Brazil are concentrated in a few products. In 1988 methanol exports alone accounted for 88.2 per cent of the total, lead waste and scrap for 7.2 per cent, and various manufactured items for 2.4 per cent.

Table 5.3
Trinidad and Tobago's trade with Brazil, 1988

Product category	Trinidad and Tobago's imports from Brazil		Trinidad and Tobago's exports to Brazil	
	Value (TT$ '000)	%	Value (TT$ '000)	%
Total	120 709.2	100.0	3 109.6	100.0
Food and live animals	2 238.7	1.9	0.2	0.0
Meat and meat preparations		(73.0)		
Beverages and tobacco	4 877.7	4.0	7.7	0.3
Tobacco, unmanufactured		(99.8)		
Crude materials, inedible				
(except fuels)	62 051.4	51.4	223.5	7.2
Iron ore and concentrate		(98.0)		
Mineral fuels	-			
Animal and vegetable oils	-			
Chemicals	2 226.0	1.8	2 742.7	88.2
Plastic resins		(30.0)		
Medicinal products		(25.0)		
Methanol				(100.0)
Basic manufactures	34 464.0	28.6	75.2	2.4
Paper and paperboards		(31.0)		
Iron and steel products		(27.0)		
Wood manufactures		(22.0)		
Machinery and transport				
equipment	12 659.6	10.5	1.0	0.0
Pumps, compressors		(19.0)		
Heating, cooling equipment		(17.0)		
Equipment for electricity				
distribution		(14.0)		
Textile, leather machinery		(11.0)		
Miscellaneous manufactured goods	2 148.9	1.8	0.1	0.0
Footwear		(72.0)		
Miscellaneous transactions	42.8	0.0	59.3	2.0

Source: Trinidad and Tobago, Central Statistical Office, *Overseas Trade* (1988)

The above discussion suggests that differences in resource endowments could provide a basis for trade between Trinidad and Tobago and Brazil. Trinidad and Tobago has a strong comparative advantage in energy intensive products, especially petrochemicals, and exports substantial amounts of those products. Brazil has a comparative disadvantage in these areas and relies to a large extent upon imports to meet domestic requirements. Further, whereas Brazilian exports to Trinidad and Tobago are large, there are limited exports from Trinidad and Tobago to Brazil. Therefore, one area which appears to have scope for the development of trade is petrochemicals. Another basis for trade can be found in the fact that Brazil has been able to upgrade its technical skills, knowledge and experience over the past few decades, and is fast emerging as an important exporter of technology. Since the country is particularly strong in the oil industry, trade in technology is another area which can be explored.

The structure and functioning of the petrochemical industries in Trinidad and Tobago and Brazil

This section examines in detail the petrochemical industries of Trinidad and Tobago and Brazil in order to (a) establish at a micro level the basis for exploring trade, and (b) to map out specific product areas in which trade can be developed. A number of areas are considered: product structure, raw materials, technology and investment, costs and pricing. The production, consumption and trading aspects of the sector in each country are also discussed.

Product structure

The petrochemical industry produces hundreds of different products which constitute a rather complicated and highly interwoven structure. These products can be classified into three major groups: *basic* or *bulk* petrochemicals, *intermediate* and *end* or final petrochemicals. Within the first group there are eight main petrochemicals – ethylene, propylene and butadiene (the olefins); benzene, toluene and xylene (the aromatics); ammonia and methanol.[9] The most important of these eight basic petrochemicals is ethylene which is the largest volume single product manufactured by the industry.

A few of the basic petrochemicals are end products in themselves. For example, ammonia is used as a liquid fertilizer in the agriculture sector. Others are directly converted into end products, as in the case of ethylene which is processed into low density polyethylene (LDPE) and high density polyethylene (HDPE) for use by the plastics industry. But the majority of basic petrochemicals are reacted with other chemicals to form hundreds of intermediate products. In terms of the end products, the major ones fall into three categories – plastics, synthetic fibres and synthetic rubber. The paths leading from the basic products to the end products are numerous and complex, but the main ones can be traced. Ethylene and propylene serve as basic inputs for the production of plastics; benzene, toluene and xylene (BTX) for the synthesis of non-cellulosic fibres; butadiene for the production of the main synthetic rubbers; and methanol for the production of formol, one of the constituents of adhesives (UNIDO, 1978a).

In most ICs the entire range of petrochemicals is manufactured at huge petrochemical complexes. These complexes normally consist of a large plant producing basic petrochemicals and surrounding downstream units producing intermediate and end products. In many DCs, production is undertaken in only a few product areas. These two cases are illustrative of the industries in Brazil and Trinidad and Tobago respectively. The bulk of petrochemicals production in Brazil is organized around three large complexes. The Sâo Paulo (SP) Complex, the first of the three petrochemical complexes to be constructed, was built over the period 1965–72 to service the growing needs of the industrial capital, Sâo Paulo. There are 22 companies at this complex, the largest of which is Petroquímica União, the basic petrochemicals plant. It produces 360,000 tons of ethylene annually and all other basic petrochemicals except ammonia and methanol.

The North East (NE) Complex is currently the largest petrochemical complex in Brazil, and was built during the period 1973–78. It is located in the north eastern state of Bahia, near to some of the country's major deposits of oil and natural gas. At the centre of the NE complex are the operations of Petroquímica do Nordeste (Copene) which supplies basic petrochemicals to over thirty downstream companies. Its annual productive capacity of ethylene is 460,000 tons. The Southern petrochemical complex is located in the southern state of Rio Grande do Sul and is the most recently constructed in Brazil (1982–87). Annual productive capacity of ethylene at its basic petrochemicals plant, Companhia Petroquímica do Sul (Copesul) is 420,000 tons. In addition to the three petrochemical complexes, there are a few petrochemical plants scattered throughout Brazil which produce varying quantities of synthetic butadiene rubber (SBR), chlorochemicals, ammonia and a few other petrochemicals.

Taking into consideration the total productive capacity of petrochemicals in Brazil, the structure of production is as shown in Table 5.4. Ethylene capacity which exceeds one million tons annually accounts for the largest share of basic petrochemicals (27.4 per cent), and ammonia for the second largest (23.3 per cent). The olefins as a whole account for a little less than one half of all basic petrochemicals, whereas the aromatics account for roughly one quarter. In terms of end products, plastics is undoubtedly the most important, for it accounts for roughly three-quarters of total end products.

The petrochemical industry in Trinidad and Tobago, unlike that in Brazil, has a very narrow product structure. There is a significant omission of olefins production, the major growth pole of any petrochemical industry, and production of the main end products – plastics, SBR and synthetic fibres – is not undertaken.[10] In fact, the industry produces only six petrochemical products –

102

ammonia, methanol, urea, benzene, toluene and xylene. The first three of these are manufactured on a very large scale. Table 5.4 shows that ammonia capacity which accounts for 75 per cent of the total petrochemical capacity in the country is 1.7 million tons. Methanol capacity, which accounts for another 21 per cent, is 470,000 tons. For each of these two products, annual productive capacity is greater than in Brazil. Trinidad and Tobago also produces fairly large quantities of urea (540,000 tons per year) and a limited amount of aromatics. All these products are produced for the export market. In 1989 Trinidad and Tobago was the world's second largest exporter of ammonia after the Soviet Union, and a significant producer of methanol and urea (FAO, 1990b). Ammonia is produced at five large scale ammonia plants and the oldest, which was built in 1959 and expanded significantly in 1968, has an annual productive capacity of 228,000 tons. The other four were constructed during 1978–88, and each has an annual productive capacity between 300,000–400,000 tons. The methanol plant which has recently expanded its levels of production currently has a capacity to produce 470,000 tons of methanol annually.

Table 5.4
Petrochemical product structure, Brazil and Trinidad and Tobago, 1990

	Brazil			Trinidad and Tobago	
Product	Capacity ('000 t/y)	% of total	Product	Capacity ('000 t/y)	% of total
Basics			**Basics**		
Olefins			*Olefins*	-	
Ethylene	1 439	27.4			
Propylene	792	15.1			
Butadiene	213	4.1			
Aromatics			*Aromatics*		
Benzene	536	10.2	Benzene	30	1.3
Toluene	407	7.8	Toluene	49	2.2
Xylene	394	7.5	Xylene	35	1.5
Ammonia	1 224	23.3	Ammonia	1 700	74.0
Methanol	248	4.7	Methanol	470	21.0
Total Basics	*5 253*	*100.0*	*Total Basics*	*2 284*	*100.0*
End			**End**	-	
Plastics	1 700	74.8			
SBR	300	13.2			
Synthetic fibres	274	12.0			
Total End	*2 274*	*100.0*			
Fertilizers[*]	1 747		Fertilizers[*]		540

Source: ABIQUIM (1989); Petroquisa; Republic of Trinidad and Tobago, Ministry of Energy and Natural Resources

[*] Includes only nitrogen fertilizers.

Choice of raw materials

The raw materials or feedstocks used by the petrochemicals industry today derive almost exclusively (about 90 per cent) from petroleum hydrocarbon resources – hence, the term 'petro-chemicals'. They are obtained either from the refining of crude oil or from natural gas production. Coal and biomass are two other feedstocks which are utilized in the industry, but at present they are used in very small amounts because of economic considerations. Biomass, obtained primarily from sugar cane, is used in Brazil and India, whereas a few coal based plants are located in Western Europe. In Trinidad and Tobago where there are abundant reserves of both oil and natural gas, and where energy demand in the domestic economy is small, the choice of raw material is relatively simple. But in Brazil where the demand for refined petroleum products far exceeds the supply, and where there is limited natural gas production, the problem is more complex. Before investigating raw material use in these countries however, some detail is given on the main types of raw materials that are generally used in the petrochemical industry.

Crude oil, once refined, yields three basic groups of products – light products, middle distillates and residue. The main product in the first group is light gasoline which is used for gasoline blending. In the second group are naphtha, kerosene and gas oil which are used as domestic fuel, diesel or jet fuel, and the third group of residue is used mainly as a heavy fuel oil. In theory, all these products can be used to produce petrochemicals. The choice of one refinery product against another depends upon both technological and economic factors. From a purely technological point of view, the lighter and more volatile fractions are preferred to the heavier ones, but from an economic standpoint, consideration has to be given to the alternative uses of the product, and in particular its value as a fuel. Those most widely used today are naphtha and gas oil.

In terms of the feedstocks produced from natural gas, there are two types: *associated* and *non-associated gas*. *Non-associated gas* is found in underground reservoirs, broadly similar to oil reservoirs, from which it is recovered by drilling gas wells. *Associated gas*, on the other hand, takes its name from the fact that it is produced in association with crude oil. While still underground the associated gas remains dissolved in the surrounding oil due to pressure. When the oil is brought to the surface, the pressure drops and the gas is released. In some oil fields, especially those in inaccessible regions, it is not economic to collect this gas, in which case it is simply flared.[11] The major difference between these two types of gas lies in their chemical composition, which in turn influences the type of petrochemicals that can be produced from them. The main constituents in natural gas are *methane* and *ethane*, but there are some other useful gases such as *butane* and *propane*. The specific composition varies from gas to gas, but in general, non-associated gas tends to be high in methane and low in other gases; while associated gas tends to contain large amounts of ethane, propane and butane. Ammonia and methanol

104

can be easily produced from non-associated gas because of its high methane content. However, only a gas that is high in ethane, propane and butane can produce ethylene, propylene and butadiene respectively. This means that associated gas is most suitable for the manufacture of the olefins. Unfortunately, the aromatics cannot be produced from natural gas. There are many uses for natural gas besides petrochemical manufacture. The major one is for re-injection in the oil fields, but it can also be used for the manufacture of products such as iron and steel, as a fuel, or it can be liquified and used for domestic and commercial heating.

Table 5.5 shows that natural gas in Brazil, both non-associated and associated, has a fairly high composition of methane as well as large proportions of ethane and other gases. Natural gas in Trinidad and Tobago has a very high methane content and small proportions of ethane and other gases. The technical composition of the natural gas in these two countries has no doubt influenced the types of petrochemicals produced by them. As noted in the previous section, Brazil's petrochemical industry is highly diversified and produces the entire range of petrochemicals, whereas in Trinidad and Tobago there is a concentration on production of ammonia and methanol.

Table 5.5
Composition of selected natural gases (% by volume)

	Country/Location					
Natural gas components	Brazil (Rio de Janeiro)	T and T[*]	Iran (Agha Jari)	Brazil (Bahia)	T and T[*] (East Coast)	UK (North Sea)
	Associated gas			Non-associated gas		
Methane	89.9	89.7	66.0	88.5	92.6	94.4
Ethane	8.5	4.0	14.0	8.4	4.3	3.1
Butane	0.5	2.1	10.5	0.3	1.5	0.5
Propane	-	1.2	5.0	-	0.7	0.2
Others	-	3.0	4.5	-	1.0	1.8

Source: Petroquisa; Republic of Trinidad and Tobago, Ministry of Energy and Natural Resources (1985); Wiseman (1986)

[*] T and T: Trinidad and Tobago.

The importance of the various feedstocks differs according to regions. In the USA and the centrally planned economies the major feedstock is natural gas, whereas in Western Europe and Japan naphtha is the major raw material.[12] Table 5.6 shows that Brazil relies heavily upon the products of oil refining, mainly naphtha, but it also uses large quantities of natural gas and small quantities of ethanol, made from sugar cane. The industry in Trinidad and Tobago is based almost exclusively on natural gas.

Table 5.6
Raw material use in the petrochemical industry in Brazil and Trinidad and Tobago, 1980 and 1990 (%)

	Brazil			Trinidad and Tobago	
Product	1980	1990	Product	1980	1990
Naphtha	90	70	Natural Gas	98	98
Others:	10	30	Others	2	2
Gas oil	..	..			
Natural gas	..	..			
Ethanol	..	..			
Total	100	100	Total	100	100

Source: Instituto Brasileiro Petróleo (1983); Petroquisa; Trinidad and Tobago, Ministry of Energy and Natural Resources

Despite its dominance in the petrochemical industry, naphtha use in Brazil has declined over time. Whereas in 1980 naphtha accounted for some 90 percent of the total raw materials used by the industry, in 1990 this share fell to 80 per cent. The growing importance of natural gas has largely contributed to this. Until 1975 natural gas production in Brazil was quite small, and its use was confined to the refineries. This was not only because of the lack of substantial natural gas reserves, but also because of their location. Most of them were located in the Upper Amazon area from where it was difficult to transport it to the main industrial areas. With the construction of the NE Complex in 1978 and new discoveries of gas in the northern state of Sergipe, natural gas began to be used for petrochemicals manufacture. In 1980–84 alone natural gas consumption in the industry more than doubled, and additional oil and gas discoveries in 1986–87 stimulated even greater use of this raw material. Despite the growing use of natural gas by the petrochemical industry only 20 per cent of total production is used by it. This is because natural gas in Brazil has many competing uses. About one half of production is used in the refineries and 30 per cent is used for domestic heating, and for the production of liquefied petroleum gas and natural gasoline.[13]

The structure of raw material use in the petrochemical industry in Trinidad and Tobago is quite different from that in Brazil. Roughly 98 per cent consists of natural gas which, because of its technical composition, is used in the production of ammonia and methanol. Oil refinery fractions are not generally used for petrochemicals manufacture in Trinidad and Tobago, despite the country's endowments of crude oil and large facilities for oil refining.[14] The

106

main reason why the use of refinery fractions was never explored was because the industry was owned by foreign TNCs who organized it in a way to suit their own needs. This type of organization meant exporting large amounts of crude oil and gearing refinery output towards the production of heavy, low-value products, mainly fuel oil (Farrell, 1977).

Until 1984, AMOCO and Texaco, two large US companies respectively dominated crude oil production and refinery activities in Trinidad and Tobago. Amoco's main aim was to provide low cost crude oil to the USA, while Texaco was interested in exporting low value refined products to that market for domestic heating. This affected the availability of raw materials to the petrochemical industry to the extent that in the first case it reduced the amount of crude oil for local processing; and in the second it constrained the availability of refined products suitable for petrochemicals manufacture. Some 56 per cent of refinery output in 1980 consisted of fuel oil, and the remaining portion comprised mainly gasoline. No naphtha production was undertaken.[15] In 1984 the government of Trinidad and Tobago purchased the Texaco refinery and all its production facilities. However, since Texaco traditionally imported large quantities of crude oil for processing at the local refinery, this development led to a cessation of oil imports and hence to excess refinery capacity. AMOCO continues to export the bulk of its output of crude oil. In 1989 the refinery capacity utilization rate was only 25 per cent compared to 70 per cent in 1980. Attempts are now being made to upgrade the refinery and to increase the processing of local as well as imported crude from neighbouring, oil producing countries such as Venezuela. These efforts have led to higher levels of refinery use. Between 1989 and 1990 alone the refinery capacity utilization rate rose by 11 per cent.[16]

Technology and investment

The technologies for petrochemical manufacture are complex and the investment requirements very large. The complexity of the technology arises not only from the fact that the chemical processes are complicated; but also because these processes can be applied to many different raw materials to produce varying combinations of products. A brief discussion of these technologies is first undertaken below, and then a comparison is made of the technologies used in Brazil and Trinidad and Tobago. The extent to which these countries have been able to acquire a technological capability in producing petrochemicals is also discussed.

The key processes in the primary petrochemical industry are *steam cracking* and *catalytic reforming*. Steam cracking utilizes fractions from both natural gas and crude oil refining, and is used in the production of olefins. Catalytic reforming utilizes either naphtha or gas oil. It is the main process used in the production of aromatics, although some aromatics may also be produced by steam cracking. The complicated nature of the technology can be observed if we consider the many ways in which ethylene can be produced, and the

107

resulting product mixes. Table C.1 shows that ethylene can be produced either through 'cracking' of ethane, butane, propane, naphtha, or gas oil. If ethane is cracked, the sole product recovered is ethylene and the yield is very high (75 per cent). By contrast, if naphtha or gas oil is cracked, the yields of ethylene are quite low (13–15 per cent), and the quantity of co-products is large. The most important co-products are propylene and butadiene which must be separated out for further processing. There are two points to note about the cracking process. One is that the heavier the feed, the more complex is the product mix. The second is that the facilities required for cracking increase with the complexity of the mixtures. This, in turn, impacts upon the scale of investments required. As Table C.1 shows, investment costs for a plant based on the cracking of ethane was $84.8 million during the mid-1980s. This was much lower than that based on the cracking of naphtha ($123.5 million) or of gas oil ($141.3 million).

Besides the processes noted above, there are two others which are used in the manufacture of ammonia and methanol – *steam reforming* and *partial oxidation*. The former utilizes methane and naphtha, whereas the latter uses fuel oil or coal. Steam reforming is by far the most widely used process for the production of ammonia and methanol. From a technological point of view it is the simplest, and it also requires the least costly investments. By contrast the partial oxidation process is more complex, uses heavier feeds and requires more extensive investments. Only a few plants use this process today.

Types of technologies used. From the above, it is clear that the selection of technologies depends critically upon the raw materials available, as well as upon the mix of products required. In Brazil the main technology used is the steam cracking of naphtha. Table 5.7 shows that roughly 85 per cent of ethylene is based on steam cracking of naphtha; 9 per cent on dehydration of sugar cane alcohol and 6 per cent on cracking of gas oil. Production of the rest of the olefins and the aromatics is based on the steam cracking of naphtha. The technologies used for ammonia and methanol production are more varied. Over one half (54 per cent) of ammonia production is based on the steam reforming of natural gas, and 12 per cent on naphtha steam reforming. Further, it is surprising to note that 34 per cent of ammonia capacity is based on the seldom used partial oxidation process, using fuel oil as feedstock. This includes the largest ammonia plant in Brazil which produces 1,200 t/d of ammonia. In the case of methanol, 30 per cent of capacity is based on steam reforming of methane, and 70 per cent on naphtha steam reforming.

Compared with those in Brazil, the technologies used in the Trinidad and Tobago petrochemical industry are the more modern and efficient ones and the sizes of plants are generally larger. Both ammonia and methanol are produced through steam reforming of methane and, except for one ammonia unit, all plant sizes exceed 1,000 t/d. These observations on the types of technologies employed in the two countries imply that production costs in

Brazil are likely to be higher than in Trinidad and Tobago. This issue is investigated more directly in the next section.

Table 5.7
Major processes used in the Brazilian and
Trinidad and Tobago petrochemical industries

Product	Country/Company	Year of start-up	Plant size (t/d)	Process
Ethylene	Brazil/PQU	1972	1 043	steam cracking of naphtha
	Copene	1978	1 125	steam cracking of naphtha (80%)
				steam cracking of gas oil (20%)
	Copesul	1982	1 217	steam cracking of naphtha
	Coperbo	..	116	dehydration of sugar alcohol
	Salgema	1982	232	dehydration of sugar alcohol
Ammonia	Brazil/Cubatão	1958	90	partial oxidation of fuel oil
	Piaçaguera	..	454	steam reforming of naphtha
	NE Complex	1978	200	steam reforming of methane
	NE Complex	1978	907	steam reforming of methane
	Araúcaria	1981	1 200	partial oxidation of fuel oil
	Laranjeiras	..	907	steam reforming of methane
	T and T*/ Norsk-Hydro	1968	680	steam reforming of methane
	Tringen I	1978	1 100	steam reforming of methane
	Tringen II	1988	1 400	steam reforming of methane
	Fertrin I	1981	1 045	steam reforming of methane
	Fertrin II	1981	1 045	steam reforming of methane
Methanol	Brazil/Alba-Química	..	100	steam reforming of naphtha
	Hoechst	..	17	steam reforming of naphtha
	Polyenka	..	17	steam reforming of naphtha
	Metanor	1978	210	steam reforming of methane
	Prosint	..	350	steam reforming of naphtha
	T and T/Methanol Co. of T and T	1984	1 400	steam reforming of methane

Source: ABIQUIM (1989); Stanford Research Institute International (1985); Petrofértil (1985); Petroquisa

* T and T: Trinidad and Tobago

Technology acquisition. Sercovich (1985) noted that Brazil is one of the few DCs that is likely to reach the technological frontiers of research in petrochemicals in the future. He attributed this to the fact that the government of Brazil has taken a very active role in the acquisition of technologies for the production of petrochemicals. In particular, it devised a unique strategy for dealing with TNCs and the acquisition of technologies. It invited foreign investors with technological expertise to participate in a three-sided joint venture arrangement involving the State (1/3), local national capital (1/3), and foreign capital (1/3). Then through a policy of skilful 'de-packaging' of technology it managed to acquire a considerable amount of technological expertise (Stauffer, 1985).

Table 5.8 shows how Brazil has progressed over time in providing technological inputs to the local industry. During the construction of the Sâo Paulo Complex (1965–72) only 50 per cent of the technological inputs were provided locally. This consisted mainly of inputs at the construction and assembly stage (100 per cent), the conduct of preliminary studies (50 per cent) and the provision of capital goods (45 per cent). But some 15 years later when construction of the Southern complex was undertaken (1978–82) the proportion of local technological inputs rose to 75 per cent. All preliminary studies, detailed engineering, and construction and assembly work were conducted locally. In addition, 75 per cent of capital goods and 30 per cent of technical assistance were obtained locally. The areas of technology in which Brazil are deficient are process licensing and basic engineering. Despite these deficiencies, Brazil has begun to export some of the technological expertise it has acquired in petrochemicals manufacture (Stauffer, 1985). This is one area which has been earmarked for development of trade with the South.[17]

Information is not available on the technological capabilities acquired by the petrochemical industry in Trinidad and Tobago. It has been suggested that some technological expertise has been acquired over the past 30 years. But it is likely that the type of technological skills acquired are those of the 'static' type – that is, those which enable the day-to-day running of the plant (De Castro, 1977). The local industry is known to be severely deficient in the types of technologies required for the construction of plants, problem solving and generation of new products. This is evidenced by the fact that during the recent expansion of the petrochemical industry, there was almost complete dependence on foreign TNCs for the supply of technology.

Table 5.8

The Brazilian petrochemical industry, local supply of technological inputs (%)

Petrochemical complex	Category of inputs						
	Preliminary studies	Process licensing	Basic engineering	Detailed engineering	Technical assistance	Construction and assembly	Capital goods	Local proportional content
São Paulo (1965-72)	50	-	-	10	5	100	45	50
North East (1972-78)	100	-	-	70	30	100	60	65
Southern (1978-82)	100	-	-	100	30	100	75	75

Source: Teixeira (1985)

Cost structure and pricing

In this section the comparative cost positions and pricing policies of the Brazilian and Trinidad and Tobago petrochemical industries are examined. This is an important discussion since it addresses the question of comparative advantage at a micro level. First, the various cost categories are examined and the factors influencing production costs are briefly discussed, together with the relationship between costs and prices. Then the specific cost structures and pricing policies of the two countries are examined.

The major cost components of petrochemicals fall into three categories: *variable costs, semi-variable costs* and *fixed costs*. The main items in the variable cost category are raw materials, utilities, catalyst and chemicals; in the semi-variable cost category they are operating labour, maintenance labour and laboratory control; and fixed costs include plant overhead, depreciation and local taxes and insurance. Of these cost elements, the most important are raw material and capital investment costs. The labour cost component is small since petrochemical production is highly capital intensive.

Prior to the oil boom, the shares of raw material and investment costs in total production costs were roughly the same, about 40–45 per cent each. However, the two oil price shocks in 1973–74 and 1979–80 radically altered the structure of costs in the petrochemical industry. In particular, they raised the share of raw materials in total costs of production, and lowered that of capital investment. In the case of ethylene production (based on naphtha), the cost of investment rose in real terms by 300 per cent during 1973–80, but investment shares declined from 48 per cent to 13 per cent. Costs of raw materials rose by 1,360 per cent, and raw material shares escalated from 46 per cent to 85 per cent (OECD, 1985a). With lower oil prices prevailing since 1986, raw material shares have declined somewhat, but the dominance of raw materials in total production costs remains.

The above example is illustrative of the general changes which have taken place in cost structures. However, the extent to which specific cost structures have been altered depends upon a variety of factors. These include the type of product, processes and raw materials used, investment requirements, plant size and location. The type of product is important since some products are more energy intensive than others, and therefore have higher energy costs. In general, the energy requirements for aromatics are greater than for the olefins or ammonia and methanol; and those for basic products and intermediates larger than for downstream products. For example, whereas the production of one ton of ammonia requires 9,900 thermies of energy, an equivalent quantity of para-xylene requires 22,350 thermies (UNIDO, 1981a).

The type of process and raw material used are also important in determining production costs. In discussing the technological aspects of the industry, it was established that the processes which use heavier feeds are more complex and generally require heavier capital outlays. In addition, the heavier feedstocks tend to be more highly priced than the lighter ones, when measured in terms of energy equivalents. Indeed, price increases of the heavier feedstocks were greater than the lighter ones in the post-1973 period. Location factors and plant size also feature prominently in production costs. UNIDO (1981a) notes that plant construction costs are, in general, higher in DCs than in ICs. The inadequacy of existing infrastructure in DCs, the need to adapt technologies to DC environments and shortage of skilled construction workers contribute to this. Finally, as far as plant size is concerned larger units tend to have lower per unit production costs than smaller ones. For example, production costs at a plant producing less than 600 t/d of ammonia are roughly 25 per cent more than those producing between 600 and 1,000 t/d (UNIDO, 1981a).

Production costs in Trinidad and Tobago and Brazil. It is clear from the above discussion that many factors have to be taken into consideration when evaluating production costs. There are additional problems when comparisons are to be made across countries. Table 5.8 shows for example that in Brazil and Trinidad and Tobago the age and sizes of plants vary widely. Further, available production cost data for the two countries are not strictly comparable. However, some general idea of costs can first be obtained by examining raw material prices, and then production cost data can be compared.

All feedstock prices in Brazil are fixed by the government. The Conselho Nacional Petróleo (CNP) or the National Petroleum Council, the governmental body responsible for policy decisions regarding oil, sets the prices for all products and users in accordance with national development goals and priorities. Since the petrochemical industry is regarded as one of the priority industries, it receives feedstocks at substantially lower prices than other users. Within the petrochemicals sector, the fertilizer industry receives especially favourable treatment. Table C.2 shows the huge disparity in energy prices charged to different users. For industrial users such as the iron and steel industry, the price of natural gas charged is $3.59 per mmBtu, whereas the basic petrochemicals sector (olefins, aromatics and methanol) is charged $2.90 per mmBtu and the fertilizer industry $0.96 per mmBtu. The differences are even more marked in the case of naphtha. The fertilizer industry is charged $42 per ton, whereas the rest of the petrochemicals industry pays $210 per ton. Naphtha for other uses (excluding fuel generation) is sold at $874 per ton.

In Trinidad and Tobago, the government also sets feedstock prices, but the situation is somewhat different. The state owned National Gas Company (NGC) is the sole supplier of natural gas in Trinidad and Tobago. However, it has first to purchase the gas from the AMOCO oil company, which is the major producer of natural gas in Trinidad and Tobago. The final price charged to consumers is set by the NGC according to criteria similar to those outlined in the case of Brazil. The specific prices charged to different users are not available, but it is known that the price charged to the fertilizer industry is lower than to methanol producers.

Table 5.9 shows feedstock prices in Brazil and Trinidad and Tobago, and also includes some international figures for comparative purposes. As a result of the subsidy, the prices of natural gas and naphtha for fertilizer production in Brazil are 64.2 per cent and 82.9 per cent respectively lower than the US or international price. The extent of the subsidy is not as great for other basic petrochemicals. Natural gas and naphta prices for the manufacture of the basic petrochemicals are 16 per cent and 14.3 per cent respectively lower than the international price. Comparing Brazil's and Trinidad and Tobago's prices, it can be seen that because of the subsidy the price of natural gas for fertilizers is the same as in Trinidad and Tobago. For other petrochemicals manufacture however, prices are 35 per cent lower in Trinidad and Tobago.

Table 5.9
Raw material prices for petrochemicals in selected countries, 1984[a]

Country	Natural gas	($/mmBtu)	Naphtha	($/ton)
Brazil	Petrochemicals	2.90	Petrochemicals	210
	Fertilizers	0.96	Fertilizers	42
Trinidad	Petrochemicals	1.89		
and Tobago	Fertilizers	0.96		..
USA	Petrochemicals	3.45[b]		..
	Fertilizers	2.68		..
Western		..	Petrochemicals	245
Europe			Fertilizers	..

Source: (1) Brazil data: Conselho Nacional Petróleo (2) Trinidad and Tobago data: *Green Markets*, 3 June, 1985, p. 71; Trinidad and Tobago Methanol Company reports (3) USA data: Serletis (1986) and Chem Systems Incorporated (1985) (4) Western Europe data: OECD (1985a)

[a] In this table 'petrochemicals' refers to all basic petrochemicals except ammonia.
[b] 1985 price

Raw material prices are only one indicator of production costs. If the types of technologies and plant sizes in the two countries are considered, one is likely to conclude that production costs in Trinidad and Tobago are much lower than in Brazil. Table 5.10 gives some indication that this is the case. The figures in this table have to be interpreted carefully, since they are not directly comparable. For example, production cost figures for ammonia in Trinidad and Tobago are for only one of the three companies. Pricing data also differ. Prices in Brazil are domestic (or ex-factory prices) ones, while those for Trinidad and Tobago and the international market are f.o.b. prices. However, these differences do not pose a serious problem for our analysis.

Two major points emerge from Table 5.10. First of all, the cost of producing petrochemicals in Trinidad and Tobago is much lower than in Brazil or in the USA. Ammonia is produced in Trinidad and Tobago at costs which are 25 per cent lower than in Brazil and 27 per cent lower than in the USA. Sufficient data are not available to make comparisons for urea and methanol, but it is likely that cost differentials are similar, or even larger. For example, controlled prices of methanol in Brazil are 62 per cent higher than international prices. This, plus the fact that a large proportion of methanol in Brazil is naphtha based and several of the plants are small, suggest that methanol production costs are also very high. This situation was noted in a report by Menezes Pereira (1984) as follows:

> The lack of methanol plants in the country using modern technology (1,000–2,000 t/d) must be noted. This has resulted in the consumer having to bear very high prices, and at the same time it has inhibited the development of the national market (p.6).

The second major point that emerges from Table 5.10 concerns the cost/price relationship. The data for Brazil show that in the case of urea, production costs are 21 per cent higher than prices, and for ammonia, costs and prices are the same. It must be noted though, that production costs are current ones, and prices are short run ones. Further, this situation prevails because the prices of

Table 5.10
Production costs and prices of ammonia, urea and methanol
in selected countries, 1984 ($/ton)

Country	Ammonia	Urea	Methanol
Trinidad and Tobago			
Costs	92	..	99
Prices	152	140	95
Cost/price ratio	0.61	..	1.04
Brazil			
Costs	123	180	..
Prices	123	149	350[a]
Cost/price ratio	1.00	1.21	..
USA			
Costs	126	..	178[b]
Prices	168	170	134
Cost/price ratio	0.75	..	1.33

Source: (1) Trinidad and Tobago data: production costs from petrochemical company reports; product prices from Trinidad and Tobago, Central Statistical Office, *Overseas Trade* (1984) (2) Brazil data: production costs and prices for ammonia and urea from Schultz and Mattos (1986); methanol price from Menezes Pereira (1984) (3) USA data: ammonia production costs from Serletis (1986); methanol production costs from *Green Markets*, 1984 issues; methanol prices from *European Chemical News*, 1984

[a] November 1983 price
[b] estimated 1985
[c] production costs based upon a 1971 plant with capacity of 299,700 t/y using natural gas

Brazilian petrochemicals are all set by the government's Interministerial Prices Council. Schultz and Mattos (1986) state that if Brazil were to fix its price of ammonia at a level which is considered to be 'adequate' according to the international organization's definitions, the price will escalate to $192 per ton (13 per cent higher than international prices). In the case of Trinidad and Tobago, the cost/price ratio for ammonia revealed that costs were only 61 per cent of prices, compared with 100 per cent for Brazil and 75 per cent for the USA. For methanol however, although costs were slightly higher than prices (4 per cent), the difference was less than that prevailing internationally (33 per cent). It must be noted that in 1984 methanol prices were particularly low because of the rapid build up of methanol capacity worldwide.

This overall discussion on costs has shown that the Trinidad and Tobago petrochemical industry is low cost when compared with that in Brazil. This is despite the fact that the Brazilian petrochemical industry benefits from large input subsidies. Trinidad and Tobago's advantage derives from its low feedstock costs, the large scale nature of its production, and modern technology. Hence, it does have a comparative advantage over Brazil in the production of petrochemicals.

The growth in production, consumption and trade

The petrochemical industry in Trinidad and Tobago has similar roots to that in Brazil, for they both started during the 1950s producing small amounts of fertilizers. However, since that time the industry in Brazil has diversified its range of products and rapidly expanded its levels of production. Today it produces over 100 products and is considered one of the Third World's largest producers of ethylene and polyethylene. Two major factors have facilitated the rapid growth of the Brazilian petrochemical industry. One has been Brazil's large domestic markets and the other the rapid growth of its economy during the 1960s and the 1970s. Indeed, it was in response to a large and growing domestic demand that the industry developed. The industry in Trinidad and Tobago on the other hand, has also experienced rapid growth, but this has been in only a few products. Since the Trinidad and Tobago market is small, local consumption of petrochemicals has been limited and almost the entire output is exported.

Table C.3 shows that whereas in Brazil production and consumption levels of petrochemicals were quite low up until 1965, they expanded tremendously from the mid-1970s onwards. The production of ethylene, the most important product in the industry, grew from 20,000 tons in 1965 to 404,000 tons in 1978 and reached 1.4 million tons in 1990. Substantial increases were registered for all the other major products, although many of them, especially the aromatics and their downstream products, are undertaken on a much smaller scale. As Brazil expanded its production of petrochemicals, consumption levels rose equally rapidly, and imports which were fairly high during the 1960s, fell dramatically over time. The decline in imports was particularly severe for ammonia and urea. Ammonia imports dropped from 224,000 tons in 1978 to 20,000 tons in 1990, and urea from 399,000 tons to 56,000 tons over the same period.

A recent development in the Brazilian petrochemical industry is the drive towards exports in a few product areas. In 1981 when local demand was depressed because of domestic recessionary conditions, small quantities of polyethylene and benzene began to be exported. Since that time this trend has continued, and Brazil now exports fairly large amounts of plastics [polyethylene (PE), polyvinyl chloride (PVC) and polypropylene (PP)] to a wide range of countries. In 1990 PE exports amounted to 248,000 tons or roughly 25 per cent of production.

Of the few petrochemicals that are produced in Trinidad and Tobago, growth has been fastest for ammonia and urea production, especially in 1980–90 (Table C.4). During the latter period ammonia and urea production more than doubled, reaching 1,859,700 tons and 504,000 tons respectively in 1990. By contrast, BTX production has not expanded over the years, largely because of feedstock and technical problems. Consumption of basic petrochemicals in Trinidad and Tobago is low, and almost the whole output of petrochemicals is exported.[18] In fact, Trinidad and Tobago is currently the world's second largest exporter of ammonia and a significant exporter of urea and methanol. There are virtually no imports of basic petrochemicals into Trinidad and Tobago, but small amounts of plastic resins such as PE, PVC and PP are imported to meet the needs of the domestic plastics processing industry. In 1990 roughly 30,000 tons of plastic resins were imported from Germany, the USA and other ICs.[19]

As far as the direction of trade is concerned, the trade of both Brazil and Trinidad and Tobago has been oriented towards the North. Table 5.11 shows that about 90 per cent of Brazilian imports of urea are from the ICs, including a little over one half from the USA. Similarly, in Trinidad and Tobago the bulk of ammonia and methanol is exported to the ICs, with roughly 50 per cent to the USA. It is interesting to note that urea exports from Trinidad and Tobago and plastics exports from Brazil go mainly to Southern countries. The reasons for these recent developments are discussed more fully in Chapter 6.

Table 5.11
Direction of trade in urea:
Brazil and Trinidad and Tobago, 1980 and 1988

Brazilian imports from:	% of total 1980	1988	Trinidad and Tobago's exports to:	% of total 1980	1988
Northern countries			*Northern countries*		
USA	55.5	11.2	USA	43.3	44.5
USSR	10.6	41.3	Canada		13.7
Netherlands	7.6		France		10.5
Germany	13.9	11.2	Belgium-Luxembourg		3.9
Italy	11.2				
Southern countries			*Southern countries*		
Venezuela	12.0		Puerto Rico	3.4	
Argentina	0.4		Costa Rica	5.0	
Nigeria	16.0		Guyana		5.6
			Belize		0.7
			Chile		3.9
			Colombia		17.1
			Rest of the world[*]		48.3
Total	*100.0*	*100.0*	*Total*	*100.0*	*100.0*

Source: Trinidad and Tobago, Central Statistical Office, *Overseas Trade* (1980 and 1988); República Federativa do Brasil, Ministério da Fazenda, *Comércio Exterior do Brasil* (1988)

[*] The data for this category were recorded in an aggregate form. They therefore include both Northern and Southern countries.

Prospective areas for trade cooperation

Having examined the structure and functioning of the petrochemical industry both in Brazil and Trinidad and Tobago, specific areas can now be mapped out for the development of trade. Two areas appear to have potential:

1 The export of selected petrochemical products – ammonia, methanol and urea – from Trinidad and Tobago to Brazil.

2 The export of petrochemical technologies from Brazil to Trinidad and Tobago for the development of the plastics industry in the latter country.

Both Trinidad and Tobago and Brazil can reap gains from trade in the above areas. Trinidad and Tobago's production costs of petrochemicals are low compared with those in Brazil, and with those in the USA from where the bulk of Brazil's imports are sourced. Therefore, one major benefit expected for Brazil is access to low cost petrochemicals. Such gains are likely to be of particular importance to the agriculture sector in Brazil, for in the past farmers have complained bitterly about the high prices of locally manufactured fertilizers. In 1990, for example, the National Confederation of Agriculture lodged complaints against Petrofértil, the state owned fertilizer enterprise, for allegedly engaging in monopolistic and 'abusive' price increases in ammonia and urea. It was held that between March and August 1990 the company raised fertilizer prices by some 60–79 per cent (*Green Markets*, 17 September, 1990).

Trinidad and Tobago can also reap benefits from the export of petrochemicals to Brazil through access to wider markets. In the past Trinidad and Tobago's petrochemicals could be imported into the Western European and US markets free of duties. This duty free status was assured through various types of trading arrangements entered into with the ICs – the Generalized System of Trade Preferences, the Lomé Agreement and the Caribbean Basin Initiative. However since the mid-1980s access to these markets has become increasingly difficult as the ICs have adopted measures to protect their domestic industries against large scale, low cost imports from oil rich countries. In July 1986 producers in the EEC lodged a dumping complaint against the exports of urea from Trinidad and Tobago and seven other countries.[20] As a result, an anti-dumping duty of 11.2 per cent was imposed on Trinidad and Tobago's urea and the country had to agree to limit its exports to the EEC. Although the extent of the quota restriction is not known, it is believed to have been around 50,000 tons.

As the ICs are becoming more protectionist, Brazil is in the process of implementing a massive trade liberalization programme. This involves the elimination of import controls and the progressive reduction of average tariffs from 32 per cent in 1990 to 14 per cent in 1994 (*GATT Focus*, 1991). These liberalization efforts augur well for potential petrochemical exports from Trinidad and Tobago. But besides freer markets Brazil is also expected to offer more high growth ones, compared with those in the ICs. The projected growth rate of nitrogen fertilizer consumption to the year 2000 in the ICs is 2.8 per cent, compared to 6.3 per cent in Brazil (UNIDO, 1978a). The former rate could be lower, depending upon limits placed on fertilizer consumption for environmental reasons, and on reduced incentives to agriculture in the EEC and the USA which may result in land being taken out of production.

Gains can also be acquired from trade in area (2) above. Through the export of its petrochemical technologies, Brazil could upgrade its skills and augment its stock of human capital. Since its technological capabilities relate specifically to the use of refinery fractions, the provision of these could lead to greater natural resource utilization in Trinidad and Tobago. Further, the establishment of an olefins plant could lead to greater product diversification in the Trinidad and Tobago petrochemical industry, and to the creation of linkages with the downstream plastics industry.

One institutional form which may be explored for the establishment of the olefins plant is a joint venture arrangement. This could involve the pooling of Trinidad and Tobago's natural resources with the technological expertise and marketing experience of Brazil. Brazil may be able to provide technologies

119

which are cheaper than those in the North, and more appropriate to the needs of Trinidad and Tobago. Also, it may provide an avenue for stimulating trade reciprocity. Indeed, one of the major factors that has motivated Brazil to develop trade with other DCs has been the prospects for exporting its manufactured goods and services to those countries.

But whereas trade in the areas outlined above are likely to benefit both trading partners, the question as to whether trade can actually take place in those areas requires detailed examination. This is because the constraints to trade, policy induced or institutional, can provide powerful obstacles to trade. These issues are investigated in the next chapter.

Summary

This chapter examines prospective trading links between Trinidad and Tobago and Brazil. Drawing upon the H–O theory, it is argued that since Trinidad and Tobago is relatively well-endowed with oil and natural gas while Brazil is relatively lacking in these resources, there exists a basis for trade in energy intensive products. Differences in levels of technological development between the two countries provide another basis for trade. Whereas Brazil is one of the most technologically advanced countries in the Third World and is fast emerging as an important exporter of technology, human capital development in Trinidad and Tobago is at a relatively low level and the country relies to a large extent upon imported technologies. Trade in technology is therefore considered to be another area to be explored. Some empirical observations indicate that the petrochemicals sector is a good choice for detailed study. An examination of RCA indices in Trinidad and Tobago and Brazil reveal that the former country has a strong comparative advantage in petrochemicals. In addition, although Trinidad and Tobago exports large quantities of petrochemicals and Brazil is geographically close to it, trade between the two countries is little developed. Brazil's import requirements are met mainly from the ICs, particularly the USA.

An examination of the functioning and operations of the petrochemical industries in Trinidad and Tobago reveals some interesting features. First of all, despite the wide availability of raw materials in Trinidad and Tobago and the scores of petrochemicals which it could produce, production on a large scale is confined to only three petrochemical products – ammonia, urea and methanol. Secondly, owing to the domestic availability of low cost raw materials in Trinidad and Tobago and the modern technologies employed there, its production costs are low compared with those in Brazil and in the USA. Thirdly, over the past few decades Brazil has developed a substantial technological capability in petrochemicals manufacture, and is anxious to develop exports in this area. Their experience has been particularly with plants utilizing refinery fractions, an area which has been relatively unexplored in Trinidad and Tobago.

In the light of the above features, two areas are selected for examination of trade potential: (a) the export of ammonia, urea and methanol from Trinidad and Tobago to Brazil, and (b) the export of technological expertise from Brazil to Trinidad and Tobago for the expansion of the plastics industry in the latter country. The organizational form envisaged is a joint venture arrangement. The likely benefits of trade in these areas are considered to be great. In area (a) above Trinidad and Tobago could reap gains from access to expanded markets, and Brazil from availability to low cost petrochemicals. In area (b) however, the likely gains are considered to be of the more dynamic type. Through its export of technologies, Brazil can upgrade its skills and augment its stock of human capital, whereas wider use of refinery fractions in Trinidad and Tobago would represent greater natural resource utilization. Wider product diversification and the creation of inter-industry linkages in the Trinidad and Tobago petrochemical industry are additional benefits.

Notes

1. See Vanek (1959) for a discussion of these.
2. USA, Bureau of Mines, Department of the Interior (1983).
3. See British Petroleum (1990) and Republic of Trinidad and Tobago (1989), *Medium-Term Macro-Planning Framework, 1989–1995*.
4. The RCA index is based upon a comparison of a country's commodity structure of exports and the structure of world exports. It is measured in the following way:

$$RCA = (x_{ij} / X_{iT}) / (x_{wj}) / X_{wT})\ 0 < EP_{ij} < \infty$$

where

x_{ij} = country i's exports of product j
x_{iT} = world exports of product j
x_{wj} = country i's total exports
x_{wT} = total world exports

5. See Hillman (1980) and UNIDO (1986a) for recent discussions of this concept.
6. See APEC (1990).
7. Republic of Trinidad and Tobago, Central Statistical Office, *Overseas Trade Report* (1988) and IMF, *Direction of Trade* (1990).
8. Ibid.
9. Ammonia is essentially an inorganic chemical, but since it utilizes technologies and raw materials that are similar to those of petrochemicals it is considered a petrochemical.
10. The reasons for this production structure are explained in the subsequent discussion on the use of raw materials.
11. In Saudi Arabia, for example, roughly 40 per cent of the non-associated gas produced is flared. See UNIDO and Gulf Organization for Industrial Consulting (1981).
12. Naphtha is increasingly being used in the USA, since natural gas reserves there are being exhausted.
13. See Instituto de Petróleo Brasileiro (1983) and Petroquisa.
14. The exceptions are the production of small quantities of benzene, toluene and xylene.
15. Republic of Trinidad and Tobago, Ministry of Energy and Natural Resources, *Annual Report* (1984).

16. Central Bank of Trinidad and Tobago, *Annual Economic Survey 1990*.
17. Interview with the Head, Technical Division, Petroquisa, December, 1985.
18. The exception is ammonia, large quantities of which are used for the domestic production of urea.
19. See Trinidad and Tobago, Central Statistical Office, *Overseas Trade* (1990).
20. Other countries included in the petition were Czechoslovakia, East Germany, Kuwait, Libya, Saudi Arabia, USSR and Yugoslavia.

6 The potential for Brazil–Trinidad and Tobago trade in the petrochemicals sector

Introduction

This chapter assesses the potential for trade between Trinidad and Tobago and Brazil in the two areas outlined in Chapter 5. This discussion is an important one since many of the issues raised in the first part of the book are investigated here at a fairly detailed level. First of all, the potential for trade in ammonia, methanol and urea is investigated by examining Trinidad and Tobago's trade competitiveness, the scope for imports by Brazil and the constraints to trade between the two countries. Secondly, an assessment is undertaken of the potential for a joint venture arrangement between the two countries for the production of plastics, together with other linkages in the downstream plastics industry. Thirdly, a summary potential for trade between the two countries is presented and a strategy outlined for facilitating its development.

The competitiveness of Trinidad and Tobago's petrochemicals in the Brazilian market

It was established before that Trinidad and Tobago has a strong comparative advantage in petrochemicals. However, having a comparative advantage does not necessarily imply having a competitive advantage. This is because trade competitiveness depends upon not only production costs, but also those of transportation and those imposed by tariffs. Since Trinidad and Tobago is geographically close to Brazil and shipping links between them are well developed, transportation costs are not likely to be very high. It is likely however that in view of the historically high trade barriers which Brazil has maintained,[1] tariffs could provide a major obstacle to trade. In the discussion below the competitiveness of Trinidad and Tobago's petrochemicals is examined both in relation to domestically produced goods in Brazil, as well as to those of its major competitor, the USA. The analysis is based on data for the 1980s, but discussion of future prospects takes into account recent trade policy reform in Brazil.

In the present investigation the landed price of Trinidad and Tobago's petrochemicals in Brazil is compared with the prevailing market prices in that country. Landed prices include direct production costs plus the rate of return on investment (ROI), as well as shipping and tariff costs. The ROI used for DCs is five per cent while that used for ICs is 25 per cent. These rates were used by UNIDO in its study of the world petrochemical industry. They are based on the assumption that DCs are normally prepared to accept a lower rate of investment than ICs (UNIDO, 1983b). Table 6.1 provides data on the competitiveness of Trinidad and Tobago's products in the Brazilian market during the 1980s. A few points should be noted about the data. Firstly, owing to the unavailability of appropriate data Trinidad and Tobago-US shipping costs were used as a proxy for Trinidad and Tobago-Brazil ones. This was considered an acceptable proxy by industry officials in Trinidad and Tobago.[2] Secondly, since production costs for Trinidad and Tobago's urea were not available, computation of the transfer price for that product was based on its f.o.b. price. This would have raised the transfer price somewhat since in 1984 urea prices were high compared with previous years.[3] Thirdly, since petrochemical prices in Brazil are controlled by the government they are likely to have been far lower than true market prices.

Table 6.1 shows that when both shipping costs and tariff barriers were considered, only Trinidad and Tobago's exports of methanol could compete against locally produced petrochemicals in Brazil. The landed price of Trinidad and Tobago's methanol was 50.7 per cent lower than Brazilian market prices, but those of ammonia and urea were 28.1 per cent and 29 per cent higher than the local prices respectively. Two important questions arise in connection with these findings. Firstly, what are the major factors that contributed to Trinidad and Tobago's lack of competitiveness in the Brazilian market? Secondly, under what conditions can Trinidad and Tobago become competitive in that market? In order to answer these questions the relative roles of shipping costs and tariffs must be examined more closely.

Our earlier prediction that tariffs provide the major constraint to trade is confirmed for all three products. For ammonia and methanol which carried the same tariff rate of 45 per cent the shares of tariff costs in the landed prices were 31 per cent each, whereas the shares of shipping costs were 11.8 per cent and 8.7 per cent respectively. In the case of urea which bore a lower tariff rate of 15 per cent, the share of tariff costs was also higher than for shipping costs – 13 per cent compared to 9.4 per cent.

The importance of tariffs in constraining Trinidad and Tobago-Brazil trade can be seen more clearly through a comparison of Trinidad and Tobago's c.i.f. prices and Brazilian market prices. When tariff costs are excluded, Trinidad and Tobago's c.i.f. prices of ammonia and methanol are 11.7 per cent and 66 per cent lower than Brazilian market prices. Similar comparisons cannot be

Table 6.1

Competitiveness of selected petrochemical products from Trinidad and Tobago and the USA in the Brazilian market, 1984

Product	Trinidad and Tobago ($/ton)					Brazil ($/ton)	USA ($/ton)				
	Prod. cost + 5 %	Shipping cost	c.i.f. price	Tariffs[a]	Landed price	Market price	Prod. cost + 5 %	Shipping cost	c.i.f. price	Tariffs[a]	Landed price
Ammonia	96.60	20.00	116.60	52.47	169.07	132	157.50	24.00	181.50	81.68	263.18
Urea	140.00[b]	17.00	157.00	23.55	180.55	140	170.00[b]	27.55	197.55	29.63	227.18
Methanol	103.95	15.00	118.95	53.52	172.47	350[c]	222.50	20.00	242.50	109.13	351.63

Source: (1) Production cost data: Table 5.10 (2) Shipping costs: Industry estimates and República Federativa do Brasil, Ministério da Fazenda, *Comércio Exterior do Brasil* (1984) (3) Brazilian market prices of ammonia and urea from Petrofértil (1985) and methanol prices from Menezes Pereira (1984) (4) Tariff rates from Brasil, *Tarifa Aduaneira do Brasil* (1984)

[a] Tariff rates for ammonia, urea and methanol are 45 per cent, 15 per cent and 45 per cent respectively.
[b] f.o.b. prices
[c] November 1983 prices

made for urea since the basis for computing c.i.f. prices is different. However the data for ammonia and methanol suggest that a removal of tariff barriers can allow Trinidad and Tobago's products to compete against Brazilian products.

From the above analysis it is clear that high nominal tariffs protect the Brazilian petrochemical industry. The question of protection however needs to be examined within a broader context. That is, subsidies have to be considered in addition to tariffs and their effects evaluated within a framework of effective protection. The concept of effective protection is extremely important in evaluating the degree to which an industry is protected. This is because it incorporates protection provided not only on the output of the industry but also on its inputs. Accordingly effective protection depends not on the nominal tariff per se, but on the extent to which a nominal tariff on the firm's output affects its value added. The effective rate of protection (ERP) is measured in the following way:

$$ERP_j = t_j - \Sigma_i t_i a_{ij}/1 - \Sigma a_{ij}$$

where

ERP_j = effective rate of protection on output j
t_j = nominal tariff rate on the output j
t_i = nominal tariff rate on the input i
a_{ij} = cost share of input i in the production of j, valued at world prices

The ERP as stated above thus measures the extent to which value added in the import substitute sector can be raised as a consequence of the imposition of tariffs. Other things being equal, a rise in the nominal tariff on the final good or a lowering of the nominal tariff on the input will raise the ERP, and for a given level of tariffs a higher intermediate input share is associated with a higher ERP. In the present case the t_i's were simply the nominal tariff rates obtained from the Brazilian Customs Tariff List. The rates for ammonia, urea and methanol were 45 per cent, 15 per cent and 45 per cent respectively. The a_{ij}'s were for only the feedstock, and in particular for gas based feedstock. Further these cost shares were valued at world prices (that is, US prices) and they were obtained from List (1986) for ammonia and methanol, and from UNIDO (1981a) for urea. The US input-output coefficients were used since they were considered to be subject to fewer distortions than the Brazilian ones. The feedstock cost shares for ammonia and methanol were 67 per cent each and for urea 45 per cent.

The non-feedstock inputs which comprised mainly non-traded items were lumped together and treated as a part of value added. The assumption made was that the protection for an activity producing a traded product represents not only protection for those primary factors intensive in that activity, but also protection for those industries producing non-traded inputs. In other words, the effect of a tariff on non-traded inputs is basically the same as the effect on primary inputs. In this respect our measure of effective protection is essentially the Corden one. This is as distinct from the one by Balassa which treats non-traded inputs like traded ones on the assumption that non-traded inputs are in infinitely elastic supply. The t_i's for the two basic petrochemicals were the input subsidy rates. These were used because the protection given on the inputs were mainly through subsidies. Since the effects of a subsidy are exactly the same as for a tariff, the subsidy rates were used, calculated in relation to world prices. These were 64.2 per cent for ammonia and 16 per cent for methanol.[4] Another assumption made was that Brazilian producers used all of the available protection. That is, there was no 'water in the tariff'.

Table 6.2 shows the ERPs for the three products together with estimates for the EEC and the USA. They indicate that the true protection given to these products is far greater than nominal tariffs suggest. In the case of ammonia, a combination of a 45 per cent tariff on the output and 64.2 per cent subsidy on the input produced an ERP of 267 per cent. The ERP was lower for methanol (169 per cent) which carried the same tariff rate on the output but a much lower subsidy rate on the input (16 per cent). The ERP for urea was negative (-11 per cent). A negative ERP suggests that tariff-distorted value added is less than free trade value added. This can result either as a consequence of $t_j < a_{ij} t_i$ or $a_{ij} > 1$. In the latter case negative protection results because the value of imported inputs exceeds the world value added of the finished product. Since value added in our case was at world prices, this was not possible. Instead the negative ERP on urea resulted because the tariff on ammonia (45 per cent) was much higher than on urea (15 per cent) – that is, $t_j < a_{ij} t_i$.

Table 6.2
Tariff rates on ammonia, urea and methanol in Brazil, USA and the EEC (%)

Product	Brazil		EEC		USA	
	Nominal	ERP	Nominal	ERP	Nominal	ERP
Ammonia	45	267	11	19	Free	0
Methanol	45	169	13	22	18	30
Urea	15	-11	11	11	Free	0

Source: Brasil, *Tarifa Aduaneira Brasileira* (1984); UNCTAD (1982).

ERPs in Brazil were also high when compared with those in the EEC and the USA. For ammonia (where the differential in ERPs was widest) the rate was 267 per cent in Brazil compared with 19 per cent in the EEC and zero per cent in the USA.

From the above discussion it is clear that the Brazilian petrochemical industry is highly protected through a combination of input subsidies and tariffs on outputs. However the existence of price controls in the industry also have to be taken into consideration. In the case of ammonia, urea and methanol the tariff equivalents of price controls were calculated to be 72.3 per cent, 44.1 per cent and 0.7 per cent respectively.[5]

Having examined the competitiveness of Trinidad and Tobago's petrochemicals against the domestically produced products in Brazil, we can now investigate it in relation to products from the USA. Some interesting points emerge from a comparison of Trinidad and Tobago's landed prices with those from the US, and the US c.i.f. prices with the Brazilian market prices. First of all, since both production and shipping costs were lower in Trinidad and Tobago than in the USA, its landed prices were much lower than those from the USA. The difference was 37 per cent for ammonia, 20.5 per cent for urea and 51 per cent for methanol. These findings imply that Trinidad and Tobago's products were far more competitive in the Brazilian market than those from the USA. The question arises as to why Brazil imports from a high cost producer like the USA and not from a low cost one like Trinidad and Tobago. Why has Trinidad and Tobago been unable to develop profitable trade with Brazil? These questions are explored more fully when the constraints to trade are discussed. Here we simply note that a combination of factors have led to such an outcome, including the influence of North based TNCs, special trading arrangements with the North, and easy access to export credit facilities.

A comparison of the US c.i.f. prices with the Brazilian market prices show that in general the former were higher than the latter. The differences were 27.3 per cent for ammonia and 29.1 per cent for urea. Hence there seemed to be a certain irrationality in the imposition of tariff barriers against products which have higher c.i.f. prices than the prevailing market prices in the domestic market. Indeed, it is likely that these tariff barriers were set up at a time when there were no price controls and therefore protection was needed against imported products.[6]

Two main conclusions arise from the above analysis: (a) tariff barriers have been a major obstacle to the development of Trinidad and Tobago-Brazil trade in petrochemicals and, (b) Trinidad and Tobago's products could compete more effectively in the Brazilian market than those from the USA. This case therefore supports the view that tariff barriers have represented a major obstacle to S–S trade.

The future prospects for trade between Brazil and Trinidad and Tobago are quite bright however, in view of the recent dismantling of trade barriers in Brazil and plans for wider trade policy reform. In 1990 the Brazilian government abolished all tariffs on ammonia imports and reduced the tariff rate on urea from 15 per cent to 10 per cent. It also expects to reduce those in methanol from 50 per cent to 20 per cent over the 1991–94 period.[7] With these changes Trinidad and Tobago will be able to compete in the Brazilian market in all three products. Its advantage is likely to be greatest for methanol where the disparity between its production costs and those in Brazil is greatest.

The scope for trade in selected petrochemical products

This section examines the quantitative potential for trade in ammonia, urea and methanol. The future demand and supply of the particular products in Brazil are first assessed and the scope for imports determined in the light of projected demand and supply balances. The ability of Trinidad and Tobago to supply the Brazilian market is then examined, and taking into consideration the situation both in the importing and exporting countries the scope for trade is determined.

The future demand and supply for ammonia, urea and methanol in Brazil and the scope for imports

Making projections about the future in a country such as Brazil which is at present undergoing dramatic changes in economic policies is a particularly hazardous undertaking. The task is even more difficult when products such as ammonia and urea are involved, the demand for which is dependent upon the growth of agriculture, and the supply of which depends on the future energy situation. For example, adverse climatic conditions may reduce the volume of agricultural output and hence the demand for fertilizers; and oil prices may change radically depending upon the influence of political factors which, in turn, will have an impact on the supply of petrochemicals. However, since our projections relate to the medium term (that is, the period 1990–2000) year to year variations do not significantly affect our analysis. Further it is assumed that although there may be short term fluctuations in oil prices, on average they are unlikely to return to the high levels of the 1970s.

The demand side. Since the factors which influence the demand for ammonia and urea are different from those for methanol, ammonia and urea are discussed separately from methanol.

Ammonia and urea. In Brazil consumption levels of both ammonia and urea have grown rapidly over the past 20 years. Ammonia consumption rose from 54,000 tons in 1970 to 1.3 million tons in 1990 or at an annual average rate of 17.2 per cent. Consumption of urea rose from 204,000 tons in 1975 to 963,000 tons in 1990 and grew on average at a rate of 10.9 per cent per year (Tables D.1 and 6.3). But although growth in consumption has been considerable over the whole period there have been variations over time.

Growth in ammonia consumption was highest during the period 1970–1974 (52.5 per cent). This occurred at a time of rapid economic expansion and buoyant growth in the agriculture sector. During 1970–74 annual growth rates of GDP and agriculture averaged 10 per cent and 12 per cent respectively (Tyler, 1981b, p. 3). Further, the price of fertilizers was low and farm credit was easily available. In 1972 international prices of ammonia and urea were $28–34 and $45–60 per ton respectively, and under the government's farm

129

Table 6.3
**Growth rates of consumption of ammonia, urea and methanol,
1970–90 and projections to 2000 (%)**

Period	Ammonia	Urea	Methanol
1970–74	52.5	..	17.9
1975–80	19.5	33.1	21.8
1980–85	10.9	4.3	–0.1
1985–90	2.4	–1.8	11.2
1970–90	17.2	10.9	12.4[a]
	Projections		
1990–2000[b]	2.7	4.1	8.5
1990–2000[c]	4.0	7.0	10.0

Source: Calculated from Table D.1

[a] 1970–89
[b] Petroquisa's projections
[c] Author's projections

credit programme farmers were entitled to 100 per cent interest free credit (Sheldrick, 1987).

The oil crisis drastically altered the above picture, however. In 1975–80 growth rates of GDP slowed down to an average of 6.5 per cent per year and in 1981–83 the economy went into a deep recession, contracting on average by 3.9 per cent annually (Tyler, 1981b; *Conjuntura*, 1981–83). The price of fertilizers also shot up, and in the light of mounting debt pressures the government's ability to extend credit facilities to farmers was severely curtailed. It was estimated that between 1973 and 1974 alone international prices of ammonia and urea rose by 282 per cent and 233 per cent respectively (Sheldrick, 1987). Further, in 1981 the farm credit programme was stopped in an attempt to reduce the growing public deficit. As a result of these developments, growth rates of ammonia consumption slowed down to 19.5 per cent in 1975–80 and further to 10.9 per cent in 1981–85. Urea consumption meanwhile grew rapidly in the 1975–80 period, at an annual average growth rate of 33.1 per cent. However, there was a drastic drop in consumption levels in 1980–85 and annual average growth for the period declined to 4.3 per cent.

In recent years the situation has worsened, largely as a result of radical economic reforms undertaken by the government and the prevalence of high fertilizer prices. As inflation soared during 1987–88, the measures taken to bring inflation down and reduce the public sector deficit hit the farming sector. In particular, a liquidity squeeze led to a sharp fall in farmers' spending power and reduced their ability to purchase fertilizers. In 1985–90 ammonia consumption grew on average by only 2.4 per cent annually while urea consumption contracted by 1.8 per cent.

Given the past trends in ammonia and urea consumption and the volatile nature of the Brazilian economy, it is difficult to make predictions about future trends. Petroquisa, the state-owned subsidiary of Petrobrás responsible for petrochemicals production, has made some projections to the year 2000 and these are shown in Table 6.3. According to its estimates, ammonia and urea consumption are expected to grow on average by 2.7 per cent and 4.1 per cent per year respectively over the period 1990–2000. These growth rates are quite low compared with previous years. The influence of two major factors could, however, raise fertilizer consumption in Brazil above the levels projected by Petroquisa. They include government's plans to bring more land into cultivation and the potential for intensifying the use of fertilizers.

Although the fertile area in the south of Brazil has been the traditional centre for agriculture, the government intends to develop the agricultural potential of the central west region of the country (which is known to respond well to the application of fertilizers) and the north east region. The central or 'cerrado' region which covers the central high plateau and pasture areas of Mato Grosso, Minas Gerais and Goiás accounts for about two-thirds of total fertilizer consumption, but only 3.5 per cent of it is currently under cultivation. The semi-arid north east region is currently receiving considerable infrastructural support through the establishment of an extensive irrigation scheme. If Brazil's plans for further development of its agricultural potential materialize, the growth of the agricultural sector and hence fertilizer consumption is likely to be far greater than in the past.

But even without expanding the acreage planted, fertilizer use could be much higher than at present since nitrogen fertilizer use in Brazil is very low. In 1988 an average of 10.4 kg of nitrogen fertilizers was applied per hectare of arable land and land under permanent crops in Brazil. This compares with a world average of 53.9 kg/ha, an average for North America of 45.9 kg/ha and for Western Europe of 113.9 kg/ha (FAO, 1990a). Further, as tariffs and NTBs against fertilizer imports are gradually removed, prices are expected to fall and this could lead to large increases in fertilizer consumption.

Based on the likelihood of more land being brought into cultivation and more intensive application of fertilizers, growth rates in ammonia and urea consumption could be around four per cent and seven per cent per annum respectively.

Methanol. Methanol has many industrial uses and growth in consumption depends largely on growth of the industrial sector. Roughly 50 per cent of methanol production is channelled into the manufacture of formaldehyde and about 25 per cent is used for dimethylterephthalate (DMT) production, a major input into the production of polyester fibres. Methanol is also a feedstock for methyl tertiary butyl ether (MTBE), a non-lead gasoline octane enhancer whose use is growing rapidly. In the past the levels of demand for methanol in

131

Brazil have been much lower than for ammonia and urea. In 1990 methanol consumption amounted to 258,000 tons compared to 1.2 million tons for ammonia and 1.0 million tons for urea. In addition, in 1970–90 it grew annually at an average rate of 12.4 per cent, compared with 17.2 per cent for ammonia and 10.9 per cent for urea (Table 6.3).

Past growth rates cannot be used to project future growth in consumption of methanol in Brazil, however. This is because since 1990 methanol has begun to be used in Brazil as an automotive fuel and this has led to a soaring of consumption. It is now being blended with gasoline to constitute 33 per cent of a fuel mix which would have otherwise been formed by 60 per cent alcohol and seven per cent gasoline (*European Chemical News*, 26 February 1990). Consumption levels of methanol are estimated to have risen to 1.1 million tons in 1991, far in excess of previous levels. Brazil's use of methanol as a fuel represents efforts to secure feedstocks for its alcohol running fleet of vehicles, in the light of alcohol shortages and the high costs of alcohol production. In 1988 roughly 33 per cent of Brazil's 11.3 million passenger vehicles ran on ethanol, 63 per cent were driven on gasohol (a mixture of ethanol and gasoline) and two per cent ran on diesel fuel. The alcohol programme has come under heavy attack however, because of the large subsidies which have been required to support it. It has been estimated that in 1988 alone economic losses of about $1.8 billion were attributable to the programme (*European Chemical News*, 26 February, 1990). If this programme is reduced in the future methanol demand is likely to be much higher than in the past.

The official projections for methanol demand show an average growth rate of 8.5 per cent, but an alternative estimate can conservatively be put at around ten per cent.

The supply side. Like consumption, production levels of ammonia, urea and methanol expanded tremendously over the period 1970–90 (See Table D.1). Ammonia production rose from a level of 29,000 tons in 1970 to 1.3 million tons in 1990, and urea from 19,000 in 1975 to 1.04 million tons in 1990. Methanol production started at a lower level of 13,000 tons in 1970 but grew to 166,000 tons in 1990. Growth of production was fastest during the 1970s when imported feedstocks were available at low cost and domestic demand rose rapidly. But expansions continued in the post-oil boom period, in response to high international petrochemical prices and additional increases in domestic consumption levels.

In the light of recent oil and gas discoveries, plans are being made to expand petrochemical production in Brazil. However, these are mainly along the olefins route, chiefly ethylene. No firm plans have been made for additional ammonia or urea plants over the next decade, so that total capacity of these two products should be 1.3 million and 1.6 million tons respectively. But two new methanol plants are expected to come on stream over the next ten years and two existing ones are being 'debottlenecked' to increase capacity. These expansions should result in a total increase in methanol capacity to 499,000 tons in the year 2000 (Petroquisa; *European Chemical News*, May/June 1990).

The scope for imports. Ammonia and urea imports were quite large until 1982, and although this situation has changed dramatically in recent years petrochemical imports are expected to surge forward in the future. In 1976–81 imports of ammonia averaged 198,000 tons per year, equivalent to 40 per cent of consumption; and urea imports averaged 340,000 tons per year or 65 per cent of consumption. Imports of methanol which averaged between 10–12 per cent of consumption, were much lower. Since 1982 imports of ammonia and urea have experienced marked decreases, as new production came on stream in 1982 and 1983 and government imposed more restrictive trade policy barriers. In 1990 ammonia and urea imports were 18,000 tons and 56,000 tons respectively (Table D.1).

In assessing the scope for imports the future demand/supply balances for the products need to be considered (Table D.2). The official projections indicate that no urea imports will be required in the medium term, but that for ammonia and methanol imports should amount to 370,000 tons and 83,000 tons respectively. Alternative projections suggest however, that in view of the gradual relaxation of trade policy barriers and potential availability of cheap imports, roughly 600,000 tons of ammonia and 700,000 tons of urea may need to be imported in the future. Methanol imports are difficult to predict since much depends on the extent to which it is used as a fuel. However, based on past trends it is predicted that imports of this product could amount to 237,000 tons of methanol in the year 2000.

The future supply of ammonia, urea and methanol in Trinidad and Tobago

In estimating the amount of petrochemicals available for export from Trinidad and Tobago to Brazil in the future, existing supply and future expansions, local demand and demand associated with export commitments have to be considered. In Trinidad and Tobago local demand for methanol and urea is negligible, but roughly 60,000 tons of ammonia are required annually for urea production. In terms of export commitments, roughly 40 per cent of ammonia, 80 per cent of methanol and 45 per cent of urea are contracted to firms in Western Europe, Japan and the USA. Many of the existing contracts are due to expire in 1993–94 but several are likely to be renewed.[8]

At present total ammonia and urea capacity in Trinidad and Tobago are 1.7 million tons and 540,000 tons per year respectively, and there are no firm plans for expansions in these areas. In the case of methanol, present capacity is 470,000 tons annually and two plants with a combined annual productive capacity of 1,150,000 tons of methanol are expected to come on stream by 1994. This will bring annual productive capacity of methanol to 1.6 million tons by the year 2000. When local demand and future export commitments are taken into consideration, roughly 960,000 tons of ammonia, 292,000 tons of urea and 324,000 tons of methanol will be available for export to Brazil (Table 6.4). These figures may be larger if additional plants which are currently being studied come on stream over the next ten years. They include a 500,000 t/y plant for urea production, and two plants to produce 1 million tons of methanol annually (*European Chemical News*, May/June 1990).

Table 6.4
Medium term availability of ammonia, urea and methanol
in Trinidad and Tobago for export to Brazil ('000 tons)

Category	Ammonia	Urea	Methanol
Present supply	1700	540	470
Medium term expansions	–	–	1150
Productive capacity	1700	540	1620
Local demand	60	5	–
Export commitments	680	243	1296
Medium term availability	*960*	*292*	*324*

Summary of scope for trade

Considering Brazil's import capacity and Trinidad and Tobago's export capability, the scope for trade appears greatest for ammonia, followed by methanol and urea. Table 6.5 shows that even under a 'high import' scenario, Trinidad and Tobago will be able to meet all of Brazil's ammonia and methanol import requirements, and roughly 40 per cent of those for urea.

Three broad conclusions emerge from the foregoing analysis:

1   Although the growth in demand for ammonia, urea and methanol in Brazil is likely to be lower than in the past, there will still be scope for large imports.

2   The supply capability of Trinidad and Tobago is sufficient to meet the needs of the Brazilian market.

3   Given the demand and supply situation in the two countries there is expected to be scope for trade.

Table 6.5
Scope for trade between Brazil and Trinidad and Tobago in ammonia, urea and methanol, 2000 ('000 tons)

Product	Brazilian import capacity		T and T's[a] export capability
	Low[b]	High[c]	
Ammonia	370	598	960
Urea	–	698	292
Methanol	83	237	324

Source: Tables 6.4 and D.2

[a] T and T: Trinidad and Tobago
[b] Based on Petroquisa's projections
[c] Based on the author's projections

Obstacles to trade

Trade policy reforms and the future growth of petrochemical consumption in Brazil suggest that the potential for its trade with Trinidad and Tobago may be far greater than in the past. However, the realization of such trade potential will depend on a range of other factors, including the existence of NTBs, the influence of North based TNCs, and the lack of adequate shipping and export credit facilities. These are discussed below.

The existence of NTBs

The range of NTBs employed in Brazil has perhaps constituted a far more serious barrier to trade between Trinidad and Tobago and Brazil than tariffs. During the 1970s and 1980s Brazil operated a vast array of import controls which included import prohibitions of selected products, quota restrictions, import licensing, taxes on financial operations and the use of local content provisions. These controls were enforced by the foreign trade arm of the Bank of Brazil (Carteira de Comércio Exterior do Banco do Brasil) and a host of other government agencies. Intermediate and capital goods had to jump additional barriers imposed by the 'law of similars'. According to this law, imports could only be made of those products for which there did not exist a 'similar' national one (Haugen, 1985).

One of the most effective ways of limiting imports of petrochemicals into Brazil has been through the discretionary import licensing programme. The discretionary tariff waiver has also been used in selected periods. These NTBs were most forcefully applied after the second oil shock, and the extent to which they were applied varied in accordance with the country's balance of payments position. Both importers in Brazil and exporters in Trinidad and Tobago claimed that the difficulties associated with obtaining an import license posed one of the most serious barriers to trade. The authorities in Brazil carefully monitored the situation and granted import licenses only when there were expected shortfalls in domestic supply. In such cases explicit import quotas were given for specified periods only. For example during March–December 1985, roughly 100,000 tons of ammonia were imported into Brazil free of customs duties (*Nitrogen*, May–June, 1985, p. 10). These duty free import quotas continued in 1986 and 1987 for specified periods (*Nitrogen*, March–April, 1987, p. 12). Approval was also given for the import of 1.3 million tons of methanol during the period January 1990–April 1991 (*European Chemical News*, 30 December, 1990).

The Brazilian trade policy reforms which began in 1990 have already led to the dismantling of many of the above mentioned NTBs. Quantitative controls have been relaxed, financing requirements eliminated and import duty exemptions under special regimes have ended. It is expected that by 1994 all quantitative restrictions will be abolished and replaced by tariffs (Fritsch and Franco, 1991). If these reforms are carried out then Trinidad and Tobago will have easier access to the Brazilian market in the future.

The influence of North based TNCs

It is difficult to assess the likely influence of North based TNCs on future Brazil–Trinidad and Tobago trade. The limited available data indicates however, that although US-based TNCs may have influenced the direction of Trinidad and Tobago's trade in petrochemicals in the past, their role may be considerably less in the future.

Until 1978 the petrochemical industry in Trinidad and Tobago was owned and controlled by the US firm, W. R. Grace & Co. The aim of that company was to produce low cost basic fertilizers in Trinidad and Tobago for export to its downstream industries in the USA. This was particularly advantageous to the TNC since it was able to reap monopoly profits via its transfer pricing operations (Parsan, 1981). In fact, until the mid-1970s the bulk of Trinidad and Tobago's petrochemical exports consisted of intra-company transfers.

During the 1980s the Trinidad and Tobago government increased its ownership of the industry. Table 6.6 shows that government shareholding at two ammonia plants constructed in 1978–81 (Tringen and Fertrin) was 51 per cent, while the remaining 49 per cent shareholding was accounted for by US TNCs (W. R. Grace & Co. and AMOCO Oil Co.). In 1983–84 a methanol plant, Trinidad and Tobago Methanol Company (TTMC), and a urea plant, Trinidad and Tobago Urea Company (TTUC), were also constructed and these are fully owned by the government.

But despite increased government ownership of the industry, US TNCs continued to dominate the marketing of its output and there was no significant change in the direction of exports. In the case of Tringen the state's role was

Table 6.6
Ownership structure of the Trinidad and Tobago
petrochemical industry

Company	Year of start-up	Ownership structure		General remarks
Fedchem	1959	100%	(F)	Wholly owned subsidiary of W. R. Grace & Co. until 1990; currently owned by Norsk-Hydro.
Tringen	1978	51% 49%	(S) (F)	Foreign partner was W. R. Grace & Co. until 1990: foreign shareholding now owned by Norsk-Hydro.
Fertrin	1981	51% 49%	(S) (F)	Foreign partner is AMOCO Oil Co.
Trinidad and Tobago Urea Co.	1983	100%	(S)	
Trinidad and Tobago Methanol Co.	1984	100%	(S)	

Source: National Energy Corporation of Trinidad and Tobago

Note: S – State; F – Foreign

limited to that of equity partner, since W. R. Grace & Co. was responsible for managing and operating the plant. The entire output was contracted to its parent company in the USA and indirect evidence suggests that W. R. Grace & Co. continued its transfer pricing practices at Tringen (Parsan, 1981). The marketing of output at Fertrin and TTUC was also undertaken by foreign TNCs through special arrangements made with those companies. Table 6.7 shows that the proportion of ammonia exports to the ICs declined from 96.3 per cent in 1977 to 89.5 per cent in 1989, but the share of urea exports to those countries rose from 58 per cent in 1981 to 61.8 per cent in 1989.

The above discussion indicates that in the early years TNC involvement in the Trinidad and Tobago petrochemical industry may have constrained its trade with other DCs, but the evidence regarding the influence of North based TNCs for the more recent period is not wholly conclusive. Indeed it would have been easier and more profitable for foreign TNCs to export to the ICs' markets during the 1960s rather than to countries such as Brazil, given the scope for transfer pricing and the well developed trading infrastructure between the USA and Trinidad and Tobago. The lack of shipping and other links between Brazil and Trinidad and Tobago, the restrictive tariff and NTBs coupled with the high costs of entering a new market would have discouraged the TNCs from developing an export trade between Trinidad and Tobago and Brazil.

It is interesting to note however, that whereas in the past Trinidad and Tobago's exports of ammonia and urea to Brazil have been extremely limited,

Table 6.7
Trinidad and Tobago's exports of ammonia and urea,
by destination, 1977, 1981 and 1989 (%)

Exports to:	Percentage of Exports			
	Urea		Ammonia	
	1981	1989	1977	1989
North	*58.0*	*61.8*	*96.3*	*89.5*
USA	58.0	34.8	96.3	55.9
UK		8.3		
France		10.4		10.2
Belgium-Luxembourg		3.9		12.2
West Germany		4.4		
Denmark				4.1
Portugal				1.0
Norway				0.7
Spain				3.8
Gibraltar				0.5
South	*41.9*	*38.2*	*3.5*	*10.0*
Guyana	18.8	5.1		0.7
Surinam	23.0			
Other Caribbean	0.1	0.6	0.6	0.2
Venezuela		1.1		
Colombia		2.8	2.9	1.2
Argentina		2.1		
Chile		8.0		
Costa Rica		2.0		0.9
Dominican Republic		9.7		
Guatemala		1.3		
Panama		2.8		
Haiti		0.4		
Brazil				1.2
Tanzania				1.2
Malawi		2.3		
Tunisia				0.8
Israel				3.3
Senegal				0.5

Source: Republic of Trinidad and Tobago, Central Statistical Office, *Overseas Trade* (1977–89 issues)

since the start of methanol production in Trinidad and Tobago small amounts of methanol have been exported to Brazil on a consistent basis. This has occurred despite prohibitively high tariffs and NTBs in Brazil. This is an area in which there has never been foreign involvement and the product is fully marketed by the state owned company. In this specific case state involvement appears to have been a major factor in the development of Trinidad and Tobago–Brazil trade. For it is unlikely that North based TNCs would have attempted to develop trade between these two countries, given the small volumes involved.

In the future the role of TNCs in the Trinidad and Tobago petrochemical industry may be considerably reduced. Several of the earlier marketing arrangements with foreign TNCs have now expired and the government has assumed a far more active role in sourcing markets. Further, the government intends to set up a joint ammonia selling company with the Norwegian firm, Norsk-Hydro (which has recently taken over W. R. Grace's shareholdings in Tringen) for the marketing of its output at Tringen when current contractual arrangements expire at the end of 1997.

Shipping barriers

Although shipping barriers may have served as an obstacle to trade between Trinidad and Tobago and Brazil during the 1950s and 1960s, they have not prevented trade between the two countries in recent years and are unlikely to do so in the future. In the pre-1970 period there were no direct shipping routes between Trinidad and Tobago and Brazil and trade between the two countries was largely underdeveloped. Since the mid-1970s however, Trinidad and Tobago has begun to import a wide range of products from Brazil (with the assistance of Brazilian ships) and this increased movement of goods has contributed to the creation of a better shipping infrastructure. There are now direct shipping links between the two countries, and the increase in incoming ships has led to greater availability of ships to export goods back to Brazil. Further, unit shipping costs are perhaps now lower than before as a result of the increased volumes of trade.[9] It appears therefore that shipping constraints no longer present an obstacle to Trinidad and Tobago-Brazil trade. Detailed investigation is required however, on the availability of ships and shipping costs for trade in the specific products concerned.

Since ammonia and methanol are liquid chemicals, their transport requires highly specialized vessels called liquid tankers. By contrast urea can be shipped in any type of bulk cargo carrier. This means that whereas urea exports from Trinidad and Tobago can be facilitated using general cargo ships from Brazil on the return voyage, the transport of ammonia and methanol trade cannot be accommodated in this way since there are no liquid tankers that come from Brazil to Trinidad and Tobago. The latter case brings into focus issues regarding the national ownership of vessels since it is often stated that S–S trade is hampered by the lack of ships. At present Trinidad and Tobago does not own any ships to transport ammonia but it has two liquid tankers for the transport of methanol. These have a combined capacity of 28,000 deadweight tons and are used to transport methanol to Western Europe, USA and Brazil. In terms of general cargo ships, Trinidad and Tobago owns several of these, either alone or jointly with other Caribbean and Central American countries.

139

There is no evidence to indicate that the lack of nationally owned ships in Trinidad and Tobago has hampered the development of ammonia exports to Brazil. However, indirect information suggests that national acquisition of methanol tankers by Trinidad and Tobago has been a major factor in influencing methanol trade with Brazil. The types of tankers owned by Trinidad and Tobago are known as 'dedicated methanol tankers', vessels which are constructed for the transport of methanol alone. Methanol can also be shipped in 'parcel tankers', vessels which are designed to carry several types of chemicals. Dedicated methanol tankers are preferred to parcel tankers since freight charges are much lower. This is largely because of their lower investment costs,[10] shorter loading time, and less staff, testing and cleaning requirements (Silver and Marple, 1990). However, there are only nine dedicated methanol tankers available worldwide (including the two owned by Trinidad and Tobago).[11]

In view of the small volumes of methanol exported from Trinidad and Tobago to Brazil, it would have been very difficult to obtain dedicated methanol tankers to service such trade. The use of parcel tankers which are widely available internationally would have entailed higher freight charges. In this specific case therefore national ownership of vessels appears to have been crucial for the development of trade between Brazil and Trinidad and Tobago.

Given the improved shipping infrastructure for Brazil–Trinidad and Tobago trade and increased ownership of vessels in both countries, shipping barriers are not likely to present an obstacle to trade in the future.

The lack of export credit facilities

Given Brazil's debt situation, a key element in developing exports to that country is the ability to offer export credit to importers, or buy an equivalent amount of its exports (including services). Since Trinidad and Tobago's debt situation is equally severe and it does not have extensive nationally supported export credit facilities, it is unlikely to be able to extend export credit to Brazil.

A national export credit scheme was established in Trinidad and Tobago only in 1986. Prior to this exporters had to rely upon financing from the commercial banks. It is not possible to establish the extent to which the lack of export credit facilities has constrained the development of trade between Brazil and Trinidad and Tobago. However, it is possible that the relative ease with which Brazil has obtained export credit finance from the USA has been a major factor in influencing Brazil's trade with that country. US suppliers are in a particularly advantageous position to offer export credit for they can obtain export financing at concessional rates from the US Export-Import Bank. One such arrangement was reported as follows:

> The Chemical Bank has set up a novel arrangement to assist Brazilian importers in buying fertilizers from US suppliers. The bank, working in

conjunction with the US Export-Import Bank and the Banco do Brasil, will confirm letters of credit for purchases totalling $20 mn, according to John Jones of the Chemical Bank's Sâo Paulo office... He went on to say that the operation does not represent a loan to Brazil, but rather a traditional letter of credit 'with one added nuance: the Ex-Im Bank guarantees the political risk while the Banco do Brasil picks up the commercial one.' By political risk, Jones explained that he meant situations such as the Brazilian government's decree some 18 months ago that suspended dollar outflows for part of the year. 'In this event, Ex-Im would come in to cover the exporter's loss', said the Chembank rep. (*Green Markets*, 7 January, 1985, p.1).

These kinds of arrangements would have undoubtedly been important in facilitating Brazil's trade with the USA.

The current export credit scheme operated by the Trinidad and Tobago government involves export credit insurance, pre- and post-shipment credit guarantees, and rediscounting facilities at concessionary rates. However, since the resources available under this scheme are extremely limited it is unlikely that Trinidad and Tobago will be able to extend large amounts of export credit to Brazil in the future, or to match the terms of credit which are currently offered by the USA. Therefore, the lack of export credit facilities is likely to present an obstacle to future Brazil–Trinidad and Tobago trade.

Trading possibilities in the plastics industry

This section explores the potential for trade in the second area identified above, that is, trade within the plastics industry. The investigation is not as detailed as that in the previous section, since we are concerned with trade in an area in which production does not yet exist. To the extent that certain key data such as costs are not available, our analysis relies upon indirect information.

This area of trade is very important for several reasons. First of all, since trade is being explored in a completely new area of production it provides an excellent example of trade expansion. Secondly, not only is trade in goods being investigated, but also in services – an area in which S–S trade is known to have great potential. Thirdly, to the extent that trade is being examined within the institutional setting of a joint venture arrangement, it is expected to highlight the existing resource complementarities among Southern countries.

In the discussion below the reasons for the development of the plastics industry in Trinidad and Tobago are first advanced. Then the scope for a joint venture arrangement for the production of plastics is examined, and the prospective linkages with the downstream plastics industry are outlined.

Establishing a case for the development of the plastics industry in Trinidad and Tobago. It was pointed out above that the promotion of a plastics industry in Trinidad and Tobago can assist the country in diversifying its production and export of petrochemicals. But there are other good reasons for establishing such an industry. An important one relates to the increased utilization of existing natural resources. Whereas the Trinidad and Tobago petrochemical industry has been oriented towards the use of non-associated natural gas, it has never explored the possibilities for the use of associated gas or oil refinery fractions. The production of plastics provides the opportunity for exploring the use of all these materials.

It is generally acknowledged that natural gas with an ethane content of three per cent or higher is worth considering for olefins manufacture. Since non-associated and associated gases in Trinidad and Tobago have an ethane content of 4.3 per cent and four per cent respectively[12] these materials can be used for the manufacture of plastics. Ethane can be obtained from: (a) stripping the non-associated gas from the East Coast or the new Pelican Fields; (b) recovering the wasted portion from the non-associated gas currently used for ammonia and methanol production; and (c) associated gas produced in the refineries. At present roughly 20 per cent of Trinidad and Tobago's associated gas is wasted through flaring.[13] If this gas can be recovered for use in plastics manufacture, it will represent a more efficient use of resources.

The potential use of oil refinery products for plastics manufacture is more complex than for natural gas, since their use for petrochemicals production must be weighed against that of directly exporting them.[14] The case for utilizing refinery products for plastics production rests on the higher value added that can be obtained from them. Much will depend therefore on the future price of oil which is especially difficult to predict. However, given the volatile nature of oil prices and the need for reducing dependence on the oil sector, there is a strong case for development of a plastics industry.

Secondly, the plastics industry is a good choice for expansion since it is currently the most dynamic branch in the petrochemicals sector and is likely to grow rapidly in the future. Whereas in 1975–79 and 1979–84 the annual rates of growth in demand of all major plastics products were 13.6 per cent and 6.1 per cent respectively, these rates were 7.5 per cent and 5.8 per cent respectively for rubber, and 9 per cent and 4.1 per cent respectively for fibres (UNIDO, 1981a). Projections on the future growth of plastics consumption also show high rates, especially in the DCs.

A third reason for establishing a plastics industry in Trinidad and Tobago relates to the forward linkages which it can create with the small, local downstream plastics industry. These linkages are discussed in detail later, but here we note that if the domestic production of plastic resins leads to lower costs to the local processing industry, this can provide a basis for expansion of the industry and its subsequent development as an export one. Indeed this is likely to be the case in view of the transport cost savings possible and the potentially lower domestic production costs, compared with those internationally. The latter can be illustrated indirectly through a comparison of Mexican production costs (a proxy for Trinidad and Tobago's) with those

142

from the USA. Table D.3 shows that in general the costs of production of Mexican plastics are lower than those in the USA. The disparities are greatest for Polypropylene (25.7 per cent) and for HDPE (16.9 per cent).

Finally, since the plastics industry is very skill intensive its establishment in Trinidad and Tobago can generate important learning benefits and encourage skill accumulation in the local economy. It ranks eighth in a list of 89 manufacturing industries, arranged in ascending order of skill intensity (UNIDO, 1986a).

Scope for a joint venture arrangement for the production of plastics

To date there are few S–S joint venture arrangements for petrochemicals production, although several studies indicate that there is considerable scope for their development (UNIDO, 1983c; Balkay, 1984; Stauffer, 1985). This is based on existing resource complementarities between DCs with raw material surpluses and those with considerable technological expertise. In the light of this, the potential for a joint venture arrangement between Trinidad and Tobago and Brazil is explored below. The relative contributions of the joint venture partners are examined in relation to their ability to provide the main inputs to a petrochemicals plant – raw materials, technology, marketing skills and finance.

Raw materials supply. Given the abundance of oil and natural gas in Trinidad and Tobago, the local joint venture partner can supply the raw materials. Different feedstock mixes had been explored in a series of studies prior to the oil boom[15] and these can be re-evaluated in the light of the existing situation. These mixes include: (a) natural gas + natural gas liquids (NGL),[16] (b) naphtha + NGL, (c) natural gas + NGL, (d) naphtha + ethane + propane + NGL, (e) NGL only, (f) naphtha only, and (g) natural gas only.

The petroleum industry in Trinidad and Tobago is now being reorganized with a view to increasing oil production, upgrading its refinery and adjusting its product mix. A considerable amount of oil exploration work started in 1990 which yielded an increase in the production of crude oil and condensates by one per cent; and a large secondary oil recovery programme is soon to be implemented. In addition, oil is now being imported from Venezuela under special contractual arrangements for processing in the local refinery, and plans being made for an upgrading of the state-owned oil refinery at the Trinidad and Tobago Oil Company. In 1990 alone refinery activity expanded by 20.6 per cent (Central Bank of Trinidad and Tobago, 1991). These developments indicate that there will be wider feedstock choices for petrochemicals manufacture. In particular, with a refinery configuration geared towards the lighter end of the barrel, possibilities will emerge for the use of refinery fractions such as naphtha. Indeed, the different raw material mixes will have to be carefully evaluated in order to ensure the most efficient use of resources in line with the country's broad development objectives.

143

Technology. Given Brazil's technological capability in petrochemicals manufacture, it is likely to be extremely important as a supplier of technology to the joint venture. The extent of its technological expertise was briefly discussed earlier but this investigation assesses its role as a potential supplier of technology by examining its ability to fulfil the main technological requirements of a typical petrochemical enterprise.[17]

1   At the centre of petrochemical production lies the 'know-how' or 'core' technology. This consists of the process design which embodies the fundamentals of a petrochemical technique. From this a basic and detailed engineering design is obtained which is further translated into specifications for equipment and components, as well as for plant location, civil construction and assembly.

Unfortunately Brazil does not have the technical know-how for petrochemicals manufacture. In the development of its industry all process licensing and basic engineering work, along with roughly one third of its technical assistance requirements were sourced from foreign TNCs (Table 6.8). Having secured these basic inputs however, it undertook all detailed engineering, construction and assembly locally.

Table 6.8
Local supply of technological inputs during the construction of the Southern petrochemical complex

Category of inputs	%
Preliminary studies	100
Process licensing	-
Basic engineering	-
Detailed engineering	100
Technical assistance	30
Construction and assembly	100
Capital goods	75
Total local content	*75*

Source: See Table 5.8

Brazil's lack of technical know-how is not likely to limit its role as a technology supplier though, given the nature of petrochemical technologies and the markets in which they are sold. The technologies for petrochemicals, both basic and end products, are mature and standardized (Fayad and Motamen, 1986). Further they are widely available internationally and the markets in which they are sold are highly competitive. For example, technologies for LDPE manufacture can be obtained from Union Carbide, ATO Chimie or ICI, for HDPE manufacture from Solvay, Hoechst, Union Carbide, Phillips, Mitsubishi, and for PVC manufacture from Solvay, B. F. Goodrich, or Sumitomo (UNIDO, 1981a). Within such a context it is more important to be able to source the most suitable technology at the cheapest possible price, rather than to 'own' the technology.

2   Another area of technology concerns the conduct of preliminary or pre-investment studies. This basically involves project feasibility work: the selection of alternative production processes and suppliers, industrial location, marketing, financing and economic viability aspects. In the light of the above discussion regarding the need to source the most appropriate technologies, the selection and contracting of technology assumes added importance. The benefits from such activities have been outlined by Teixeira (1985) as follows:

> Previous experience not only in negotiating contractual agreements, but also in investment projects and operating petrochemical facilities is essential for obtaining more suitable techniques and more favorable contractual conditions... the firm tends to obtain better results not only because the staff becomes more experienced but mainly because the firm has acquired more information about the market in which it is immersed... As a result, the firm may manage better contractual conditions and probably will need to buy less comprehensive packages, being able to, if advantageous, split the package and buy from different suppliers (p. 80).

Table 6.8 shows that during the construction of the Southern petrochemical complex all preliminary studies were undertaken locally. In the past Brazil has pursued an aggressive policy in acquiring technological expertise and this has contributed to a considerable amount of technological learning. Further, as learning progressed in the industry it was able to improve its negotiating skills and obtain more favourable deals. This was confirmed by the Head of the Technical Division at Petroquisa when he commented that:

> A 'high price' had to be paid in the installations of the first petrochemical plants... Only experience allowed us to improve upon subsequent contracts. So much so that various firms in operation contracted technology from abroad with the right to free use (*Petro e Química*, November 1985, p. 39).

Given Brazil's wide experience in sourcing technologies for petrochemicals manufacture (particularly those based on naphtha) and its strong negotiating skills in obtaining favourable technology 'packages', it is likely to be extremely important as a joint venture partner.

3   In addition to the above requirements technologies will be required for the start-up and operation of the plant. This should not present a problem for Brazil in view of its wide experience in setting up and maintaining large scale petrochemical complexes. Indeed, given the similarities in environments between Brazil and Trinidad and Tobago, it is likely that changes or adjustments

made in petrochemical equipment and processes for Brazilian production will also be suitable for those in Trinidad and Tobago.

4   The stimulation of innovative activity which involves both minor and major technical change is an important part of a petrochemical firm's activities. Minor technical change is closely related to the operation of production systems and usually results in changes in operational conditions. Major technical change involves the development of skills and related resources for the creation of new production systems and requires the work of specialized R & D structures. Over the past few decades there have been no major technical changes in petrochemicals manufacture worldwide, but some minor technical changes have taken place. These include mainly energy saving measures, product upgrading, abatement of pollution control and changes in equipment specifications.

Brazil does not have the extensive R & D structures necessary for facilitating technical change in the petrochemical industry. However, over the past two decades it has gradually built up its R & D facilities and succeeded in making some outstanding technological achievements. Petrobrás's R & D unit has pioneered the ethanol-to-ethylene technology which uses chemical feedstocks based on alcohol (derived from sugar cane). It is especially suitable for small scale units, and countries like India and Pakistan which have large sugar cane plantations have benefited from this technological innovation.

Some minor technical change has also recently been instituted in Brazil. In 1989 the Brazilian firm Nitrocarbono developed a new catalyst for the manufacture of caprolactam, a feedstock for nylon 6. The company claims that the new catalyst which is based on technology from the Rhône-Poulenc subsidiary Procatalyse, improves productivity and reduces maintenance costs. Over the period 1987–88 it saved $3.6 million per year with the catalyst. As a result, the company is now expanding output levels and intends to construct other units for caprolactam production (*European Chemical News*, 1 May, 1989). Given these technological advances it is likely that Brazil can, indeed, reach the technological frontiers of petrochemical production in the future.

In light of the above Brazil is likely to be particularly valuable as a joint venture partner, given its expertise in sourcing technology, its experience in operating petrochemical plants in a similar environment, and its potential for reaching the technological frontiers of petrochemical technology.

Marketing.   Since the domestic market in Trinidad and Tobago is small and the bulk of plastics production will have to be exported, international marketing will form an important part of the joint venture. New producers may find it quite difficult to enter international markets however, because of the strong competition globally and growing protectionism in the ICs. It will therefore be important to source markets not only in the traditional IC markets, but also in the DCs where rates of growth in demand are expected to be most rapid.

Given the above objectives, Brazil is well placed to provide marketing expertise to the joint venture since it has managed to penetrate a wide range of markets, including those in the DC region. Table 6.9 shows that in 1985 when plastics exports peaked in Brazil, it marketed 217,049 tons of LDPE in 41 countries. Roughly three-quarters of these exports were to 28 DCs and the remaining portion was to 13 ICs. The development of such an extensive export network was facilitated by the state owned international marketing corporation, Interbrás which was responsible for the export marketing of all Brazilian petrochemicals. Interbrás maintained offices in New York and other DCs including China, India, Nigeria, Algeria, Singapore and Hong Kong in order to develop sales to those markets. It also arranged countertrade deals with several countries in order to facilitate sales of its plastics products. Although there are no official statistics on these arrangements, it is known that a large part of Brazil's exports of LDPE to China is on a countertrade basis.[18] In 1985 China absorbed roughly 57 per cent of Brazilian LDPE exports, the largest amount for any single country.

Table 6.9
Brazil's exports of LDPE by country of destination, 1985 ('000 tons)

Country	Quantity	Country	Quantity
Northern countries			
West Germany	2 010	Colombia	2 837
Belgium	1 414	Costa Rica	50
Spain	1 000	Ecuador	7 412
USA	5 068	United Arab Emirates	1 000
Finland	108	Guatemala	50
Italy	6 550	Honduras	104
Japan	6 288	Hong Kong	7 470
Netherlands	12 377	India	1 050
Portugal	236	Indonesia	6 500
UK	428	Iran	1 790
Sweden	90	Nigeria	5 582
Switzerland	1 000	Pakistan	500
Australia	10	Panama	360
Southern countries			
Saudi Arabia	1 770	Paraguay	1 742
Bolivia	678	Peru	1 320
Cameroon	63	Kenya	428
Chile	4 475	Dominican Republic	376
China continent	122 789	Salvador	404
Surinam	128	Uruguay	8 138
		Argentina	854

Source: República Federativa do Brasil, Ministério da Fazenda *Comércio Exterior do Brasil* (1985)

Given Brazil's capabilities to market plastics internationally, especially in the high growth areas of the South, it is likely to be particularly valuable to the joint venture.

Finance. The most serious obstacle to the development of a joint venture arrangement is likely to be the lack of finance. Since Brazil is a capital deficient country with large external debts, it cannot be considered a suitable joint venture partner from the point of view of providing finance. Trinidad and Tobago's debts are not as large as Brazil's, but as pointed out earlier, when viewed on a per capita basis its debt burden is perhaps more onerous. Therefore, it will also be unable to provide finance to a large scale industrial undertaking. In the light of the existing situation the joint venture will have to rely largely upon loan financing. Indeed, this appears to have been the practice in recent petrochemical joint ventures involving Northern TNCs and the government of Trinidad and Tobago. In the planned petrochemical ventures the bulk of financing is also being sourced from abroad. For example, for the new 495,000 t/y methanol plant at Point Lisas, Trinidad some two-thirds of financing will come from external sources (*European Chemical News*, 15 May, 1989).

Scope for linkages with the Trinidad and Tobago downstream plastics industry

One of the arguments put forward for establishment of a plastics plant in Trinidad and Tobago is the linkages which it can create with the small downstream plastics industry. In this section key aspects of that industry are examined[19] and ways in which Brazil can aid in its expansion.

The Trinidad and Tobago plastics processing industry is small, depends entirely on imported raw materials and operates at low levels of capacity. This combination of characteristics suggests that it is high cost and levels of X-inefficiency are high. Of the 50 firms in the industry roughly 80 per cent employ between 4–50 persons, and they manufacture various plastic products ranging from toothbrushes to boats and water tanks. The major types of raw materials used are PE and PVC, about 20,000 tons of which are imported annually from the USA and Canada. Output is geared principally to the domestic market but small amounts of plastic products are exported to the Caribbean region.

Detailed information is not available on production costs in the industry, but during the 1970s and 1980s these were considered to be high on account of high wages and high resin prices. Wages which accounted for between 35–50 per cent of total costs were deemed to be high as a result of the Dutch Disease effects of the oil boom. Such costs however, may have fallen in recent years as the economy has largely returned to a pre-boom situation. Resin prices were considered high partly because of the small orders made by individual manufacturers, but also because of high domestic tariffs (45 per cent) on imported resins.

Given the above characteristics of the plastics processing industry there appears to be a strong case for its reorganization and expansion. Indeed, possibilities can be explored for streamlining production towards a narrow range of products in order to benefit from economies of scale and specialization. By undertaking production on a larger scale, costs per unit can be reduced and higher levels of efficiency achieved. Other benefits could be gained through a lowering of resin costs if raw materials are obtained locally. Indeed, increased local availability of cheaper resins strengthens the case for expansion of the local industry.

Assuming that a major expansion of the Trinidad and Tobago plastics processing industry is to be undertaken, the discussion below explores various ways in which Brazil can assist Trinidad and Tobago in this exercise.

Potential trade in goods and services. In view of Brazil's emerging comparative advantage in capital goods and its increasing technological capabilities, it could provide assistance to Trinidad and Tobago in two ways: (a) through the provision of technology, and (b) through the supply of machinery and equipment. For most branches of the plastics industry, including those in which the local industry is involved, the technologies required are mature and simple. If production is to be based on these simple technologies Brazil will be in a strong position to provide technological expertise. But if more sophisticated products are to be produced, such as engineering and other specialty plastics, Brazil may be unable to provide the requisite technologies since these are all firmly under the control of North based TNCs. The plastics plants which currently manufacture specialty products in Brazil are largely under TNC control (Haguenauer, 1986). Given the large pool of unskilled labour in Trinidad and Tobago however, and the low levels of skill formation there, it is unlikely that the local industry will manufacture sophisticated products such as engineering plastics.

In addition to technology, Brazil can also provide machinery and equipment to the Trinidad and Tobago plastics processing industry. Brazil produces all major types of machinery and equipment required for the basic processes of injection moulding, extrusion, blow moulding and thermoforming. In addition, it produces complementary machines for cutting and welding, printing and electric welding, as well as auxiliary equipment such as automatic feeders, temperature controllers and plastic cutters. Although output levels in the Brazilian plastics equipment industry are low compared with major producers like the USA and West Germany, they have expanded considerably over the past decade.

Two important questions arise in connection with the potential supply of plastics machinery and equipment to Trinidad and Tobago: (a) to what extent can Brazil provide up-to-date machinery and equipment for the industry? and (b) are Brazilian prices competitive with those internationally? The 'state of the art' technology in the plastics industry involves the production of highly computerized equipment which is not available in Brazil. This may not be a disadvantage for Trinidad and Tobago however, since it may not wish to employ labour-saving machinery in view of its high unemployment situation. But in order to be internationally competitive it will have to install machinery which embodies new technology. In the end a choice will have to be made as to the most appropriate type of machinery, given the development objectives of the country.

Information on the prices of Brazilian plastics machinery and equipment were not available, and it was therefore not possible to determine the price competitiveness of these products. Fairly detailed data are normally required to make appropriate price comparisons given the particular products being considered. For example, prices of injection moulding machines may differ considerably depending on factors such as the life of the machine and its clamping force capacity. Indirect information indicates that Brazilian plastics machinery may be price competitive with those from the ICs. An early study by Tyler (1981b) showed that, in general, the Brazilian capital goods sector can compete with those of other countries. Prices of 17 products (which included machine tools, textile machinery and agricultural machinery) produced in Brazil were found to be similar to those produced in the ICs.

But whereas Brazil may be able to supply the Trinidad and Tobago plastics processing industry with machinery and equipment at favourable prices, non-price factors such as the availability of export credit facilities are likely to provide a powerful barrier to trade. Officials at the Brazilian Association for the Machinery and Equipment Industry cited this as the most important barrier to its trade with the South.

Summary

This chapter examines the potential for trade between Brazil and Trinidad and Tobago in respect of: (a) Trinidad and Tobago's exports of ammonia, methanol and urea to Brazil, and (b) prospective trade linkages in the establishment of a plastics industry in Trinidad and Tobago. In general, it is found that there is considerable potential for trade in these two areas but the realization of trading possibilities would require policies to help overcome existing financial constraints.

A number of factors favour the future development of petrochemical exports from Trinidad and Tobago to Brazil. An important one relates to the potential trade competitiveness of Trinidad and Tobago's products in the Brazilian market. It is found that whereas in the past Trinidad and Tobago's petrochemicals could not compete against Brazilian products because of high tariffs, this situation is likely to be substantially different in the future given trade policy reforms currently being undertaken in Brazil. Since 1990 tariffs on urea and methanol have been progressively reduced, and those on ammonia removed. Therefore it is expected that in the future Trinidad and Tobago's products will be able to compete effectively against both Brazilian products and those of its major competitor, the USA.

A second factor favouring prospective expansions in Trinidad and Tobago–Brazil trade is the future import capacity of Brazil for petrochemicals. Despite recent expansions in Brazilian petrochemical production, future growth in demand for ammonia, urea and methanol is likely to outstrip supply of these products. Therefore, there is likely to be scope for sizeable imports. Trinidad and Tobago has the capacity to fulfil these import requirements, given its large and growing export capabilities of petrochemicals. Further, it is likely to be anxious to develop trade with Brazil, given its need for market diversification in the light of growing protectionism in the ICs.

With respect to (b) above it is found that there is great potential for the establishment of a joint venture arrangement for plastics production between Trinidad and Tobago and Brazil. There are also prospects for linkages with the plastics processing industry in Trinidad and Tobago. Potential contributions of the two joint venture partners involve the supply of raw materials by Trinidad and Tobago and the provision of technology and marketing expertise by Brazil. The bulk of financing would have to be sourced externally however, given the debt problems currently facing both countries. Other potential trade linkages include the export of technology, machinery and equipment from Brazil to Trinidad and Tobago for the upgrading and expansion of the small plastics processing industry in Trinidad and Tobago. Brazil's contribution to the joint venture is likely to be particularly significant on account of its ability to source low cost technology 'packages'; its willingness to transfer technology; experience in operating plants based on both natural gas and refinery fractions; ability to stimulate technological innovations in petrochemical technology, and to source important markets in the South. Further, in the light of Trinidad and Tobago's experience with joint venture partners from the ICs, its contribution is likely to be far greater than a North based TNC.

The barriers to the above trade are investigated and it is found that whereas in the past the influence of North based TNCs, existence of powerful NTBs and the lack of shipping facilities have constrained the development of trade between the two countries, they are unlikely to provide barriers to trade in the future. All NTBs in Brazil are gradually being removed, national fleets have been developed by the two countries and transportation networks between them are now firmly established. In addition, arrangements with TNCs now involve more arms length agreements. However, the major barrier likely to hamper trade in the future is the lack of finance. The limited availability of export credit facilities in Trinidad and Tobago could pose a problem for its exports of ammonia, urea and methanol to Brazil. Similar barriers could adversely affect Brazil's exports of machinery and equipment to Trinidad and Tobago. Further, the lack of finance by both countries could reduce the chances for the development of a joint venture. It is pointed out, however, that possibilities for loan financing could be sought for this latter venture.

In order to overcome the financial barriers, countertrade possibilities could be explored in the above arrangements. That is, Trinidad and Tobago's exports of ammonia, urea and methanol could be linked to Brazilian imports of technology, machinery and equipment for the plastics industry. Indeed, there is a strong case for selective countertrade, given the potential for fruitful, trade expanding possibilities between the two countries.

Notes

1. See, for example, IBRD (1984) and Haugen (1985).
2. Most studies calculate transportation costs from trade statistics as the difference between f.o.b. and c.i.f. values. (e.g. Yeats, 1981b; Prewo, 1978; Langhammer 1983). However, this method could not be used since Trinidad and Tobago–Brazil trade in petrochemicals was little developed, and the limited available data appeared unreliable since they were not comparable across countries.
3. Average urea prices per ton were $130 in 1983, $168 in 1984 and $140 in 1985 (Sheldrick, 1987, p. 226).
4. See Chapter 5.
5. In computing these tariff equivalents the US c.i.f. price was considered to be representative of the world price.
6. The tariff barriers for ammonia and methanol in 1975 were the same as those in 1984.
7. Brasil, *Tarifa Aduaneira do Brasil* (1991).
8. Pantin (1986) and *The Financial and Petroleum Times of Trinidad and Tobago*, January, 1991.
9. For goods shipped on the back haul it is usually possible to have greater cost savings.
10. The basic cost of a dedicated tanker is about half that of a parcel tanker (Silver and Marple, 1990).
11. The other seven are owned by Japan/Canada (2), Chile (2) and Saudi Arabia (3). See Silver and Marple (1990).
12. See Table 5.5.
13. This is low compared with countries like Saudi Arabia and Iran which flare about 50 per cent of their natural gas, but high compared with Venezuela and Mexico whose gas loss is less than ten per cent of production.
14. This choice does not arise in the case of natural gas since the cost of liquefying and transporting it is large in relation to its production cost.
15. See Japan Gasolene Company (1970) and De Castro (1977).
16. NGL includes all natural gas components excluding methane, ethane and non-hydrocarbons.
17. These requirements are outlined by Teixeira (1985).
18. Interview with official, Interbrás, December 1985.
19. See Cupid (1987).

7   Summary and conclusions

This study sheds light on a number of controversial issues regarding the adoption of a S–S trade strategy and its role within a changing global context. Three major conclusions emerge. Firstly, although there is great potential for trade among Southern countries its realization will require the implementation of certain policy measures to remove existing constraints to trade. Secondly, in view of the special developmental gains to be derived from a S–S trade strategy it should be accorded high priority in a country's development plans. However, the relative importance which countries may wish to attach to it may differ depending upon the economic features and conditions of those countries. Thirdly, in view of the growing interdependence in the world economy S–S and S–N trade should not be viewed as mutually exclusive trading options but complementary to each other. These conclusions which are drawn from the general analysis of S–S trade are also supported in the case study of trade between Trinidad and Tobago and Brazil.

Several writers emphasize the potential for trade among the more industrialized countries of the South based on their rapid growth, large export capabilities and import capacities. In particular, trade in agricultural goods and raw materials is considered to have the greatest scope for expansion on the grounds that it can assist DCs to exploit their 'natural' comparative advantages. However, this study finds that although the potential for trade varies among different groups of countries within the South, in general it extends to a far wider range of countries and goods than is generally acknowledged. Given the heterogeneous nature of the South, trading possibilities could be explored along different theoretical bases and opportunities created for countries to change their comparative advantage over time.

There is scope for trade between the more industrialized countries in the South and those which are less advanced, based upon differences in factor endowments and levels of technological advancement. NICs, for example, could export capital and skill intensive goods to LDCs, and the latter in turn export primary products and simple, labour intensive manufactures back to them. In addition, DCs which are more technologically advanced could export technology intensive goods to those which are not able to stimulate innovations, while the latter group can export back to the former goods which are fairly standardized.

Both large and small countries at all levels of development could produce and export scale economy goods to other DCs, based either on their large market size or on long production runs. Large countries could trade in differentiated goods such as motor vehicles or electronic equipment, while smaller ones could mass produce and export standardized products. Further, countries which are at similar levels of development and hence have similar taste patterns could trade in various types of consumer and producer goods. For example, low income, labour abundant countries could export to other low income DCs relatively inexpensive, labour intensive machinery and equipment. In general then, both small and large countries, and those at different as well as similar levels of development have great potential for trade.

The goods and services which could be traded among Southern countries cover a wide variety. They include resource based products, principally food items and raw materials such as oil, copper, wood and iron ore; capital and scale intensive goods such as motor vehicles and electrical machinery; skill intensive ones like chemicals and computers; labour intensive items such as footwear, textiles and clothing; and technology exports in the form of industrial project exports, direct foreign investment, licensing, consultancy and technical services. Among this range of products however, those which appear to have the most dynamic potential for future growth are manufactured goods. They currently account for over one-half of S–S trade and have been the fastest-growing in recent years. This is in contrast to agricultural goods and raw materials, the proportion of which has declined considerably over time.

Besides trade potential, the 'gains from trade' issue occupies a central part of the study. Much of the debate in this area stems from the fact that whereas some analysts evaluate the benefits from trade in terms of its static effects, others emphasize the more long run, dynamic ones. The main argument of the former group is that S–S trade, owing to its capital intensive nature, has a relatively small impact on overall employment and growth in DCs. S–N trade, because of its potential to absorb labour intensive exports, could assist DCs in realizing their 'natural' comparative advantage. It is pointed out, however, that S–S trade must be evaluated not only in terms of employment generation but within a wider framework of the developmental needs of the South. Accordingly, the study emphasizes the dynamic benefits of trade.

Drawing from theoretical analyses of S–S trade the main dynamic gains are considered to be the accumulation of skills and technological learning; the realization of scale economies and improvement in the terms of trade including those for technology resources; and the provision of goods more appropriate

154

to Southern environments and income levels. An empirical investigation into the factor content of DCs' trading patterns shows that the types of goods currently traded among Southern countries enable the realization of a major part of these dynamic gains. In particular, skill intensive goods feature prominently in S–S trade and this contributes greatly to human capital development in DCs. This is in contrast to S–N trade which contains a high proportion of labour intensive goods and therefore promotes unskilled labour formation in the South.

The above finding on the factor content of S–S/S–N trade carries important implications for the pursuit of a S–S trade strategy. Since S–S and S–N trade are associated with different types of benefits, a country can pursue a trade strategy that contains elements of both. In other words, S–S and S–N trade are actually complementary to each other and should not be viewed as alternatives. However, since S–S trade has more 'development-promoting' properties than S–N trade, it should be accorded a relatively higher priority in a country's development plans. The mix of policies will depend on the specific economic features and conditions in a country. For example, in the short run a NIC may be in a better position to pursue an aggressive S–S trade policy and derive gains through skill accumulation than a LDC whose exportables consist mainly of simple, labour intensive manufactures. But, given the potential of a S–S trade strategy to assist LDCs in changing their comparative advantage over time, it should constitute an important element in their long run development programmes.

Despite the potential for S–S trade and gains associated with it, certain barriers are found to constrain its development. The identification of these barriers and assessment of their influence pose particular problems for the study. For example, whereas the impact of tariff barriers can be easily measured, institutional barriers such as those arising from the system of finance and shipping do not lend themselves to quantification. In spite of these difficulties however, attempts are made to evaluate the extent to which both policy-induced and institutional barriers impede the development of S–S trade. It is found that trade policy barriers pose some of the most serious constraints to trade among DCs. High tariffs erected by Southern countries coupled with the imposition of a range of NTBs (particularly quotas and import licensing) reduce the DCs' competitive position in Third World markets. This is compounded by the fact that the structure of protection in these countries discriminates against goods in which DCs have their greatest comparative advantage (such as simple, labour intensive manufactures and agro-processed goods), but provides little incentive for the domestic production of items such as capital goods in which there is great potential for S–S trade.

Among the institutional barriers to trade, financial constraints are the most severe. These stem largely from the fact that DCs rely heavily on the currencies and financial network of the North to finance their intra-trade, which in turn renders them vulnerable to changes in the monetary policies of the ICs. In particular, the adoption of highly restrictive monetary and fiscal policies by the Northern countries worsen the structural foreign exchange constraints of the DCs, and hence their ability to finance their intra-trade. The lack of adequate export credit facilities also contribute to the DCs' financial constraints. Whereas exporters in the ICs benefit from government supported export credit schemes, those in the DCs have limited access to such facilities and are frequently unable to match the volume and attractive terms of payment offered by the North. As a result, the DCs are often in a disadvantageous position when competing against ICs' exporters in Southern markets.

Other barriers to S–S trade include those arising out of the system of shipping, marketing and distribution, the presence of North based TNCs and tied aid. Existing shipping routes favour S–N trade and the ICs which dominate world shipping do not encourage the transport of goods between DCs. S–S freight rates are considered to be disproportionately higher than S–N ones, and this is not only because of costly transhipment arising from the lack of direct shipping routes to service S–S trade, but also because of the pricing policies of Northern conference liners which discriminate against S–S trade. This bias against S–S shipping is difficult to verify empirically, but indirect evidence indicates that it does, in fact, exist.

The dominance of North based TNCs in the DCs' production and trading structures reinforces S–N/N–S trading patterns and therefore indirectly constrains the development of S–S trade. The subsidiaries of these corporations located in DCs source their main inputs from their parent companies or other firms in the ICs, whilst directing the bulk of their exports to them. This pattern is being reinforced at present through the production of parts or components of manufactured items in DCs from where they are exported to the ICs for assembly into finished items. Other barriers to S–S trade include the lack of well-developed marketing and distribution networks in the DCs, and the practice by ICs of tying their aid to procurement of goods and services in the donor country or other ICs.

The presence of the above barriers to trade undoubtedly limits the extent to which a S–S trade strategy can be successfully pursued. The removal of many of the institutional obstacles will require major reviews of the entire international trading and monetary system. This in turn will necessitate cooperation at a global level, an exercise in which the Northern countries have shown themselves unwilling to participate. Despite the difficulties in pursuing this 'first best' option however, appropriate policy measures can be adopted to facilitate the removal of existing obstacles to trade. These involve a set of second-best policies requiring action at the national, regional and international levels.

An important policy recommendation relates to the removal of trade policy barriers. Some countries have taken steps recently to dismantle their trade policy barriers unilaterally, but for various reasons this is not an option open to all DCs. This plus the fact that DCs trade in a less than 'first best' world where Northern trade policy barriers are high suggest that some form of discriminatory liberalization is required. Therefore, it is recommended that negotiations for a more comprehensive GSTP be continued where DCs can exchange mutual trade preferences among themselves.

In the area of finance, policy prescriptions include a strengthening of regional payments and credit arrangements; an expansion of government supported, subsidized export credit facilities; and the selective use of countertrade. Payments and credit arrangements could help to alleviate the problems associated with the use of convertible currencies, while increased availability of low cost export credit could help DCs' exporters to increase their competitiveness in Third World markets. Given the shortage of financial resources in the South, export credit facilities could be expanded greatly if ICs were to channel additional resources into regional or national development finance agencies. Countertrade has the potential to generate foreign exchange savings for DCs, but it should be used selectively for specific areas of trade and under certain conditions. That is, its use should be confined to the financing of genuine trade expansion.

In order to overcome their shipping constraints, countries could develop their own fleets or in cooperation with others establish joint shipping lines; improve their port management; upgrade training of shipping personnel; and change the valuation base of their tariffs from a c.i.f. to a f.o.b. one. Other policy measures include the promotion of TWTNCs and wider establishment of STOs. TWTNCs have an important role to play in raising the level of technological development of DCs, and STOs could assist in building marketing and distribution networks among them. Finally, it is recommended that DCs urge the Northern countries and international agencies to untie bilateral aid partially and multilateral aid completely.

The case study of S–S trade is a specific one which deals with two countries and trade in a particular sector. But despite its limited focus it illustrates quite clearly how countries at different levels of development could engage in mutually beneficial trade in both goods and services. Differences in factor endowments and in levels of technological development provide the bases for trade between Brazil and Trinidad and Tobago. Trinidad and Tobago is relatively well endowed with oil and natural gas, and manufactures products such as petrochemicals on a large scale which make intensive use of these resources. It is also at a low level of technological development and depends almost entirely on imported technological inputs for its petrochemical industry. Brazil is relatively lacking in oil and natural gas and imports large quantities of petrochemicals. However, it possesses considerable technological expertise in a number of areas, especially in the oil and petrochemical industries. Therefore, there seems to be potential for exports of petrochemical products from Trinidad and Tobago to Brazil, and exports of petrochemical technologies from Brazil to Trinidad and Tobago.

A close examination of the organization and functioning of the petrochemical industries in Brazil and Trinidad and Tobago reveals that these industries operate at varying levels of efficiency. The Brazilian one is large and highly diversified, but its production costs are high since it utilizes the more expensive

157

naphtha as raw material and older technologies. By contrast, Trinidad and Tobago's industry is narrowly based on the production of ammonia, urea and methanol but is one of the lowest cost internationally since it benefits from relatively inexpensive natural gas and uses modern technologies. In the light of the strong comparative advantage displayed by this industry, potential for the export of ammonia, urea and methanol from Trinidad and Tobago to Brazil is examined. Other areas which are deemed to have trade potential include a joint venture arrangement for the establishment of a plastics industry in Trinidad and Tobago, and the expansion of existing facilities in that country for the processing of plastics products. The joint venture involves combining Brazilian machinery and equipment, technological and marketing expertise with Trinidad and Tobago's raw materials.

Detailed investigations into the above areas highlight several issues relevant to the pursuit of a S–S trade strategy. Firstly, whereas in the past trade policy and other barriers posed a major constraint to Brazil-Trinidad and Tobago trade, this is unlikely to be so in the future. Until recently Brazil maintained a complex array of high tariff and NTBs and these rendered most of Trinidad and Tobago's petrochemicals uncompetitive in the Brazilian market. At present however, Brazil is dismantling its trade policy barriers, reducing import duties on many of its petrochemical products and removing NTBs. These changes, along with others in the areas of shipping and TNCs, are expected to facilitate Brazil-Trinidad and Tobago trade in the future. However, financial obstacles are likely to be a major problem. The lack of export credit facilities could affect adversely Brazil's exports of machinery and equipment and Trinidad and Tobago's exports of petrochemicals. Further, the possibility of a joint venture for plastics production could be jeopardized by the inability of both partners to provide financing for its development.

Secondly, an evaluation of the gains from trade reveal that both Brazil and Trinidad and Tobago could reap larger benefits from their intra-trade than from trade with their current major trading partner, the USA. The landed prices of Trinidad and Tobago's petrochemicals in the Brazilian market are much lower than those from the USA. This implies that trade between Brazil and Trinidad and Tobago is likely to be trade creating rather than trade diverting. Brazil can enjoy large consumption gains through cheaper imports, and Trinidad and Tobago benefit from having access to larger markets and diversifying their market risks. The latter gain is particularly important in view of the increasingly restrictive trade barriers being imposed on Trinidad and Tobago's petrochemicals in Northern markets.

The exploitation of trading possibilities in the plastics industry can also yield benefits to Brazil and Trinidad and Tobago, but these are likely to be more of the dynamic type. The joint venture for plastics production, for example, could facilitate greater resource utilization in Trinidad and Tobago through enhanced use of both natural gas and refinery fractions; enable foreign exchange savings through access to a cheaper technology package; effect a more favourable terms of technology transfer; permit a greater diversification of trade, given Brazil's extensive marketing networks in the South; and allow linkage creation with other industries. The major gains for Brazil are likely to arise from opportunities to upgrade its stock of skills, to contribute to technological learning and stimulate technical change.

In order to facilitate trade in the above areas, two major policy measures are suggested: countertrade possibilities be explored for trade in petrochemicals, capital goods and services, and loan financing be sought for the joint venture arrangement.

APPENDICES

Appendix A

Table A.1
Major Third World economic integration groupings

Organization	Year of establishment	Member countries
A. Africa		
West African Economic Community (CEAO)	1973	Cote d'Ivoire, Mali, Mauritania, Niger, Senegal, Burkina Faso, Benin
Mano River Union (MRU)	1977	Liberia, Sierra Leone, Guinea
Economic Community of West African States (ECOWAS)	1975	CEAO members, MRU members, Nigeria, Cameroon, Gabon
Central African Customs and Economic Union (UDEAC)	1964	Congo, Gabon, Cameroon
Economic Community of the Great Lakes (CEPGL)	1976	Burundi, Rwanda, Zaire
Economic Community of Central African States (CEEAC)	1983	Members of UDEAC and CEPGL, Chad, Equatorial Guinea, Sâo Tomé e Principe
Preferential Trade Area for Eastern and Southern African States (PTA)	1982	Burundi, Comoros, Djibouti, Ethiopia, Kenya, Lesotho, Malawi, Mauritius, Rwanda, Somalia, Swaziland, Tanzania, Uganda, Zambia, Zimbabwe
Southern African Development Co-ordination Conference (SADCC)	1979	Angola, Botswana, Lesotho, Malawi, Mozambique, Swaziland, Tanzania, Zambia, Zimbabwe
B. Latin America and the Caribbean		
Latin American Integration Association (ALADI) formerly Latin American Free Trade Association (LAFTA)	1966	Argentina, Bolivia, Brazil, Chile, Colombia, Ecuador, Mexico, Paraguay, Venezuela
Andean Group	1969	Bolivia, Colombia, Ecuador, Peru, Venezuela
Central American Common Market (CACM)	1961	Costa Rica, El Salvador, Guatemala, Honduras, Nicaragua
Caribbean Community (CARICOM)	1973	Antigua and Barbuda, Bahamas, Barbados, Belize, Dominica, Grenada, Guyana, Jamaica, Montserrat, St Christopher and Nevis, St Lucia, St Vincent and the Grenadines
Organization of Eastern Caribbean States	1981	Antigua and Barbuda, Dominica, Grenada, Montserrat, St Christopher and Nevis, St Lucia, St Vincent and the Grenadines
C. Asia		
Association of South East Asian Nations (ASEAN)	1967	Brunei, Indonesia, Malaysia, Philippines, Singapore, Thailand
Bangkok Agreement	1975	Bangladesh, India, South Korea, Sri Lanka, Lao People's Democratic Republic
Cooperation Council for the Arab States of the Gulf (GCC)	1981	Bahrain, Kuwait, Oman, Saudi Arabia, the United Arab Emirates
South Asian Association for Regional Cooperation (SAARC)	1985	Bangladesh, Bhutan, India, Maldives, Nepal, Pakistan, Sri Lanka

Source: UNCTAD (1989a, 1990a)

Appendix B

Table B.1
Partnerships identified for increased S–S trade in 15 industrial branches

Exporting Region	Product and Importing Region				
	Latin America	Tropical Africa	Near East	Indian Sub-Continent	East Asia
Latin America	Food products	Food products	Food products		
	Textiles	Textiles	Textiles		
		Wood products			
	Paper	Paper	Paper	Paper	Paper
	Metal products	Metal products	Metal products	Metal products	
	Glass	Glass	Glass	Glass	
	Industrial chemicals	Industrial chemicals	Industrial chemicals		Industrial chemicals
	Other chemicals	Other chemicals	Other chemicals	Other chemicals	
	Rubber products	Rubber products	Rubber products		
	Iron and steel	Iron and steel	Iron and steel		Iron and steel
	Non-metallic mineral products	Non-metallic mineral products	Non-metallic mineral products		Non-metallic mineral products
		Non-ferrous metals	Non-ferrous metals	Non-ferrous metals	Non-ferrous metals
	Non-electrical machinery	Non-electrical machinery	Non-electrical machinery	Non-electrical machinery	Non-electrical machinery
	Electrical machinery	Electrical machinery			
East Asia	Food products	Food products			
	Textiles	Textiles	Textiles	Textiles	
	Paper	Paper		Paper	Paper
	Rubber products	Rubber products	Rubber products	Rubber products	
		Metal products		Metal products	Metal products
		Industrial chemicals	Industrial chemicals	Industrial chemicals	Industrial chemical
				Other chemicals	
	Glass	Glass		Glass	
			Iron and steel	Iron and steel	Iron and steel
		Non-ferrous metals		Non-ferrous metals	
		Non-electrical machinery	Non-electrical machinery	Non-electrical machinery	Non-electrical machinery
	Electrical machinery	Electrical machinery	Electrical machinery	Electrical machinery	Electrical machinery
	Transport equipment	Transport equipment	Transport equipment	Transport equipment	Transport equipment

164

Exporting Region	Product and Importing Region				
	Latin America	Tropical Africa	Near East	Indian Sub-Continent	East Asia
Indian Sub-Continent		Food products			
	Rubber products	Rubber products	Rubber products	Rubber products	
				Paper	
		Textiles			
			Glass	Glass	
				Metal products	
				Industrial chemicals	
				Iron and steel	
				Non-ferrous metals	
	Non-metallic mineral products		Non-metallic mineral products		
		Non-electrical machinery	Non-electrical machinery	Non-electrical machinery	
				Electrical machinery	
				Transport equipment	
Tropical Africa	Rubber products		Rubber products	Rubber products	
		Non-ferrous metals	Non-ferrous metals		Non-ferrous metals
Near East		Food products			
		Metal products			Metal products
			Iron and steel		
			Industrial chemicals		
		Non-electrical machinery			Non-electrical machinery
	Electrical machinery			Electrical machinery	

Source: UNIDO (1985a)

165

Appendix C

Table C.1
Typical yields and investment costs for a 200,000 t/y olefins plant using different raw materials

Raw Material (t/y)	Ethane 266 373	Propane 463 957	Butane 574 698	Naphtha 701 995	Gas oil 919 282	Alcohol 352 000
Investment costs ($mn)	84.8	94.3	96.6	123.5	141.3	50
Typical yields (%)						
Ethylene	75.1	43.1	34.8	28.5	21.8	56.3
Co-Products:						
Propylene	-	15.5	17.5	14.5	12.9	-
Butadiene	-	2.2	2.0	4.1	4.2	-
LPG	3.4	1.5	7.2	4.7	5.1	-
Benzene	-	-	-	6.3	5.1	-
Toluene	-	-	-	3.7	3.8	-
Gasoline	-	-	. .	10.8	11.4	-
Fuel oil	3.6	7.8	11.5	10.1	22.6	-
Residual oil	17.9	29.9	27.0	17.3	13.1	-

Source: Petroquisa

Table C.2
Prices of naphtha and natural gas in Brazil, 1984

Category	Price of natural gas ($/mmBtu)	Category	Price of naphtha ($/ton)
Fuel	3.59	Petrochemicals	210
Iron and steel	3.59	Fertilizers	42
Domestic heating	2.52	Fuel generation	115
Petrochemicals	2.90	Other uses	874
Fertilizers	0.96		

Source: Conselho Nacional Petróleo

Table C.3
Production, consumption and trade of major petrochemical products, Brazil, 1965–90 ('000 tons)

Product	1965	1975	1978	1985	1990
Basics					
Ethylene					
Consumption	20	300	404	1 231	1 432
Production	20	300	404	1 302	1 485
Imports	-	-	-	-	-
Exports	-	-	-	71	53
Propylene					
Consumption	2	86	214	643	717
Production	2	86	214	738	826
Imports	-	-	-	-	-
Exports	-	-	-	95	109
Benzene					
Consumption	7	107	175	416	538
Production	7	100	174	516	587
Imports	-	7	-	-	-
Exports	-	-	-	100	49
Ammonia					
Consumption	28	279	471	1 140	1282
Production	28	201	247	1 157	1262
Imports	-	78	224	17	20
Exports	-	-	-	34	-
Methanol					
Consumption	..	57	98	176	258
Production	..	48	95	155	166
Imports	..	9	3	21	92
Exports	..	-	-	-	-
End Products					
Polyethylene					
Consumption	20	207	322	450	696
Production	18	182	262	771	931
Imports	12	25	56	-	..
Exports	-	-	-	326	248
SBR					
Consumption	31	97	149	151	168
Production	36	98	155	188	182
Imports	-	1	56	-	..
Exports	-	-	21	38	18
Urea					
Production	..	204	510	1053	962
Consumption	..	77	113	1044	1148
Imports	..	127	399	16	56
Exports	..	-	-	-	..

Source: Instituto de Planejamento Econômico e Social (1974); Petroquisa

Table C.4
Production and export of major petrochemical products,
Trinidad and Tobago, 1960–90 ('000 tons)

Product	1960	1970	1980	1985	1990
Ammonia					
Production	28.1	425.4	559.1	1 322.9	1 859.7
Export	..	386.7	579.3	1 120.2	1 548.4
Methanol					
Production	-	-	-	360.1	402.5
Export	-	-	-	334.8	395.4
Benzene					
Production	-	14.6	11.3	-	14.7
Export	-	12.2	10.6	-	7.5
Toluene					
Production	-	31.8	46.7	-	52.1
Export	-	32.7	45.1	-	30.2
Xylene					
Production	-	3.0	9.4	-	13.1
Export	-	2.9	8.8	-	7.3
Urea					
Production	12.7	58.1	56.7	388.5	504.0
Export	..	58.8	54.0	350.9	490.7

Source: Republic of Trinidad and Tobago, Ministry of Energy and Natural Resources, *Annual Report* (1980–90 issues); Republic of Trinidad and Tobago, Central Statistical Office, *Quarterly Agricultural Report* (1960–1990 issues)

Appendix D

Table D.1
Production, consumption, and imports of selected petrochemical products, Brazil 1970–1990 and projections to 2000 ('000 tons)

Year	Ammonia			Urea[a]			Methanol		
	Prod.	Cons.	Imp.	Prod.	Cons.	Imp.	Prod.	Cons.	Imp.
1970	29	54	25	..	..	..	13	25	12
1972	147	177	30	..	..	..	34	38	4
1974	204	292	88	..	..	..	53	66	13
1975	201	279	78	78	204	127	48	57	9
1980	444	679	235	273	852	579	142	153	11
1981	463	623	175	292	595	303	126	130	4
1985	1 157	1 140	17	1 044	1 053	16	155	176	21
1990	1 262	1 282	18	1 148	963	56	166	258	92
Projections									
2000[b]	1 300	1 670	370	1 560	1 440	-	499	582	83
2000[c]	1 300	1 898	598	1 560	2 258	698	499	736	237

Source: ABIQUIM (1989); Petroquisa.

[a] Prior to 1975, figures for urea were lumped together with other nitrogenous fertilizers such as ammonium sulphate, di-ammonium sulphate and di-ammonium phosphate.

[b] Petroquisa's projections

[c] Author's projections

Note: Prod. – Production; Cons. – Consumption; Imp. – Imports

Table D.2
The future demand/supply balance of ammonia, urea and methanol in Brazil, 2000 ('000 tons)

Year			Product		
			Ammonia	Urea	Methanol
I[a]	2000	Demand	1 670	1 440	582
		Supply	1 300	1 560	499
		Balance	370	-120	83
II[b]	2000	Demand	1 898	2 258	736
		Supply	1 300	1 560	499
		Balance	598	698	237

Source: Calculated from Table D.1

[a] Petroquisa's projections
[b] Author's projections

Table D.3
Mexico and US production costs of major thermoplastics, 1980 ($/ton)

Product	USA	Mexico
	Production costs (25% ROI)	*Production costs (25% ROI)*
High density polyethylene	1 061	988
Low density polyethylene	979	958
Polypropylene	986	733
Polystyrene	1 068	911
Polyvinyl chloride	1 090	1 497

Source: Stauffer (1985); UNIDO (1981b)

Bibliography

Abbott, George (1986), 'Private Capital and the Proposal for a South Bank', *World Economy*, No. 3, September, 1986, pp. 275–94.

ABIQUIM (1989), *Anuário da Indústria Química Brasileira 1989*, ABIQUIM, Sâo Paulo.

Amsden, Alice (1976), 'Trade in Manufactures Between Developing Countries', *Economic Journal*, Vol. 86, No. 344, December, pp. 778–790.

Amsden, Alice (1980), 'The Industry Characteristics of Intra-Third World Trade in Manufactures', *Economic Development and Cultural Change*, Vol. 28, No. 4, October, pp. 181–219.

Amsden, Alice (1986), 'The Direction of Trade – Past and Present – and the "Learning Effects" of Exports to Different Destinations', *Journal of Development Economics*, Vol. 23, pp. 249–274.

APEC (1990), *A Economía Brasileira e Suas Perspectivas*, APEC, Rio de Janeiro.

Avramovic, Dragoslav (1983), *South-South Cooperation, Approaches to the Current Crisis – the Jamaican Papers*, St Martin's Press, New York.

Balassa, Bela (1965), 'Trade Liberalization and "Revealed Comparative Advantage" ', *Manchester School of Economic and Social Studies*, Vol. 33, pp. 99–123.

Balassa, Bela (1971), *The Structure of Protection in Developing Countries*, John Hopkins Press, Baltimore.

Balassa, Bela (1977),' "Revealed" Comparative Advantage Revisited: An Analysis of Relative Export Shares of the Industrial Countries, 1953–1971,' *Manchester School of Economic and Social Studies*, Vol. 45, pp. 327–344.

Balassa, Bela (1979a), 'A "Stages" Approach to Comparative Advantage', in Adelman, Irma (ed.), *Economic Growth and Resources*, Vol. 4, Macmillan, London.

Balassa, Bela (1979b), 'Intra-Industry Trade and the Integration of Developing Countries in the World Economy', in Giersch, Herbert (ed.), *On the Economics of Intra-Industry Trade: Symposium 1978*, J. C. B. Mohr, Tübingen, pp. 245–270.

Balassa, Bela (1979c), 'The Changing Pattern of Comparative Advantage in Manufactured Goods', *Review of Economics and Statistics*, Vol. 61, No.2, pp. 259–266.

Balkay, B. (1984), *South-South Cooperation in Mineral Resource-Based Industries*, UNIDO, Vienna.

Banco do Brasil, *Relatório Anuário* (1982–89 issues), Banco do Brasil, Brasília.

Banco do Brasil, Carteira de Comércio Exterior do Banco do Brasil (1985), *Brasil – 1985. Comércio Exterior. Séries Estatísticos*, Banco do Brasil, Brasília.

Baron, David (1983), *The Export-Import Bank: An Economic Analysis*, Academic Press, New York.

Barros de Castro, Antonio (1987), 'The Brazilian Energy Policy at a Crossroad', in Maillet, P., Hague D. and Rowland C. (eds.), *The Economics of Choice Between Energy Sources*, Macmillan, London.

Bennathan, Esra and Walters, A. A. (1969), *The Economics of Ocean Freight Rates*, Praeger, New York.

Bennett, Karl (1982), 'An Evaluation of the Contribution of CARICOM to Intra-Regional Caribbean Trade', *Social and Economic Studies*, Vol. 31, No. 1, pp. 74–88.

Bergsman, Joel (1970), *Brazil: Industrialization and Trade Policies*, Oxford, Oxford University Press.

Bhaduri, Amit (1985), 'Financial Reconstruction for North–North and South–South Trade', *Industry and Development*, No. 14, pp. 37–45.

Bhagwati, Jagdish (1964), 'The Pure Theory of International Trade: A Survey', *Economic Journal*, Vol. 74, pp. 1–84.

Bhagwati, Jagdish (1967), 'The Tying of Aid', in Bhagwati, J. and Eckaus, R. S. (eds.), *Foreign Aid*, Harmondsworth, Middlesex.

Blomstrom, Magnus (1990), *Transnational Corporations and Manufacturing Exports from Developing Countries*, UNCTC, New York.

Boyd, J.H. (1982), 'Eximbank Lending: A Federal Program That Costs Too Much,' *Federal Reserve Bank of Minneapolis Quarterly Review*, Winter, pp. 1–17.

Brasil, *Tarifa Aduaneira do Brasil* (1984 and 1991 issues), Editora Agenco Ltda, Rio de Janeiro.

Brau, Edward and Puckahtikon, Champen (1985), *Export Credit Policies and Payments Difficulties*, IMF Occasional Paper No. 37, IMF, Washington.

British Petroleum Statistical Review (1988–91), British Petroleum, London.

Byatt, I. C. R. (1984), 'Byatt Report on Subsidies to British Export Credits', *World Economy*, Vol. 7, No. 2, June, pp. 163–178.

Carey, Sarah and McLean, Sheila (1986), 'The United States, Countertrade and Third World Trade', *Journal of World Trade Law*, Vol. 20, No. 4, pp. 441–473.

Carlsson, Jerker (1982), *South–South Relations in a Changing World Order*, Scandinavian Institute of African Studies, Uppsala.

Carlsson, Jerker and Shaw, Timothy (1988), *Newly-Industrializing Countries and the Political Economy of South–South Relations*, Macmillan, London.

Caves, Richard (1974), 'The Economics of Reciprocity: Theory and Evidence on Bilateral Trading Arrangements', in Sellekaerts, W. (ed.), *International Trade and Finance: Essays in Honour of Jan Tinbergen*, Macmillan, London.

Central Bank of Trinidad and Tobago (1991) *Annual Economic Survey 1990*, Central Bank of Trinidad and Tobago, Port of Spain.

Chem Systems Incorporated (1985), *Methanol Annual 1985*, Chem Systems Incorporated, New York.

Chen, Edward (1983), *Multinational Corporations, Technology and Employment*, St Martin's Press, New York.

Chidzero, Bernard and Gauhar, Altaf (1986), *Linking the South*, Third World Foundation, London.

Chudnovsky, Daniel (1989), 'South–South Trade in Capital Goods: The Experiences of Argentina and Brazil', in Ventura-Dias V. (ed.), *South–South Trade*, Praeger, New York.

Cline, William (1978), *Economic Integration in Central America*, Brookings, Washington DC.

Cline, William (1982), 'Can the East Asian Model of Development be Generalized?' *World Development*, Vol. 10, No. 2, pp. 81–90.

Collins, Paul (1985), 'Brazil in Africa: Perspectives on Economic Cooperation Among Developing Countries', *Development Policy Review*, Vol. 1, No. 1, May, pp. 21–49.

Conjuntura, 1981–83 issues.

Cooper, St G. C. and Bacon, P. R. (1983), *The Natural Resources of Trinidad and Tobago*, Edward Arnold, London.

Cupid, Janet (1987), 'Entering New Horizons with Graphics – an Indepth Study of the Plastics Industry in Trinidad and Tobago and its Export Potential for the Caricom Region', MSc Thesis, University of the West Indies, Trinidad.

De Castro, Steve (1977), *Petrochemicals Sector Study*, Caribbean Technology Studies Project Report, Institute of Social and Economic Research, Jamaica.

De Silva, Leelananda (1983), 'The Non-Aligned Movement and the Group of 77 – Issues in Monetary and Financial Cooperation, With a Case Study of the Non-Aligned Solidarity Fund for Economic and Social Development', in Avramovic, D. (ed.), *South–South Financial Cooperation, Approaches to the Current Crisis – the Jamaican Papers*, St Martin's Press, New York.

De Witt and Company (1985), *Methanol Annual 1985*, De Witt and Company, Texas.

Deardorff, Alan (1979), 'Weak Links in the Chain of Comparative Advantage', *Journal of International Economics*, Vol. 9, pp. 197–209.

Deardorff, Alan (1980), 'The General Validity of the Law of Comparative Advantage', *Journal of Political Economy*, Vol. 88, pp. 941–957.

Deardorff, Alan (1982), 'Testing Trade Theories and Predicting Trade Flows', in Jones, R. W. and Kenen, P. (eds.), *Handbook in International Economics*, North-Holland, Amsterdam.

Deardorff, Alan (1985), 'The Direction of Developing Country Trade: Examples from Pure Theory', Paper presented at Conference on 'South–South vs South–North Trade: Does the Direction of Developing Country Exports Matter?', Brussels, Belgium, 28 February – 1 March 1981.

del Castillo, Graciana (1989), 'The Role of Transnational Corporations in South–South Trade: Issues and Evidence', in Ventura-Dias V. (ed.), *South–South Trade*, New York, Praeger.

Dell, Sidney (1966), *A Latin American Common Market?*, Oxford University Press, Oxford.

Diaz-Alejandro, Carlos (1974), 'Some Characteristics of Recent Export Expansion in Latin America', in Giersch, H. (ed.), *The International Division of Labour: Problems and Perspectives*, J. C. B. Mohr, Tübingen.

Dixit, Avinash and Norman, V. (1980), *Theory of International Trade*, Oxford University Press, Oxford.

Drèze, Jacques (1960), 'Quelques Réflexions Sérieuses sur L' Adaptation de L'Industrie Belge Au Marché Commun', *Comptes Rendus Des Travaux De La Société Royale D'Economie Politique De Belgique*, No. 275, December.

Dutt, Srikant (1980), 'South–South Patterns of Exploitation: India's New Relationship with Developing Countries', *Journal of Contemporary Asia*, Vol. 10, No. 4, pp. 434–443.

Erzan, Refik, Laird, S. and Yeats, A. (1988), 'On the Potential for Expanding South–South Trade Through the Extension of Mutual Preferences among Developing Countries', *World Development*, Vol. 16, No. 12, pp. 1441–1454.

Erzan, Refik et al (1987), *The Profile of Protection in Developing Countries*, UNCTAD Discussion Paper No. 21, UNCTAD, Geneva.

Erzan, Refik and Yeats, Alexander (1991), 'Tariff Valuation Bases and Trade Among Developing Countries: Do Developing Countries Discriminate Against Their Own Trade?', *Journal of Development Studies*, Vol. 27, No. 4, July, pp. 64–83.

Ethier, Wilfred (1979), 'Internationally Decreasing Costs and World Trade', *Journal of International Economics*, Vol. 9, pp. 1–24.

Ethier, Wilfred (1982), 'National and International Returns to Scale in the Modern Theory of International Trade', *American Economic Review*, Vol. 72, pp. 389–405.

European Chemical News, 1983–1992 issues.

Evans, David (1989), *Comparative Advantage and Growth*, Harvester Wheatsheaf, London.

Evans, Peter (1979), *Dependent Development: The Alliance of Multinational, State and Local Capital in Brazil*, Princeton University Press, Princeton.

Evans, Peter (1985), 'Trends in the United States Manufacturing Industry and Their Possible Implications for Latin American Industrialization: Case Studies of Steel, Electronics and Petrochemicals', *Industry and Development*, No. 14, pp. 47–98.

Fahny, John (1985), 'The South Bank: An Economic Assessment', *Inter-Economics*, Vol. 20, No. 1, January/February, pp. 36–42.

FAO (1990a), *Fertilizer Yearbook*, FAO, Rome.

FAO (1990b), *Trade Yearbook*, FAO, Rome.

Farhadian-Lorie, Ziba and Katz, Menachem (1988), *Fiscal Dimensions of Trade Policy*, IMF Working Paper No. 43, IMF, Washington DC.

Farrell, Trevor (1977), *The Multinational Corporations, the Transfer of Technology and the Human Resources Problem in Trinidad and Tobago Petroleum Industry*, Caribbean Technology Policy Studies Project, University of the West Indies, Institute of Social and Economic Research, Jamaica.

Fashbender, Karl and Wagner, W. (1973), *Shipping Conferences, Rate Policy and Developing Countries*, Verlag Weltarchiv, Hamburg.

Fayad, H. and Motamen, H. (1986), *The Economics of the Petrochemical Industry*, Frances Pinter, London.

Fishlow, Albert (1976), *Foreign Trade Regimes and Economic Development: Brazil*, National Bureau of Economic Research, Washington DC.

Fleisig, Heyward and Hill, C. (1984), *The Benefits and Costs of Official Export Credit Programs of Industrial Countries: An Analysis*, World Bank Staff Working Paper No. 659, World Bank, Washington DC.

Fleming, Marcus (1971), *Essays in International Economics*, Allen and Unwin, London.

Forrest, Tom (1982), 'Brazil and Africa: Geopolitics, Trade, and Technology in the South Atlantic', *African Affairs*, January, pp. 3–20.

Fritsch, Winston and Franco, G. (1991), 'Trade Policy Issues in Brazil in the 1990s', Report prepared for UNCTAD under the Project Trade Policies for Developing Countries in the 1990s', Rio de Janeiro (mimeo).

Gall, Norman (1986), 'Petroleum and Economic Development in Brazil', in *Brazil and Peru: Social and Economic Effects of Petroleum Development*, ILO, Geneva.

GATT (1990), *International Trade 89–90*, GATT, Geneva.

GATT Focus (1991), Vol. 83, August, pp. 1, 8.

Gauhar, Altaf (1983), *South–South Strategy*, Third World Foundation, London.

Goldstein, Morris and Khan, Mohsin (1982), *Effects of Slowdown in Industrial Countries on Growth in Non-Oil Developing Countries*, IMF Occasional Paper No. 12, Washington, DC.

Green Markets, 1982–91 issues.

Greenaway, David and Milner, C. (1990), 'South–South Trade: Theory, Evidence and Policy', *The World Bank Observer*, Vol. 5, No. 1, January, pp. 47–68.

Grubel, Herbert and Lloyd, P. J. (1975), *Intra-Industry Trade : The Theory and Measurement of International Trade in Differentiated Products*, Macmillan, London.

Grundmann, H.E. (1978), 'The Effects of Development Aid', *Intereconomics*, Vol. 13, pp. 242–245.

Guimaraes, Eduardo Augusto (1986), 'The Activities of Brazilian Firms Abroad', in Oman, Charles (ed.), *New Forms of Overseas Investment by Developing Countries*, OECD, Paris.

Haguenauer, Lia (1986), *O Complexo Químico Brasileiro Organizaçâo e Dinâmica Interna*, Texto Para Discussâo, No. 86, Universidade Federal do Rio de Janeiro, Rio de Janeiro.

Hahn, Albert (1970), *The Petrochemical Industry*, Mc Graw-Hill, London.

Hansen, Harold (1981), *The Developing Countries and International Shipping*, World Bank Staff Working Paper No. 502, IBRD, Washington DC.

Hanson, John (1980), *Trade in Transition. Exports from the Third World 1840–1900*, Academic Press, New York.

Haugen, Maria (1985), 'The Economic Development of Brazil', University of Texas at Austin, Texas (mimeo).

Havrylyshyn, Oli (1982), 'Promoting Trade among Developing Countries: an Assessment', *Finance and Development*, Vol. 19, No. 1, March, pp. 17–21.

Havrylyshyn, Oli (1985), 'The Direction of Developing Country Trade: Empirical Evidence of Differences Between South–South and South–North Trade', *Journal of Development Economics*, Vol. 19, No. 3, December, pp. 225–281.

Havrylyshyn, Oli and Civan, Engin (1983), 'Intra-Industry Trade and the Stage of Development: A Regression Analysis of Industrial and Developing Countries', in Tharakan, P. K. M. (ed.), *Intra-Industry Trade: Empirical and Methodological Aspects*, North-Holland, Amsterdam.

Havrylyshyn, Oli (1985), 'Intra-Industry Trade Among Developing Countries', *Journal of Development Economics*, Vol. 18, No. 2–3, August, pp. 253–275.

Havrylyshyn, Oli and Wolf, Martin (1981), *Trade among Developing Countries: Theory, Policy Issues, and Principal Trends*, World Bank Staff Working Paper No. 479, Washington, IBRD.

Helleiner, Gerald (1990), *The New Global Economy and the Developing Countries*, Edward Elgar, Aldershot.

Helpman, Elhanan (1981), 'International Trade in the Presence of Product Differentiation, Economies of Scale and Monopolistic Competition: A Chamberlin-Heckscher-Ohlin Approach', *Journal of International Economics*, Vol. 11, pp. 305–340.

Hughes, Helen (1980), 'Inter-Developing Country Trade and Employment', in Burton, Weisbrod and Hughes, Helen (eds.), *Human Resources, Employment and Development*, Vol. 3, Macmillan, London.

176

Huque, K. A. (1985), 'Implementation of Aid projects: A View from The Other Side', Report R3, Building Function Analysis, The Royal Institute of Technology, Stockholm.

Hillman, Arye (1980), 'Observations on the Relation Between "Revealed Comparative Advantage" and Comparative Advantage as Indicated by Pre-Trade Relative Prices', *Weltwirtschaftliches Archiv*, Vol. 116, pp. 315–321.

IBRD, *World Development Report* (1980–91 issues), IBRD, Washington DC.

IBRD (1979), *Brazil. Human Resources Special Report*, IBRD, Washington DC.

IBRD (1984), *Brazil. Economic Memorandum*, IBRD, Washington DC.

IBRD, *World Debt Tables* (1990), IBRD, Washington DC.

IMF, *Direction of Trade Statistics* (1970–1990 issues), IMF, Washington DC.

IMF, *International Financial Statistics* (1972–89 issues), IMF, Washington DC.

IMF, *Monthly Bulletin of Statistics* (1980–1990 issues), IMF, Washington DC.

Instituto Brasileiro de Geografía e Estatística (IBGE) (1989), *Auário Estatístico do Brasil*, IBGE, Rio de Janeiro.

Instituto Brasileiro de Petróleo (1983), *A Indústria Petroquímica Brasileira*, Instituto Brasileiro de Petróleo, Rio de Janeiro.

Instituto de Planejamento Econômico e Social (1974), *Perspectivas da Indústria e Petroquímica no Brasil*, Série Estudos para o Planejamento, No. 9, Instituto de Planejamento Econômico e Social, Brasília.

Japan Gasolene Company (1970), 'Draft Report on Programming of Studies including a Macroscopic Market Survey and an Evaluation of Export Possibilities for Petrochemicals from Trinidad & Tobago', Japan Gasolene Company, Tokyo.

Jepma, Catrinus (1988), 'The Impact of Untying Aid of the European Community Countries', *World Development*, Vol. 16, No. 7, pp. 797–805.

Jepma, Catrinus (1991), *The Tying of Aid*, OECD, Paris.

Jones, S. F. and Jagoe, A. (1988), *Third World Countertrade. Analysis of 1,350 Deals Involving Developing Countries, 1980–87*, Produce Studies, Newbury.

Jones, Ronald and Neary, P. (1984), 'The Positive Theory of International Trade', in Jones, R. and Kenen, P. (eds.), *Handbook of International Economics*, Vol. 1, North-Holland, Amsterdam.

Kahnert, F., Germidis, D. and Stier, H. (1971), *Aid Tying and Export of Nitrogenous Fertilizers from the Persian Gulf*, Development Centre of the OECD, Paris.

Keesing, Donald (1966), 'Labour Skills and Comparative Advantage', *American Economic Review*, Vol. 56, No. 2, May, pp. 249–258.

Kelly, Margaret et al (1988), *Issues and Developments in International Trade Policy*, IMF Occasional Paper No. 63, IMF, Washington DC.

Kenen, Peter (1965), 'Nature, Capital and Trade', *Journal of Political Economy*, Vol. 73, October, pp. 437–460.

Kenen, Peter (1975), *International Trade and Finance: Frontiers for Research*, Cambridge University Press, Cambridge.

Khan, Khushi (ed.) (1986), *Multinationals of the South*, German Overseas Institute and Frances Pinter, London and Hamburg.

Khanna, Ashok (1985), 'A Note on the Dynamic Aspects of the Heckscher-Ohlin Model: Some Empirical Evidence', *World Development*, October/November, Vol. 13, No. 10/11, pp. 1171–1176.

Kiljunen, Kimmo (1985), *Industrialisation in Developing Countries and Consequent Trade-Related Restructuring Constraints in Finland*, Labour Institute for Economic Research, Helsinki.

Kleiman, Ephraim (1976), 'Trade and the Decline of Colonialism', *Economic Journal*, Vol. 86, pp. 459–480.

Kostecki, M. M. (1982), *State Trading in Industrial Markets*, Macmillan, London.

Krueger, Anne (1977), *Growth, Distortions, and Patterns of Trade Among Many Countries*, Princeton Studies in International Finance No. 40, Princeton University Press, Princeton.

Krueger, Anne (1978), 'Alternative Trade Strategies and Employment in LDCs', *American Economic Review, Papers and Proceedings*, Vol. 68, pp. 270–274.

Krueger, Anne (1983), 'Alternative Trade Strategies and Employment',in Weisbrod, Burton and Hughes, Helen (eds.), *Human Resources, Employment and Development*, Vol. 3, Macmillan, London.

Krueger, Anne et al (eds.) (1981), *Trade and Employment in Developing Countries – Individual Studies, Vol. 1: Individual Studies*, University of Chicago Press, Chicago.

Krugman, Paul (1979), 'Increasing Returns, Monopolistic Competition and International Trade', *Journal of International Economics*, Vol. 9, pp. 469–479.

Krugman, Paul (1980), 'Scale Economies, Product Differentiation, and the Pattern of Trade', *American Economic Review*, Vol. 70, No. 5, December, pp. 950–959.

Krugman, Paul (1981), 'Intra-Industry Specialization and the Gains from Trade', *Journal of Political Economy*, Vol. 89, pp. 959–973.

Lall, Sanjaya (1982), *Developing Countries As Exporters of Technology*, Macmillan, London.

Lall, Sanjaya (ed.) (1983), *The New Multinationals: The Spread of Third World Enterprises*, John Wiley and Sons, Chichester.

Lall, Sanjaya (1984a), 'South–South Economic Cooperation and Global Negotiations,' in Bhagwati, J. N. and Ruggie, J. (eds.) *Power, Passion and Purpose: Prospects for North–South Negotiations*, MIT Press, Cambridge (Mass.).

Lall, Sanjaya (1984b), 'Exports of Technology by Newly-Industrialising Countries: An Overview', *World Development*, Vol. 12, May/June, pp. 471–480.

Lall, Sanjaya (1984c), 'India',*World Development*, Vol. 12, May/June, pp. 535–565.

Lall, Sanjaya (1985a), 'South–South Economic Cooperation: Lessons from the Indian Experience', in Lall, Sanjaya (ed.), *Multinationals, Technology and Exports*, Macmillan, London.

Lall, Sanjaya (1985b), 'Trade Between Developing Countries', *Trade and Development*, No. 6, pp. 1–16.

Lall, Sanjaya, Ray, A. and Ghosh, S. (1989), 'The Determinants and Promotion of South–South Trade in Manufactured Products', in Ventura-Dias, V. (ed.), *South–South Trade*, Praeger, New York.

Lancaster, Kelvin (1980), 'Intra-Industry Trade Under Perfect Monopolistic Competition', *Journal of International Economics*, Vol. 10, pp. 151–175.

Lancaster, Kelvin (1984), 'Protection and Product Differentiation', in Kierskowski, H. (ed.), *Monopolistic Competition and International Trade*, Oxford University Press, Oxford.

Langhammer, Rolf (1980), 'Multilateral Trade Liberalization Among Developing Countries', *Journal of World Trade Law*, Vol. 14, November/December, pp. 508–515.

Langhammer, Rolf (1983), 'The Importance of 'Natural' Barriers to Trade Among Developing Countries: Some Evidence from the Transport Cost Content in Brazilian Imports', *World Development*, Vol. 11, No. 5, pp. 417–425.

Leontief, Wassily (1954), 'Domestic Production and Foreign Trade: the American Position Re-Examined', *Economia Internazionale*, Vol. 7, pp. 3–32.

Lewis, Arthur William (1980), 'The Slowing Down of the Engine of Growth', *American Economic Review*, Vol. 70, No. 4, September, pp. 555–564.

Linder, Staffan Burenstam (1961), *An Essay on Trade and Transformation*, Almqvist and Wiksell, Stockholm.

Linnemann, Hans and Verbruggen, Harmen (1991), 'GSTP Tariff Reductions and its Effects on South–South Trade in Manufactures', *World Development*, Vol. 19, No. 5, pp. 539–51.

Lipsey, R.G. (1960), 'The Theory of Customs Union: A General Survey', *Economic Journal*, Vol. 70, pp. 496–513.

List, H.L. (1986), *Petrochemical Technology*, Englewood Cliffs, Prentice-Hall, New Jersey.

Livingstone, Ian (1986), *International Transport Costs and Industrial Development in the Least Developed Countries*, UNIDO, Vienna.

Maizels, Alfred (1976), 'A New International Strategy for Primary Commodities', in Helleiner, G. K. (ed.), *A World Divided: The Less Developed Countries in the International Economy*, Cambridge University Press, Cambridge.

Marin, Dalia (1990), 'Tying in International Trade: Evidence on Countertrade', *World Economy*, Vol. 13, No. 3, September, pp. 445–462.

Matthies, Volker (1979), 'Collective Self-Reliance: Concept and Reality', *Intereconomics*, No. 2, March/April, pp. 75–79.

Meade, J. (1955), *The Theory of Customs Unions*, North-Holland, Amsterdam.

Medina, Tomas Alfonso (1983), 'Monetary and Payments Agreements Among Developing Countries', in Pavlic, Breda et al (eds.), *The Challenges of South–South Cooperation*, Westview Press, Colorado.

Menezes Pereira, Vicente (1984), 'Oportunidades de Produçâo de Metanol no Brasil', Petroquisa, Rio de Janeiro (mimeo).

Meyers, Kenneth and McCarthy, F. (1985), *Brazil. Medium-Term Policy Analysis*, World Bank Staff Working Paper No. 750, IBRD, Washington DC.

Nayyar, Deepak (1978), 'Transnational Corporations and Manufactured Exports from Poor Countries', *Economic Journal*, Vol. 88, March, pp. 59–84.

Nayyar, Deepak (1979), 'Limits and Obstacles to South–South Trade', in *Industry 2000 – New Perspectives. Collected Background Papers*, Vol. 4, UNIDO, Vienna.

Newson, Mary and Wall, David (1985), *Policy and Institutional Obstacles to South–South Trade in Manufactures*, UNIDO, Vienna.

Nitrogen, 1982–91 issues.

Norman, W. S. (1980), 'The LNG "Economy"', Society of Petroleum Engineers of T and T Conference, Dept. of Chemical Engineering, University of the West Indies, St. Augustine, Trinidad (mimeo).

Nugent, Jeffrey (1985), 'The Potential for South–South Trade in Capital Goods Industries', *Industry and Development*, No. 14, pp. 99–41.

OECD (1985a), *The Petrochemical Industry*, OECD, Paris.

OECD (1985b), *Countertrade: Developing Country Practices*, OECD, Paris.

OECD (1990), *World Economic Outlook*, OECD, Paris.

OECD (1991), *Development Cooperation 1990 Report*, OECD, Paris.

Ohlin, Bertil (1933), *Interregional and International Trade*, Harvard University Press, Cambridge (Mass.).

Ohlin, Bertil (1977), *The International Allocation of Economic Activity: Proceedings of a Nobel Symposium Held at Stockholm*, Macmillan, London.

Oil and Gas Journal, 1982–91 issues.

Oman, Charles (1984), *New Forms of International Investment in Developing Countries*, OECD Development Centre, Paris.

Ordoñez, Ramona and Lobo, Tereza (1985), 'Petroleum', in *Guía da Indústria Brasileira de Petróleo, Gás e Petroquímica – 1984/1985*, ABIQUIM, Sâo Paulo.

Overseas Development Administration (1984), *Report 1984*, London.

Pantin, Dennis (1986), 'The Economics of Natural Gas Development in Small Oil-Exporting Economies with Special Reference to Trinidad and Tobago', *OPEC Review*, Vol. 10, No. 3, pp. 345–368.

Parsan, Elizabeth (1981), 'An Evaluation of the Organization and Development of the Fertilizer Industry in Trinidad and Tobago', MSc Thesis, University of the West Indies, St. Augustine, Trinidad.

Parsan, Elizabeth (1988), 'An Investigation into the Potential for South–South Trade: A Case Study of Trinidad and Tobago–Brazil Trade in Petrochemicals', DPhil Thesis, University of Sussex, Sussex.

Pavlic, Breda et al(eds.), *The Challenges of South–South Cooperation*, Westview Press, Colorado.

Pereira da Silva Filho, Amilcar and Cardoso, Pinto Maurício Jorge (1973), *Mercado Brasileiro de Produtos Petroquímicos*, Série Estudos Para o Planejamento No. 3, Instituto de Planejamento Econômico e Social, Brasília.

Pereira da Silva Filho, Amilcar and Ribeiro, Antonio Carlos da Motta (1974), *Perspectivas da Indústria Petroquímica no Brasil*, Instituto de Planejamento Econômico e Social, Brasília.

Petro e Química, 1983–88 issues.

Petrobrás, *Annual Report* (1984–90 issues), Petrobrás, Rio de Janeiro.

Petrobrás (1984), *A Indústria Petroquímica No Brasil*, Cadernos Petrobrás 7, Petrobrás, Rio de Janeiro.

Petrobrás (1985), *The Brazilian Petrochemical Industry*, Petrobrás, Rio de Janeiro.

Petrobrás (1986), *Brazil 1986*, Petrobrás, Rio de Janeiro.

Petrofértil (1985), *Anuário de Informaçoes*, Petrofértil, Rio de Janeiro.

Petroleum Economist, 1985–91 issues.

Petroquisa, *Annual Report* (1984–88 issues), Petroquisa, Rio de Janeiro.

Posner, Michael (1961), 'International Trade and Technical Change', *Oxford Economic Papers*, Vol. 13, pp. 757–778.

Prewo, Wilfred (1978), 'The Structure of Transportation Costs on Latin American Exports', *Weltwirtschaftliches Archiv*, Vol. 114, April, pp. 305–327.

Republic of Trinidad and Tobago, Ministry of Energy and Natural Resources (1985), *Natural Gas in Trinidad and Tobago*, Ministry of Energy and Natural Resources, Port-of-Spain.

Republic of Trinidad and Tobago (1989), *Medium-Term Macro-Planning Framework, 1985–1995*, CSO Printing Unit, Port of Spain.

Republic of Trinidad and Tobago, Ministry of Energy and Natural Resources, *Annual Report* (1980–87 issues), Government Printing Unit, Port of Spain.

Republic of Trinidad and Tobago, Central Statistical Office, *Overseas Trade Report* (1965–1990 issues), CSO Printing Unit, Port of Spain.

Republic of Trinidad and Tobago, Central Statistical Office *Quarterly Agricultural Report* (1960–90 issues), CSO Printing Unit, Port of Spain.

República Federativa do Brasil (1985), *I Plano Nacional de Desenvolvimento da Nova República – 1986–1989*, Secretária de Planejamento da República do Brasil, Brasília.

República Federativa do Brasil, Ministério da Fazenda, *Comércio Exterior do Brasil* (1984–1989 issues), Ministério da Fazenda, Brasília.

República Federativa do Brasil, Ministério das Minas e Energía (1985), *Balanço Energético Nacional 1985*, Ministério das Minas e Energía, Brasília.

Research and Information System for the Nonaligned and Other Developing Countries (1987), *South–South Economic Cooperation*, Sangam Books, London.

Richards-Loup, Anne (1984), 'Multilateral Trade in Manufactured Goods: A South–South, South–North Comparison', PhD thesis, George Washington University, Washington.

Riedel, James (1984), 'Trade as the Engine of Growth in Developing Countries Revisited', *Economic Journal*, Vol. 94, March, pp. 56–73.

Roemer, John (1977), 'The Effect of Sphere of Influence and Economic Distance on the Commodity Composition of Trade in Manufactures', *Review of Economics and Statistics*, Vol. 59, pp. 318–327.

Sabolo, Yves (1983), 'Trade Between Developing Countries, Technology Transfers and Employment', *International Labour Review*, Vol. 122, No. 5, September/October, pp. 593–608.

Sagafi-nejad, Tagi (1986), 'Third World Transnationals: Recent Literature', *The CTC Reporter*, No. 21, Spring, pp. 65–67.

Sauliners, Alfred (1981), 'State Trading Organisations: A Bias Decision Model and Applications', *World Development*, Vol. 9, No. 7, pp. 679–694.

Sauvant, Karl (1982), 'Organizational Infrastructure for Self-Reliance: The Non-Aligned Countries and the Group of 77', *Development and Peace*, Vol. 3, Spring, pp. 12–39.

Schultz, Knud and Mattos, Jorge (1986), 'Fertilizer Pricing in Brazil', in Segura, Edilberto, Shetty, Y. T. and Nishimizu, M. (eds.), *Fertilizer Pricing in Developing Countries*, Industry and Finance Series, Vol. 11, IBRD, Washington DC.

Sercovich, Francisco (1984), 'Exports of Technology by Newly-Industrializing Countries: Brazil', *World Development*, Vol. 12, No. 5/6, May/June, pp. 575–600.

Sercovich, Francisco (1985), *State-Owned Enterprises and Dynamic Comparative Advantage in the World Petrochemical Industry: the Case of Commodity Olefins in Brazil*, Development Discussion Paper No. 96, Harvard Institute for International Development, Cambridge, (Mass.).

Serletis, William (1986), 'Ammonia Plant Retrofitting: Increased Gas Efficiency and World Competitiveness', *Nitrogen*, No. 159, January – June, pp. 18–22.

Sheldrick, William (1987), *World Nitrogen Survey*, World Bank Technical Papers, Industry and Finance Series, IBRD, Washington DC.

Silver, Mitchell and Marple, Kent (1990), 'Using Dedicated Methanol Tankers', *OPEC Bulletin*, October, pp. 9–11.

Singer, Hans (1983), 'North–South and South–South: The North and ECDC', in Pavlic, Breda (eds.), *The Challenges of South–South Cooperation*, Westview Press, Colorado.

Singer, Hans (1986), 'South–South Trade Revisited in a Darkening External Environment', *Development and South–South Cooperation*, Vol. 2, No. 2, June, pp. 26–30.

Singh, Rana (1986), 'Technology Transfer and Technological Cooperation Among Developing Countries', *Development and South–South Cooperation*, Vol. 2, No. 2, June, pp. 134–155.

South Commission (1990), *The Challenge to the South: The Report of the South Commission*, Oxford University Press, Oxford.

Stanford Research Institute International (1985), *World Petrochemicals*, Stanford Research Institute International, Stanford.

Stauffer, Thomas (1985), 'Energy–Intensive Industrialization in the Middle East', *Industry and Development*, No. 14, pp. 1–35.

Stern, Robert (1975), 'Testing Trade Theories', in Kenen, P. (ed.), *International Trade and Finance*, Cambridge University Press, Cambridge.

Stewart, Frances (1976), 'The Direction of International Trade: Gains and Losses for the Third World', in Helleiner, Gerald (ed.), *A World Divided: The Less Developed Countries in the International Economy*, Cambridge University Press, Cambridge.

Stewart, Frances (1982), 'South–South Monetary Cooperation', in Al Shaikhly, Salah (ed.), *International Financial Cooperation*, Frances Pinter, London.

Stewart, Frances (1984), 'Recent Theories of International Trade: Some Implications for the South', in Kierskowski, H. (ed.), *Monopolistic Competition and International Trade*, Oxford University Press, Oxford.

Stewart, Frances (1987), 'Money and South–South Cooperation', *Third World Quarterly*, Vol. 9, No. 4, October, pp. 1184–1205.

Stewart, Frances and Stewart, Michael (1980), 'A New Currency for Trade Among Developing Countries', *Trade and Development*, No. 2, Autumn, pp. 69–82.

Stiglitz, Joseph (1970), 'Factor Price Equalization in a Dynamic Economy', *Journal of Political Economy*, Vol. 78, No. 3, May/June, pp. 456–488.

Suarez, Richard Acosta (1986), 'State Trading in International Markets: A Multinational Strategy for developing countries', in Khan, Khushi (ed.), *Multinationals of the South*, German Overseas Institute and Frances Pinter, London and Hamburg.

Technical Documentation for the Study of the Feasibility of a Bank for Developing Countries (1983), UNCTAD Secretariat, Geneva.

Teixeira, Francisco (1985), 'The Political Economy of Technological Learning in the Brazilian Petrochemical Industry', PhD thesis, University of Sussex, Science Policy Research Unit, Sussex.

Tharakan, P. K. M. (1983), *Intra-Industry Trade: Empirical and Methodological Aspects*, North-Holland, Amsterdam.

The Financial and Petroleum Times of Trinidad and Tobago, January 1991.

Thomas, Harmon (1988), *A Study of Trade Among Developing Countries, 1950–1980: An Appraisal of the Emerging Pattern*, North-Holland, Amsterdam.

Thomas Reed Publications Ltd (1981), *Reed's Marine Distance Tables*, Century Press, Sunderland.

Tran-Nguyen, A. N. (1989), 'The Monetary and Financial Aspects of South–South Trade', in Ventura-Dias, V. (ed.) *South–South Trade*, Praeger, New York.

Tyler, William (1972), 'Trade in Manufactures and Labour Skill Content: The Brazilian Case', *Economia Internazionale*, Vol. 45, No. 2, March, pp. 314–334.

Tyler, William (1978), *Manufactured Expansion and Industrialisation in Brazil*, J. C. B. Mohr, Tübingen.

Tyler, William (1981a), 'Advanced Developing Countries as Export Competitors in Third World Markets: The Brazilian Experience', in Georgetown University Center for Strategic and International Studies, *World Trade Competition: Western Countries and Third World Markets*, Praeger, New York.

Tyler, William (1981b), *The Brazilian Industrial Economy*, Lexington Books, Lexington.

Ul Haq, Mahbub (1980), 'Beyond the Slogan of South–South Cooperation', *World Development*, Vol. 8, pp. 743–751.

UN (1950), *The Economic Development of Latin America and its Principal Problems*, UN, New York.

UN (1985b), *Trade Relations Between Brazil and the United States*, UN, ECLAC, Santiago, Chile.

UN, ECLAC (1985a), *Economic Survey of Latin America and the Caribbean*, UN, ECLAC, Santiago, Chile.

UN, ESCAP (1985), 'Level and Structure of Liner Freight Charges in the Asian and Pacific Region, 1978–84', *Economic Bulletin for Asia and the Pacific*, Vol. XXXVI, No. 1, June, pp. 62–85.

UNCTAD (1969), *Level and Structure of Freight Rates, Conference Practices and Adequacy of Shipping Services*, UN, New York.

UNCTAD (1970), *Handbook of Trade and Development Statistics 1970*, UN, New York.

UNCTAD (1972), *The Intra-Trade of Developing Countries*, Research Memorandum No. 47, UNCTAD, Geneva.

UNCTAD (1982), *International Trade in the Petrochemical Sector: Implications for Developing Countries*, UNCTAD, Geneva.

UNCTAD (1983a), *Trade and Development Report*, UN, New York.

UNCTAD (1986), *Strengthening the Weakest Link*, UN, New York.

UNCTAD (1987), *Cooperation Among Developing Countries in Shipping, Ports and MultiModal Transport*, UNCTAD, Geneva.

UNCTAD (1989a), *Review of Developments in the Area of Trade and Monetary and Financial Cooperation Among Developing Countries*, UNCTAD, Geneva.

UNCTAD (1989b), *Trade and Development Report 1989*, UNCTAD, Geneva.

UNCTAD (1989c), *Cooperation Among State Trading Organizations of Developing Countries*, UNCTAD, Geneva.

UNCTAD (1990a), *Trade Expansion Among Developing Countries: Constraints and Measures to Overcome Them*, UNCTAD, Geneva.

UNCTAD (1990b), *Trade and Development Report 1990*, UNCTAD, Geneva.

UNCTAD (1990c), *Economic Integration Among Developing Countries: Trade Cooperation, Monetary and Financial Cooperation and Review of Recent Developments in Major Economic Cooperation and Integration Groupings of Developing Countries*, UNCTAD, Geneva.

UNCTAD (1990d), *Review of Maritime Transport 1989*, UNCTAD, Geneva.

UNCTAD (1991), *Report of the Review Conference on the United Nations Convention on a Code of Conduct for Liner Conferences on its Resumed Session*, UNCTAD, Geneva.

UNCTC (1983), *Transnational Corporations in World Development*, UN, New York.

UNCTC (1988), *Transnational Corporations in World Development*, UN, New York.

UNDP (1990), *Human Development Report 1990*, Oxford, UNDP and Oxford University Press.

UNESCO, *Statistical Yearbook* (1970–90 issues), UNESCO, Paris.

UNIDO (1978a), *First World-Wide Study on the Petrochemical Industry: 1975–2000*, UNIDO, Vienna.

UNIDO (1978b), *Second World-Wide Study on the Fertilizer Industry 1975–2000*, UNIDO, Vienna.

UNIDO (1981a), *Second World-Wide Study on the Petrochemical Industry: Process of Restructuring*, UNIDO, Vienna.

UNIDO (1981b), *Long-Term Arrangements for the Development of the Petrochemical Industry in Developing Countries Including Arrangements for Marketing Petrochemical Products Produced in Developing Countries*, UNIDO, Vienna.

UNIDO (1982a), *International Trade in the Petrochemicals Sector: Implications for Developing Countries*, UNCTAD, Geneva.

UNIDO (1982b), *Emerging Petrochemicals Technology: Implications for Developing Countries*, UNIDO, Vienna.

UNIDO (1983a), *Changing Patterns of Trade in World Industry: An Empirical Study of Revealed Comparative Advantage*, UNIDO, Vienna.

UNIDO (1983b), *World Demand for Petrochemical Products and the Emergence of New Producers from the Hydrocarbon Rich Developing Countries*, Sectoral Studies Series, No. 9, UNIDO, Vienna.

UNIDO (1983c), *Opportunities for Cooperation Among the Developing Countries for the Establishment of the Petrochemical Industry*, Sectoral Working Paper Series No. 1, UNIDO, Vienna.

UNIDO (1984a), *Industrial Development and South–South Cooperation*, UNIDO, Vienna.

UNIDO (1984b), *World Demand for Petrochemical Products and the Arab Petrochemical Industry*, Sectoral Working Paper Series No. 20, UNIDO, Vienna.

UNIDO (1985a), *Global Report 1985*, UN, New York.

UNIDO (1985b), *The Petrochemical Industry in Developing Countries: Prospects and Strategies*, Sectoral Studies Series No. 20, Vol. 1, UNIDO, Vienna.

UNIDO (1985c), *The Petrochemical Industry: the Sector in Figures*, Sectoral Studies Series, No. 20, Vol. II, UNIDO, Vienna.

UNIDO (1985d), *Tariff and Non-Tariff Measures in the World Trade of Petrochemical Products*, UNIDO, Vienna.

UNIDO (1986a), *International Comparative Advantage in Manufacturing*, UNIDO, Vienna.

UNIDO and Gulf Organization for Industrial Consulting (1981), *The Industrial Uses of Associated Gas*, UNIDO, Vienna.

University of São Paulo, Instituto de Pesquisas Econômicas (1983), *Estatísticas Básicas do Setor Agrícola no Brasil*, Vol. 1, University of São Paulo, São Paulo.

USA, Bureau of Mines, Department of the Interior (1983) *Mineral Commodity Profiles*, US Government Printing Office, Washington DC.

Vaitsos, Constantine (1978), 'Crisis in Regional Economic Cooperation Among Developing Countries: A Survey', *World Development*, Vol. 6, pp. 719–769.

Vanek, Jaroslav (1959), 'The Natural Resource Content of the Foreign Trade, 1870–1955, and the Relative Abundance of Natural Resources of the United States', *Review of Economics and Statistics*, Vol. 41, pp. 146–153.

Vanek, Jaroslav (1968), 'The Factor Proportions Theory: the n-Factor Case', *Kyklos*, Vol. 21, No. 4, pp. 749–756.

Ventura-Dias, Vivianne (1989), 'The Structure of South–South Trade', in Ventura-Dias, V. (ed.), *South–South Trade*, Praeger, New York.

Ventura-Dias, Vivianne and Sorsa, Piritta (1985), 'Historical Patterns of South–South Trade', Paper Presented at Informal Symposium on 'South–South Trade: Obstacles to its Growth', UNCTAD, Geneva (mimeo).

Verbruggen, Harmen (1989), 'GSTP, the Structure of Protection and South–South Trade in Manufactures', *UNCTAD Review*, Vol. 1, No. 2, pp. 23–40.

Vernon, Raymond (1966), 'International Investment and International Trade in the Product Cycle', *Quarterly Journal of Economics*, Vol. 80, pp. 190–207.

Vernon, Raymond (1971), *Sovereignty at Bay: The Multinational Spread of US Enterprises*, Penguin Books, Harmondsworth, Middlesex.

Vernon, Raymond (1979), 'The Product Cycle Hypotheses in a New International Environment', *Oxford Bulletin of Economics and Statistics*, Vol. 41, November, pp. 255–67.

Villela, Annibal (1983), 'Multinationals from Brazil', in Lall, Sanjaya (ed.), *The New Multinationals: The Spread of Third World Enterprises*, John Wiley and Sons, Chichester.

Viner, Jacob (1950), *The Customs Union Issue*, Carnegie Endowment for International Peace, New York.

Wells, Louis, Jr. (1983), *Third World Multinationals*, MIT Press, Cambridge (Mass.).

Willmore, Larry (1976), 'Trade Creation and Trade Diversion in the Central American Common Market', *Journal of Development Studies*, Vol. 12, No. 4, July, pp. 396–414.

Wirth, John (1985), *Latin American Oil Companies and the Politics of Energy*, University of Nebraska, Lincoln.

Wiseman, Peter (1986), *Petrochemicals*, Ellis Horwood, Chichester.

World Bank (1990), *Lessons in Trade Policy Reform*, Policy and Research Papers No. 10, World Bank, Washington DC.

Yeats, Alexander (1980), 'Tariff Valuation, Transport Costs and the Establishment of Trade Preferences Among Developing Countries', *World Development*, Vol. 8, pp. 129–136.

Yeats, Alexander (1981a), *Trade and Development Policy: Leading Issues for the 1980s*, Macmillan, London.

Yeats, Alexander (1981b), *Shipping and Development Policy*, Praeger, New York.

Index

188

Global System of Trade Preferences
(GSTP), 59, 157
Group of 77, 4, 59
Grubel, Herbert, 23
Grundmann, H.E., 86

Haguenauer, Lia, 149
Hanson, John, 27, 51n
Haugen, Maria, 135, 152n
Havrylyshyn, Oli, 37, 39–41, 43–4
Heckscher–Ohlin (H–O) theory, 9, 25,
120
extended version, 13–4, 17–8, 37,
39–40
simple version, 12–3, 24, 37–8
see also factor endowment theory
Helleiner, Gerald, 6, 8
Helpman, Elhanan, 23
Hillman, Arye, 23, 121n
Hong Kong, 8, 41, 43, 53, 59, 73, 75–6,
78, 80, 82, 147
human capital 13, 17, 20, 33, 40–1, 44,
51, 94–5, 98, 119–21, 155
see also skills
Huque, K.A., 86

import licensing, 54, 57, 87, 135, 155
import substituting strategy of
industrialization (ISI), 53, 83
India, 5, 9, 27, 36, 41–3, 73, 75–6, 82, 86,
96, 104, 146–47
International Association of State Trading
Organizations of Developing
Countries (ASTRO), 84
interregional trade, 33–5, 47, 50
intra-industry trade (IIT), 22–3, 25n, 43–5
intraregional trade, 11, 27, 34–5, 47, 62,
65–6, 68

Jagoe, A., 70
Jepma, Catrinus, 85–6, 89n
joint venture, 109, 119, 121, 123, 141,
143–48, 151, 158–59
Jones, Ronald, 25n
Jones, S.F., 70

Kahnert, F., 86
Kelly, Margaret, 54
Kenen, Peter, 13
Khan, Khushi, 82, 89n
Khanna, Ashok, 16
Kiljunen, Kimmo, 25n

Kostecki, M.M., 84
Krueger, Anne, 11, 14–5, 17, 24, 25n,
37–40, 44, 53
Krugman, Paul, 23, 25n

labour intensive goods, 3, 9, 12–3, 15, 17,
24, 33, 46, 87, 154–55
labour intensive trade, South–South, 38,
40, 42, 154–55
Laird, S., 59–60
Lall, Sanjaya, 41–6, 82–3
Lancaster, Kelvin, 23
Langhammer, Rolf, 75, 152n
Latin America, 5, 62
foreign investment in, 78–81
trade of, 29, 34–8, 46–7, 50–1
shipping in, 68–9, 73, 89n
tariffs in, 58
see also South America
Latin American Free Trade Area
(LAFTA), 5, 38–9, 41, 66
Latin American Integration Association
(ALADI), 35, 65–8
learning-by-doing, 18, 46
Leontief, Wassily, 13
Lewis, Arthur, 3, 6–7, 10n
Linder, Staffan, 21–2
liner conferences, 73, 76–7, 88, 89n
Linnemann, Hans, 59
Lipsey, R.G., 11
List, H.L., 143
Lloyd, Peter, 23
Lomé Agreement, 119

Malaysia, 8, 36, 43, 68, 78, 82
manufactured goods 5, 7–8, 12, 14, 18–9,
21, 23–4, 32–4, 36, 45–7, 50, 55–6,
58–9, 61, 70, 78–9, 99–100, 120,
154–55, 157
Marin, Dalia, 71
marketing, 139, 146
of petrochemicals, 136–37
marketing barriers, 4, 10, 52, 88, 156
marketing expertise/skills, 82, 143, 147,
151, 158
marketing networks/systems, 60, 157, 159
Marple, K., 140, 152n
Meade, J., 11
Menezes Pereira, Vicente, 115, 125
methanol,
consumption of, 130, 132

costs and prices of, 113–16, 124–25, 128

production and trade in, 100, 112, 117–18, 120–21, 123–24, 128, 132–35, 138, 150–52, 158

productive capacity of, 102–3, 132–33

technical aspects of production, 104–6, 108–9, 112, 142

Mexico, 4–5, 8, 41, 43, 58, 68, 70, 74, 78, 80, 82

Middle East, 8, 62, 69, 75

see also Near East

monopolistic competition and product differentiation, theories of, 12, 23, 25n

Motamen, H., 144

multinational corporations *see* transnational corporations

natural gas,
endowments of, 95, 102, 120, 121n, 142–3, 157

in the petrochemical industry, 104–9, 113–15, 151, 152n, 157–58

Nayyar, Deepak, 60

Near East, 46–7, 50–51

see also Middle East

Neary, Peter, 25n

neo-technology theory, 18, 20, 24, 94

newly-industrializing countries (NICs), 4, 7–8, 10n, 17–8, 25n, 29, 40, 43–6, 50, 79–80, 93, 153

Nigeria, 78, 118, 147

nontariff barriers (NTBs), 9, 79, 85

in industrialized countries (ICs), 3, 7

in the petrochemical industry, 93, 131, 135–38, 151, 158

in South–South trade, 52–3, 57–9, 87, 155

see also protectionism, tariffs, trade policy barriers

Norman, W.S., 23, 121n

North–North (N–N) trade, 20, 22, 30, 63

North–South (N–S) trade, 6, 13, 17, 20, 22, 26–7, 29–30, 36, 40, 57, 60, 74–6, 156

Ohlin, Bertil, 9, 25n

oil exporting countries, 8, 55

oil imports, 107

oil refinery, 106, 142–43

oil reserves, 95

Oman, Charles, 78, 89n

Pantin, Dennis, 152n

Parsan, Elizabeth, 97, 136–37

payments arrangements, 64–6

see also credit arrangements

petrochemical industry,
in Brazil, 101–41

in Trinidad and Tobago, 101–29, 133–41

see also ammonia, methanol, urea

Petrobrás Química (Petroquisa), 103, 105–6, 109, 131, 133, 135, 145

Petróleo Brasileiro (Petrobrás), 82, 95, 131, 146

Philippines, 8, 43, 59, 68, 73, 76

plastics industry, 101, 118, 119, 121, 123, 141–43, 148–50, 152, 158

plastics processing, 117, 148–51

Posner, Michael, 18

preference similarity theory, 12, 21–2, 24

Preferential Trade Area for Eastern and Southern Africa (PTA), 65–8

Prewo, Wilfred, 74, 152n

product differentiation, 22, 24, 37, 41, 43, 82

see also monopolistic competition and product differentiation

protectionism, 3, 7, 31, 146, 151

see also nontariff barriers, tariffs, trade policy barriers

Ray, A., 41–3

regional integration, 3, 5, 10n, 11, 35, 44, 50, 58

research and development (R & D), 43, 146

revealed comparative advantage (RCA)
see comparative advantage

Richards-Loup, Anne, 17–8, 37, 39–40

Roemer, John, 60, 89n

Sabolo, Yves, 44

Sagafi-nejad, Tagi, 82

Sauliners, Alfred, 84

Sauvant, Karl, 5

scale economy theory, 21

see also economies of scale

Schultz, Knud, 115–16

self-reliance, 6

Sercovich, Francisco, 98, 109

192